Untold Stories of Small Boats at War

Coastal Forces
Veterans Remember

Untold Stories of Small Boats at War

Coastal Forces Veterans Remember

Compiled by
Harold Pickles
A/Ldg Seaman D.S.M.

Consort Print Services
5a High Street
Fareham
Hants
PO16 7AN

To my wife, Sybil

©Harold Pickles 1996

First published in 1994
by The Pentland Press Ltd
1 Hutton Close
South Church
Bishop Auckland
Durham
Reprinted by Consort Print Services
5a High Street
Fareham
Hants PO16 7AN
in 1996

ISBN 1-85821-176-X

Contents

Foreword

Within these pages you have the opportunity to read of the exploits, achievements, comradeship, organisation and sheer courage of a small arm of the Royal Navy, the Light Coastal Forces—young men who fought in small wooden vessels in almost every theatre of war during the Second World War. The officers and men who manned these small warships, some no longer than the length of the famous Spitfire, can and will be likened to the Battle of Britain pilots who held fast whilst England was on the edge of catastrophe. After Dunkirk, these little ships harried the enemy in the Channel, North Sea and the Mediterranean to such an effect that Winston Churchill singled them out with his words of wisdom and congratulated the little ships and their crews for their part in bringing this holocaust to a successful conclusion and victory.

The reader will gain an insight to this part of the war. The Coastal Forces Veterans Association members publish a quarterly Newsletter, and the tales which unfold in this book are stories submitted to the Newsletter over a number of years. They have been collated to tell the great story of the Light Coastal Forces.

Should you be one of the fortunate people who served in this arm of the Royal Navy ashore or afloat, including WRNS, you have the opportunity of joining this select band by contacting the Secretary of the Coastal Forces Veterans Association, Mr Len Bridge, 15 Henning Street, Battersea, London SW11 3DR.

Notes and Abbreviations

CFVA	The Coastal Forces Veterans Association	SGB	Steam Gun Boat
		SO	Senior Officer (of a flotilla)
CMB	Coastal Motor Boat	HDML	Harbour Defence Motor Launch
MTB	Motor Torpedo Boat	RML	Rescue Motor Launch
MGB	Motor Gun Boat	'Dogboat'	D Class Fairmile MTB/MGB
ML	Motor Launch	BPB	British Power Boat
MA/SB	Motor Anti/Submarine Boat	RNVR	Royal Navy Volunteer Reserve
		HO	Hostilities only

Acknowledgement

I would like to thank G. M. Hudson, Honorary Historian of the CFVA, for supplying the pictures and captions in this book.

Harold Pickles DSM

Unknown US Build Vosper, in the Mediterranean., 20th MTB Flotilla (MTBs 287-290, 295-298). Note camouflage and that she has been re-armed with a single 20mm Oerlikon for'd and a twin aft, in place of the original turret with twin 0.5inch Vickers.

Introduction

The pages which follow tell some stories of those who served in the Navy's Light Coastal Forces in the Second World War. Many who read them will themselves have served in the boats, but perhaps others will need some background.

The idea for this compilation comes from the success of the quarterly Newsletter of the Coastal Forces Veterans Association—the CFVA—which was founded by a few stalwarts in 1974 and now has 2,000 members in many branches throughout the UK and the world. By the very nature of things, all the veterans who manned our boats are now close to seventy years young, and many passed that milestone some years ago.

Our typical Coastal Forces Veteran is unquestionably a proud man. He is proud to have served in our boats, and he believes that in them we achieved a team spirit which was rarely equalled in other units of the fighting services. This stemmed perhaps from the small numbers, the confined spaces and the intensity of the operations, all of which combined to breed loyalty for boats and flotillas and shipmates.

It is not therefore surprising that, after fifty years, the members of the CFVA demonstrate that loyalty and affection in abundance.

To help those who come to this story with only a hazy idea of the boats and the operations, a glossary is provided. Even members of CFVA will accept that they only really knew what was going on in their own boat or flotilla or base; those in the Med knew very little of the North Sea and Channel operations—and vice versa!

This introduction presents a potted history of the Coastal Forces in the Second World War. The trouble with potted histories is that they leave out more than they can include. Any mention of a particular flotilla or Senior Officer should be taken as a representative example

1

of the whole service. Indeed, many will add their own examples to make the record complete.

The particular value of Coastal Forces in war is clearly the fact that small boats of shallow draught and low silhouette can operate close to an enemy coast or in areas where larger ships would be vulnerable. Our boats were obviously of comparatively low cost and speedy construction, and to some extent were therefore expendable. Inevitably that leads to the possibility of close action, often against superior forces: and of such confrontations are legends created!

So, in the First World War, the Thornycroft CMBs and a variety of MLs earned the respect of the Royal Navy, and established traditions—enhanced by the award of several VCs for attacks on the Russian fleet in 1919.

We began the Second World War with just two flotillas of Scott-Paine boats based in Malta and Hong Kong, and with a handful of experimental Vospers and Thornycrofts similar to the CMBs. A commercial battle to secure Admiralty contracts for the development of new boats was resolved when Vospers largely built the MTBs, British Power Boats the MASBs and MGBs and the Fairmile Marine Company the ubiquitous ML—and later the Cs and Ds. Production in the USA under lease-lend was a tremendous help as the fleet expanded rapidly. The number of SGBs and the MGBs built by Camper and Nicholson added variety, and HDMLs belied their name, finding their way into invasions and combat far from their bases.

These then were the boats—what of the men and bases and the areas of operations? In 1940 and 1941 the early boats were often unreliable and certainly very modestly armed, but even so achieved great results, often under RN officers and with a high proportion of 'active service' coxswains and crew. Leaders like Nigel Pumphrey, Stewart Gould, Dickie Richards and Chris Dreyer, all operating from Dover, led the way. Soon the RNVR officers and HO ratings began largely to take over: Robert Hichens became a gunboat legend, and led the way for a new breed of RNVR leaders. His 6th and 8th Flotillas, operating mainly from Felixstowe, captured the public imagination. Peter Dickens—our first President—led his 21st MTB Flotilla with distinction.

2

Out in the Med, the 10th Flotilla operated along the desert coast, lost most of its boats at Crete, and another lot at Tobruk, but still went on to Sicily and the Aegean with tremendous spirit; the 7th Flotilla too had a three-year history of achievements in the Med.

By 1942 the demands of special operations like Dieppe and St Nazaire (where the MLs carved their name in history, and A/B William Savage in MGB314 gained our only VC of the war) had increased, and many clandestine landings, especially by C class MGBs, led to the formation of the 15th MGB Flotilla with its distinguished history.

The Fairmile MLs were everywhere: mine laying and mine sweeping, on anti-submarine patrols and convoy escorts, as RMLs in air sea rescue, and even mounting torpedoes at one time in Gibraltar.

By the end of 1942 the Dogboats were entering operations: over two hundred were built and made a huge impact because of their armament and range; they joined new Vosper and BPB flotillas with increased firepower. Patrols were continuous in the North Sea and Channel and contact with the enemy became ever more frequent. New leaders emerged—New Zealander George Macdonald and Mark Arnold Forster were examples in the short boats, and Ken Gemmell with his 'Norwegian' flotilla, and Donald Bradford (the Shark's Teeth 55th) in the Ds. The Poles, Dutch, Norwegians, Free French and Canadians all had their own crews in several flotillas, and many of the operations were building towards the expected landings of the Second Front.

Out in the Med, the force was built up to four D boat flotillas (a fifth joined in 1944) and six 'short' flotillas with Vospers, Elcos and Higgins all represented. They all played a major part as the Army drove the German army out of Africa, and then in the Sicily landings, before dispersing to operate from advanced bases in Augusta, Taranto, Maddalena, Bastia and Leghorn.

Others were in the Adriatic and Aegean where camouflage netting and island hopping were normal. The operations along the Yugoslav coast in support of Tito's partisans, with its opportunities for boarding and taking prizes at one period, were particularly significant. Flotilla leaders like Tim Bligh, Tom Fuller, and the Canadians Doug Maitland and Corny Burke in the Ds and Tony Blomfield in the 7th became legendary.

By the autumn of 1943, most of the MGBs in home waters were given tubes and redesignated as MTBs. And in 1944, especially in the Channel, the use of directing frigates to vector boats towards radar targets had changed the nature of operations—so did the improved torpedoes which dramatically improved the success ratio of firings.

The Normandy landings of 1944 involved most of the home-based flotillas in a multitude of tasks, and proved that Coastal Forces could maintain high standards of availability over many months of continuous operations.

The boats of the Coastal Forces—affectionately known as the Navy's "Little Ships"—served with distinction throughout the Second World War.

From Dunkirk to VE Day they fought over a thousand actions, and sank 500 enemy vessels including many E-boats. Of 81 enemy midget submarines destroyed, 32 were claimed by Coastal Forces.

Having fired 1,169 torpedoes, their percentage of hits and probable hits bettered that of the submarine service. In addition, 32 enemy aircraft were shot down and twice as many mine-laying operations were carried out than were credited to other mine-laying forces.

By 1944, Coastal Forces, numbering some 3,000 officers and 22,000 ratings, were operating from Norway to the Aegean. By the close of hostilities, 1,700 boats had been built and 170 had been sunk or destroyed.

Winston Churchill sent an open message to the men of Coastal Forces in which he said:

'*I have noted with admiration the work of the light coastal forces in the North Sea, in the Channel and in the Mediterranean. Both in offence and defence the fighting zeal and the professional skill of officers and men have maintained the great tradition built up by many generations of British seamen.*'

Those of us who were privileged to serve our Commonwealth and

Country in the Royal Navy will never understand why by the early 1960s all that tradition and experience was lost when the Admiralty decided to build no further boats.

How sad!

Leonard C. 'Rover' Reynolds, DSC, OBE, DL, JP

Little Ships of Britain

Of all the stories of the war at sea, there is none more thrilling than that of the Little Ships. Many times in these past six years have we seen them return to port after an engagement in the Channel, or off the then enemy-held coasts of France, Belgium and Holland. It was days after that we learned all we were allowed to know of what had occurred, but always it was also a tale that convinced us of our superiority at sea and made us glad in the thought that we too came from the same stock. It was revealed this week that these 'Little Ships', the MTBs, the MGBs and the MLs of the Coastal Forces, fought no fewer than 780 actions and sank more than 500 vessels.

The story began at Dunkirk and for the four following years they were continually in action, night as well as day, their operations extending to the Norwegian fjords, the Adriatic and the Aegean.

Their spirit of adventure and an almost reckless disregard of the dangers they ran put such a fear into the enemy that there were periods when the Germans were afraid to leave the safety of their harbours.

In 1944 they averaged one action a day and even the midget U boats—which were meant to stop their capers—made themselves scarce when our MTBs were on the prowl.

Their losses were heavy at times; all told 170 tiny craft now lie on the bottom of the sea, and some hundreds of brave lads have paid the price of admiralty, but German losses were more than two to one of ours.

Now all is over they can rest on their laurels with pride and satisfaction and the knowledge that they are honoured by a grateful country for the part they played in hastening the final victory.

This newspaper cutting, carefully folded, has again been stowed carefully away.

M.M.

The Motor Gun Boat 318

Motor Gun Boat 318 was commissioned during July 1941 and her first Commanding Officer was Lieutenant (later Lieutenant Commander) K. T. Kemsley RNVR. She was one of the boats designated to make up the 12th MGB Flotilla of eight boats, working out of Great Yarmouth, the base being known as HMS *Midge*. Motor Gun Boat 318 was a 'C' class gun boat. She was built by Aldous Successors Ltd. at the shipyard, Brightlingsea, Essex, England. Her statistics were: Length 110 ft.; Beam 17 ft. 5 in.; Draught For'ard 5 ft.; Aft 6 ft; Freeboard 6 ft.; Displacement 72 tons; Engines: three Hall Scott Defender (supercharged petrol-driven high octane fuel). Total max. BHP 2,700; Total maximum continuous BHP 1,800; Speed maximum 26.6 knots: continuous 23.6 knots; Fuel capacity 1,800 gallons; Consumption 130 gallons per hour; Range 500 nautical miles at 12 knots. Construction: all wood (double diagonal mahogany, most girders 2¾" plywood). Armament: For'ard, 2 pounder Mk VIII Gun on a Mk XV power mounting; Midships, mounted port and starboard, two twin 0.5" Vickers Machine Gun in Mk V powered mountings; Aft, single 20 mm. Oerlikon (manually operated) plus two twin .303" Vickers GO machine guns on the bridge, plus small arms and 4 depth charges; two CSA smoke floats mounted at the stern of the vessel. MGB 318 commenced her clandestine operations late in 1941 with an abortive trip to the Dutch coast from Yarmouth and within ten months of commissioning with a new Skipper, Lieutenant C. E. C. Martin, she left Great Yarmouth and the 12th MGB Flotilla for Dartmouth—the first boat to form up the 15th MGB Flotilla in March 1942 with MA/SB 36 to commence clandestine operations for SOE.

Officers and Crew

I joined HM Motor Gun Boat 318 under the then Commanding Officer

Lieutenant H. Tom Kemsley on 26 November 1941 as an A/Ldg Seaman after training at HMS *St Christopher*, Fort William, Scotland and I served on board under successive COs until 1 April 1945; in fact, all my active service was spent on this one boat. During her commission she had five Skippers: Kemsley, mentioned above; Lieutenant Commander C. E. C. (Pincher) Martin, DSC, RNVR from March 1942 to July 1943, followed by Lieutenant Commander Jan T. McQuoid-Mason, SANF(V) from July 1943 to November 1944, then, for a short period, Lieutenant Lloyd Bott (I cannot recall him) and, finally, Lieutenant Andrew Smith, RNVR to July 1945. HM MGB was paid off to reserve in July 1945 after an illustrious commission.

After leaving 318 on 1 April 1945 I attended a Navigation course at HMS *Dryad*, qualified as a Navigator's Yeoman and was released from the Navy on 15 March 1946.

We had a motley crew throughout the commission, and under the direction of two time-served petty officers (as opposed to Hostilities Only personnel), we blended as a team at all times. Petty Officer 'Paddy' Boyle served under Lieutenant Commander Martin, and Petty Officer 'Nigger' Mould, DSM and Bar under Lieutenant Commander McQuoid-Mason. In 1981, as an epitaph to Petty Officer 'Nigger' Mould I wrote an appreciation for time-served Petty Officers in Coastal Forces for the Coastal Forces Veterans Association Newsletter. It read:

> My experience of time-served Petty Officers during the war years was that they were the backbone of the Navy and I believe this was as true in Nelson's day as it is in the Navy today. What better epitaph could anyone bestow on the likes of Petty Officer H. E. Mould, DSM and Bar than to acknowledge that by their experience and seamanship they increased the chances of survival for the 'Hostilities Only' officers and ratings in the Coastal Forces.

The crew of 318 came from most parts of the United Kingdom with the exception of Northern Ireland, and we had our fair share of Cockneys, Scousers and Geordies mingled with Welsh and Scots in the complement of twenty-two men, plus a Petty Officer Coxswain and a Petty Officer Motor Mechanic; there were two officers: the

8

Skipper and the First Lieutenant. Whilst our complement frequently changed, the numbers increased as more equipment such as radar was introduced and required constant manning whilst at sea. This created accommodation problems in our closely-knit community. When the final count was made we had sixteen men sleeping on the main messdeck with two regularly sleeping on the two mess deck tables; an extra berth was allocated to the radar operator in the wheelhouse. One might say 'he slept on the job' as the radar equipment was housed there. In the for'ard mess deck where there were four cots, an extra berth was provided by the slinging of a hammock from each of the ladders which gave access to the deck.

Because of the limited space on small boats life was uncomfortable both in harbour and at sea. The compensations were both the companionship and fellowship these close quarters created and the fact that we all had to rely on each other's vigilance when on watchkeeping duties at sea.

After fifty years, this companionship and fellowship is still shown by the Coastal Forces Veterans Association to this day.

Morale

On 318 morale was of the highest order. This was due to the quality of the officers and coxswain, and most of all to the type of operations we were engaged upon. But more of that later—let me first dwell on some of the foolhardy, downright stupid and potentially dangerous escapades these matelots perpetrated in the name of fun or escape from boredom.

On Christmas Eve, the number one Gunner AA3 decided whilst we were in harbour tied up alongside the jetty at Newhaven that he would awaken the crew by dropping Mills bombs over the side for a lark. The resultant effect (apart from a dull thud) was that the boat rocked from side to side at an alarming rate. I cannot remember the sequel to this event; I guess his misdemeanour was covered up by the coxswain.

Dhobi-ing

It was a regular malpractice to 'dhobi' oil overalls in a bucket of petrol. As our engines were propelled by high octane petrol, the supply from the 1,800 gallons we carried presented no problem. The day dawned when our inoffensive Stoker 1st Class was busy dhobi-ing his overall when our dim 'Scouse' came along with his box of matches and with the determination of a man with suicidal tendencies threw the lighted matches towards our unfortunate stoker. Within seconds there was an almighty 'flash', and the stoker literally kicked the bucket which spread blazing petrol down the ship's side. We had a fire on our hands; the several layers of paint on the ship's side and deck burnt furiously until we manned the fire hose and brought the fire under control. Our Scouse 'Ginger' was given fourteen days stoppage of leave and ordered to scrape and paint the ship's side, which didn't prove to be an easy job as most of the operation was performed from a dinghy tied up alongside. The crew and his immediate 'oppos' were given strict instructions that no help whatsoever should be given to him.

Careless Talk

In our training session we were instructed never to speak of our 'clandestine voyages' to the Brittany coast of France, and indeed posters throughout the country warned that 'CARELESS TALK COSTS LIVES'. However, our matelot who hailed from Oxford was home on leave and his father took him to the 'local' pub for a drink. During the conversation at the bar he explained the operations which we undertook on behalf of SOE with the 15th MGB Flotilla. Of course, the inevitable happened—alongside them, apparently taking little notice of their conversation, was an Army major who at once realised the significance of his 'careless talk' and immediately made a report. By the time our 'matelot from Oxford' returned to 318, he was arrested and charged and spent the next 180 days in the 'glasshouse'. I often wonder what happened to him!

Absent Without Leave

Every flotilla has someone who goes 'absent without leave' at some time or other. In our case it was a bright young Cockney on 318 who had all the contacts for identity card, ration books, civilian gas mask and all the accoutrements to abscond from the Navy without a trace.

He openly discussed his intentions on the mess deck, relating his brother's experiences on the Russian convoys and his immediate switch to tropical waters, then back again to Murmansk. His brother couldn't stand the rigours of that life and had already gone AWOL. Armed with all his brother's experience it was only a matter of time before our bright young Cockney disappeared without trace. Until ... I found him when he joined the Coastal Forces Veterans Association. I visited him at his home on the 'Isle of Dogs' in 1983 shortly after he joined the CFVA and found him in failing health but quite chirpy. The authorities did catch up with him and he was sent to prison for a time. After the war, in spite of his prison record, he got a job with HM Customs and Excise Service and worked for them for thirty-five years—his prison record (which he didn't declare) never caught up with him. Unfortunately he died in 1985. I was sorry to lose another crew member of 318 as we are thin on the ground.

Enter the Entrepreneurs

The two entrepreneurs on board 318, 'Taffy' Bartlett and yours truly 'Percy' Pickles decided to go into business as 'bookmakers'—with £15, my life savings, and Taffy's £15, we were ready to accept bets. From small beginnings with bets ranged from 6d. each way to ten shillings each way, over the successive months we made a modest profit. We decided to expand, and found a 'runner' who would act as a collecting agent on board the base ship HMS *Aberdonian*, anchored in mid-stream on the River Dart at Dartmouth, our operational base. This proved a successful move until the fateful day in June 1944— Derby Day. It was our first big chance to make a big 'killing'; bets poured in from all directions, until we were ordered to start engines and move to the fuelling jetty at Kingswear (opposite Dartmouth) about an hour before the 'off'. We left instructions with our 'runner' to continue to take bets and we would collect them immediately we came back from the fuelling operation. Imagine our concern when the fuelling was delayed and, on our way back to the base ship, the race was running. By the time we were tied up alongside the Aberdonian, the race was over and the winner announced! Both Taff and I dashed

11

up the gangway to find our 'runners' list was for the winner Ocean Swell at £1 0s. 0d. each way. Ocean Swell was returned at 28–1 which meant a pay-out of £37 0s. 0d.—all our takings for the day plus a goodly amount of our capital—we had been well and truly taken to the cleaners! It was a lesson I shall never forget—where money is concerned, don't take anyone on trust. I resigned as the co-partner of the 15th MGB Flotilla bookmaker's business.

Firearms yet again

Two more incidents with firearms occurred aboard 318. One day one of the crew was larking in the mess deck with one of the ship's revolvers and fired a round into the deck head. A more serious event happened on deck, when our 'Ginger' of firelighting fame was given too many 'sippers' of rum on his birthday. In his cups, he went on deck, loaded the single Oerlikon aft and fired several rounds into the air. In no time the air raid siren was sounded in Dartmouth, and as the sound echoed across the water consternation reigned supreme with all aboard 318! Ginger was eventually given a draft chit and that was the last I saw of him.

Chore of Dhobi-ing

Dhobi-ing was always a chore, but the morale of the crew and the well-being and cleanliness of the individual was dependent on this chore being performed on a regular basis. The consequence of not adhering to the basic rules was an outbreak of the infestation of crab-louse known as 'crabs': an insect which burrows under the skin on the human body and is attributed to the lack of facilities for washing, rinsing and drying. We had a stoker aboard 318 who was most meticulous with his personal cleanliness, but each time an outbreak was reported, he was sure to catch them. One wonders how we survived.

A Tot Tale

No story about the Navy would be complete without a 'tot tale'. At 11:30 each day, come rain, hail, blow or shine, the Coxswain dispensed with monotonous regularity our daily tot. As one of the 'perks' of serving aboard MGBs and the like, we were allowed 'neaters rum'

12

with no water added; naval regulation decreed that two parts water should normally be added to the daily ration of one fourth of a gill. Strictly against regulations, this did allow an individual to save his daily ration for a special occasion. It wasn't unknown throughout the flotilla for the dispenser of the rum (usually the PO Coxswain) to be in arrears with his stock and the only time the day of reckoning came due was when the Coxswain handed over the responsibility to a new Coxswain. Such a situation occurred on 318. 'Nigger' Mould was leaving and found on checking his stock that he was fourteen tots short. As I was the only person of the old crew still on board who could help out I was the one 'asked', 'coaxed' or detailed to go without my tot for the next fourteen days—what a wrench! I nearly died during the next fortnight and the incoming Coxswain didn't even offer me 'sippers'!

Preparation and Training

Training was probably more acceptable and kept the adrenalin going longer for the officers of the flotilla than for those of us who performed our duties from the lower deck.

To do our job of landing on foreign territory, often when the surf was dangerously high, we needed specialized surf boats. Boats of an accepted Australian design were provided, and practice and training were required to overcome the elements, being swamped, waterlogged, deluged or simply getting soaked to the skin by the running surf. An ideal beach was found in the south-west area near Parr Sands and Falmouth, where 318 and three other boats of the 15th MGB Flotilla practised in conditions similar to those found on the coast of Brittany. Whilst these exercises took place the 'boffins' attached to the 15th MGB Flotilla and employed by SOE made their recommendations. At one time a one-man canoe was used as an experiment to overcome the surf, but I cannot remember this method being used to any success.

Innovations

Innovations were the order of the day. 318 on occasion was swarming with these 'boffins' dressed in bowler hats or trilbys and bow ties, and thick glasses—entirely out of keeping with the officers and matelots surrounding them. One particular invention which intrigued us was a device in the form of an Aldis lamp with a lens. A cable was plugged into the electrics, and the second part of the contraption was carried in the surf boat and took the form of a long post with a circular dome fixed on top, which contained perhaps a dozen prisms. The idea was that the surf boat, after making landfall and during the return to the mother ship, could look through the prism and pick up a reflection, thereby giving a directional 'fix' to facilitate a safe return!

The Launch and Recovery

Launching and recovering the surf boats was regularly exercised, with all the rowlocks bound with material to minimize the noise of rowing, and each launching had to be expedited with quiet precision and the recovery after the operation made with speed and efficiency. Training was the answer.

Though we were designated the 15th MGB Flotilla, each boat was an autonomous unit and the necessity to work at close contact with one another at sea did not arise as would have been the case with a flotilla hunting in packs. So training in this area was not quite vital to the success of our operations.

My Own Personal Contribution—in harbour and at sea

I served on board 318 for three years, four months and fifteen days, and my duties were divided into sea duties and harbour duties. I performed most of the harbour jobs on board 318 during my service, with the exception of the engine room. These included painting, cleaning and servicing guns, cook, mess caterer, flunkey, postman and supplies collection and some navigator yeoman duties, plus the hundred and one daily chores which were handed out by the coxswain. At sea, I was coxswain's relief on the wheel; bridge lookout; number two on the two-pounder pom-pom, and boat's crew reserve.

Perhaps it is apt to recall the job of 'mess caterer'. Each man had a victualling allowance of 1s. 10½d. per day; officers 2s.4d. per day. Should the allowance be overspent, each and every member of the crew had to contribute to the overspent kitty. We were overspent when

14

I took over, hence the reason I got the job. I must also point out that we also received an allowance of tea, sugar, kye and tinned fruit (for hard layers) which was based on the number of hours seatime we put in each month. It was therefore an advantage to the well-being of the mess kitty to have as much sea time as possible. It was fairly easy to work out: each man had so many ounces or part of an ounce for each hour at sea—all clever stuff provided you extracted every ounce out of the system. The mess caterer also had the job of planning the menu, and this was dependent on the monies available in the kitty. Generally with a well run mess the only time one could go into debt would be after December when Christmas dictated many extra goodies. On the credit side I must point out that should a profit be made this was equally distributed in cash to the crew members. Much to the surprise of everyone my first act as mess caterer was to take the tins of Libby's condensed milk off the breakfast table. We were using a case a day 'neaters' on cornflakes, and I replaced it by a mixture of two and one—it almost caused a riot! But we were soon in the black. My time as mess caterer coincided with the arrival of the tank landing craft of the US Navy, I visited these craft on the pretext of cementing Anglo-American relations but I usually came back with a couple of cases of bully beef or some such items of tinned goods.

Then as Cook

My decision to take over the job as cook, one of the worst jobs on board, was purely because it was paid an extra shilling a day, and after my finances had taken a bad turn through the misadventure I had suffered by taking a half share in the 'bookie' business.

When the 'C' class boats were commissioned they were fitted with a paraffin stove with oven, but how the devil any cook made a hot meal on that contraption I will never know. After a short while we were fitted with a coal burning stove, similar to the present day Aga. The only snag was that we had to coal ship and take down the chimney whilst at sea on operations and erect it when we came back into harbour. There were advantages in being cook: I had 'galley slaves' peeling potatoes, mess deck dodgers washing up the greasy dishes and,

15

best of all, no watchkeeping in harbour. I particularly remember baking bread—it never did rise all that well but was always eaten with gusto by the crew!

At Sea

At sea during the first eighteen months of my service on 318 was perhaps the most instructive and rewarding. Under the guidance of Petty Officer Boyle I took over as his relief on the 'wheel', and, being on the bridge where the 'conning' of the boat took place, I was always in a position to know just what was happening at any given time. Usually the Coxswain would take 318 out of harbour and take part of the first two-hour watch, generally from 1800 to 2000 hours. I would then take over from 2000 to 2200 hours by which time we would be in mid English Channel. The Coxswain would then take the 2200 to 2400 and by this time 'action stations' would be sounded and all the crew would be called to their station. I would normally take over as bridge look-out. We would do our landings or observations and, as soon as we were outside enemy territorial waters, we would revert to normal watchkeeping procedure, two hours on and two hours off. It was a pretty taxing and tiring routine, particularly if your harbour duties happened to be cook of the mess, and cooking breakfast and preparation for a mid-day meal had to follow on after the two-hour early morning watchkeeping routine.

Aground on the First Clandestine Operation

The first clandestine operation 318 was involved in entailed contacting members of the Dutch underground on enemy territory and bringing them back to the UK. It was at the end of 1941 or early 1942. This particular night everything appeared to be going according to plan: we made landfall and used the pre-determined lamp signal and awaited a reply. Nothing happened, so the Skipper decided to move along the coastline and check the 'plot' with his navigator. Still no success—and then it happened. There was an almighty shudder (though we couldn't have been steaming at more than five knots)—we had run aground! Consternation was rife and immediately the Skipper ordered full astern

16

on the single engine which was silenced by the 'dumb flow', a device which worked on the same principle as a car silencer: but we were firmly stuck on a sandbank and didn't budge.

Unfortunately for us we had gone aground at about half an hour before high tide, so as the night progressed the tide receded and we took a list of about 30 degrees to port. It was now a time for waiting and preparing for the next high tide which was due at about 0530 hours.

Looking back after fifty years, we appeared to be kept busy. First of all we were ordered to pump out the water tanks. I have since discovered they contained 350 gallons. All the ammunition for the two pounder pom-pom, 0.5" and .303 which was stowed in the for'ard magazine was brought on deck and placed amidships on the starboard side, and ready to jettison over the side. We launched the dinghy, unlashed the ship's anchor, all in preparation to help to pull the ship off the sandbank. Our 'Sparks' had the honour of dismantling most of his radio equipment ready to dump over the side.

When all these preparation were complete the Coxswain persuaded the Skipper to give the order 'splice the mainbrace': a tot in the early hours of the morning with a cold damp mist swirling around the boat was a tonic indeed—we were ready for anything—though I must admit the possibility of being a POW didn't occur to me at that moment.

Dawn came, the tide rose, we could just make out cars and lorries passing by on the occupied coast road. First of all we tried our kedge anchor with all the crew heaving in unison on the grass rope, but this was to no avail—we were firmly stuck! Next we tried rocking the boat. The first lieutenant stood on the meat locker amidships and at his signal all the crew who were congregated on the starboard side rushed over to the port as one man. This performance, hilarious if we could see ourselves now, was repeated for the best part of half an hour. Next we started the silent engine and, revving up to maximum torque in astern gear, all the crew tugged on the grass rope but still we didn't budge an inch. Finally, in desperation and fear of capture, the decision was taken to start the remaining two engines; the noise broke the silence of daybreak, the seagulls, their peace shattered, squawked and rose into the morning sky from the beach in unison. With apprehension we tugged on the rope, praying that the tension would ease and we would be free of our bond at last. At the eleventh hour, with all three engines at maximum revolutions, we finally felt movement; the sand was churning in a mixture of boiling sea water under our stern. We slipped noisily from our bondage amidst a great cheer, and a course for home and safety was ordered on the bridge.

With no radio contact with our base at Great Yarmouth and a mountainous sea running we finally made visual contact with the English coastline, south of Yarmouth, in the late afternoon and as dusk began to fall we entered the harbour mouth to be greeted by the Senior Officer of the Base who had been hurriedly informed of our arrival. He freely admitted to have given us up as lost. Our screw drive shafts were twisted. The seamen were the lucky ones to have seven days leave; but the chief motor mechanic and his stokers stayed behind to oversee the repairs.

Whilst this operation was an utter disaster, the Skipper was lucky to save his ship and this operation must have influenced the SO to agree to the transfer of 318 to start the formation of the 15th MGB Flotilla for future clandestine operation from a permanent base at Dartmouth, Devon.

On our way to form the 15th MGB Flotilla

After spending a pretty awful winter with snow, ice and gales on the East Coast, it was a relief to hear we were going to Dartmouth, Devon to form up with another flotilla; in fact we with MA/SB 36 were the 15th MGB Flotilla. We were shortly to be joined by MGB 501 whose service with the 15th was unfortunately shortlived. She was commissioned from Camper & Nicholsons yard, Gosport in April 1942. Her CO was the then Lieutenant Duncan Curtis, DSC and her 1st Lieutenant was Jan Mason, a South African who eventually became CO of 318.

In the words of Ken Davidson a crew member of 501:

> We arrived at Dartmouth during May 1942 and tied up alongside the *Killoran*, a name well known to the 15th Flotilla which was formed later that year. During our time at Dart-

18

mouth we enjoyed the company of MGB 318 and MA/SB 36. Unfortunately this all came to an abrupt end at midday on 27 July 1942 when midway between Lands End and the Scillies she, for no apparent reason, blew up and sank. Fortunately we were in the company of 318 and 36 who soon picked up survivors and landed them at Newlyn, Cornwall. It was a short but happy commission lasting 110 days; 501 I believe was destined to become flotilla leader of the 15th had she survived.

With Paddy Boyle on the bridge of 318, I witnessed the explosion aboard 501, steaming ahead of us with 36 between. Paddy turned to me and said, 'How many do you think have been killed?'

I replied, 'Perhaps three or four.'

He said, 'Could be five or six.'

We launched our dinghy and brought survivors aboard and fortunately no one was killed or missing. There were broken bones, and many ratings suffered burns caused by the explosion and the galley fire. For the second time since I joined 318 the Coxswain persuaded the Skipper to 'splice the mainbrace', for the injured and survivors of 501 of course! By the time we arrived in Newlyn harbour the uninjured were having a 'whale of a time' and were reluctant to leave 318.

Heavily armed

Though 318 was heavily armed for her size, when we were on agent dropping and retrieval operation in occupied Europe, the Commanding Officer had strict orders not to open fire except in extreme circumstances of self defence. As demand increased we were joined by MGBs 502 and 503, boats of the same class as 501, more than doubling the capabilities of the 15th Flotilla; also joining us for a short time was MGB 718, a 'D' class boat commanded by Lieutenant Ron Seddon supported by Sub Lieutenant Guy Hamilton and Pilot John Townend. When the 15th Flotilla was fully formed the Senior Officer was Lieutenant Commander Peter Williams, DSC, and the director of the operations and liaison with Captain Frank A. Slocum was Commander E. A. G. (Ted) Davis, DSO and Bar, RNR.

Many boats have been named as participants in the clandestine operations and the 15th Flotilla at Dartmouth but I have no knowledge of them. At a later stage of these operations we were joined by a couple of American PT boats but I cannot rate their success.

Our Bay of Biscay Contacts

More than the normal activity surrounded 318 when she was ordered to Falmouth where we took on board fifty gallon petrol drums on the upper deck and the dockyard staff came aboard and fitted extra loud hailers to the bridge and mast. Buzzes abounded on the mess deck— 'What, where and when?' We loaded cases of revolver ammunition and small arms, coffee, soap, cigarettes, tobacco, rum and boxes of leaflets packed in cylindrical cardboard containers. When all this was completed we made passage from Falmouth around the headland to the Helford River where we knew the 'French type fishing boats' attached to the DDOD (1) organization were at anchor.

From one of these boats we took on board two French army officers, immaculately dressed with their distinctive headgear. We cast off and made course for the Scilly Isles at an economical speed, excited by the prospects of the operation to hand. On arrival at the port of St Mary's we proceeded to replenish the boat's six fuel tanks from the quayside—this was a time-consuming and boring job using hand pumps to make the transfer.

Fully victualled and fuelled, complete with a full crew, an extra navigating officer and two Frenchmen, we set sail on what proved to be a rewarding round trip to the Bay of Biscay over a period of 2½ days and nights. With the galley fire out we survived on ship's biscuits marked 'Spratts' and cheese with bully beef, bread and tinned soup, which we heated up by lighting a central cylinder which was primed and when lit created tremendous heat down the centre of the tin and thereby provided hot soup which was our only means of a hot drink.

The object of this operation was to contact as many Breton fishing boats as possible whose port was Brest or in the surrounding area, to warn them that within the next fourteen days Brest would be subject to a massive air raid by the Royal Air Force on the dock installations and shipping in the harbour and advising the civilian population by means of these leaflets to evacuate Brest. Whilst every endeavour would be made to pin-point the harbour area some bombs would inevitably go astray and other areas would be hit. We contacted several fishing vessels. The fishermen were offered passage to England to fight the war on behalf of the Free French but volunteers were thin on the ground; in fact we didn't bring anyone back. We discharged the small arms and ammunition, the leaflets and all the creature comforts we had brought and gave them to the fishermen, and they in turn gave us four large tuna fish each measuring three feet in length! We tied these to the guard rail for our next hot meal! The 'recce' was completed with no brush with the enemy; we had only one scare when the motor mechanic reported we were almost out of fuel which caused consternation on the bridge and it was back to the drawing board. How could they have miscalculated? Fortunately, after further consultation the motor mechanic reported with a red face he had found that one tank hadn't been switched on!

'Splice the Mainbrace'

For the third time in a period of twelve months, Paddy Boyle our Coxswain persuaded the Skipper, Lieutenant Charles (Pincher) Martin, DSC, that the crew were deserving an extra 'tot' the day we berthed in Plymouth harbour after a harrowing experience at the end of one of our clandestine operations to the L'Aber Vrac'h, Brittany, on the north coast of France.

On our return from the operation we ran into a force seven gale in mid-Channel; the mountainous seas and gale force winds coming from the south-east and the tide against our course pushed us westwards so instead of reaching our home port of Dartmouth we made landfall west of Bigbury Bay. I was taking the early morning watch on the 'wheel' and the Coxswain was taking a rest in his cabin below when the Skipper realised that to avoid running aground in Wembury Bay he would have to change course, bringing the boat round on a new westerly heading. The Skipper explained to me what he intended doing and gave me precise instructions that at his command I must immediately put the wheel over to 'hard-a-port' and as soon as the boat

21

responded to the rudder I was to steady her on a new course of 30 degrees to port. A suitable wave and trough appeared, the command was given and 'hard-a-port' ordered. The boat shuddered, she started to come round and then appeared to stop and with an almighty crash heeled over at an angle of about 50 degrees. Everyone on the mess deck in the bunks on the starboard side of the ship was literally thrown out onto either the mess deck tables or the deck.

The Coxswain was on the bridge post-haste and raved at me with a mouthful of choice words and told me in no uncertain terms, never to take on such a manoeuvre again without first calling him! The sequel to this tale came ten minutes later when the steering hydraulics collapsed under the strain and we had to rig the hand steering from the stern of the boat and orders from the bridge were given by word of mouth.

So ended an operation with a sting in the tail—and with the mainbrace spliced once more!!

Able Seaman Harold Pickles, DSM

FAIRMILE 'C' M.G.B. 318

The L'Aber-Vrac'h Saga

The furthest west of our pin-points and, to my mind, by far the most difficult to reach[1] from the French mainland and from seawards was a minute islet—a patch of coarse green grass edged by craggy outcrops in the L'Aber Vrac'h Estuary. Ile Guennoc was a mere three hundred yards long and a hundred yards wide, inhabited only by seabirds, at the landward end of the rock-fringed L'Aberbenoit Channel—over a mile in length and, in places, less than a hundred yards wide. The whole area was flat and completely unprotected from the south-west winds blowing in from the Atlantic, often reaching gale force in an alarmingly short time.

The first indication of approaching land, if luck was on our side, was a sudden lessening of the echo-soundings as the MGB passed over the western tip of the Le Libenter bank and then, with more luck, the appearance of La Petite Fourche Buoy marking the seaward end of the L'Aberbenoit Channel—left there by the Germans to guide local fishing boats, though night fishing was not allowed. From the buoy, the gunboat had to wend its way, often with breaking water on either side, to the rendezvous anchorage a few hundred yards off the south-west tip of Ile Guennoc.

Access to and from the Finisterre mainland at Presque-Sainte-Marguerite was by boat from Ile Guennoc for the six hundred metres to the neighbouring islet Tariec, and then by foot across a sandbar a mile and a half wide which was uncovered for a short time at low water. Three enemy Coastal Defence Batteries commanded an uninterrupted view of Ile Guennoc, Tariec and their approaches to the mainland

---

1 It was 110 miles from Falmouth—the furthest of our pin-points from England—and under favourable conditions took six or seven hours steaming time. The double journey plus waiting time off the pin-point could take up to twenty-five hours if conditions were foul as on Envious IIB or Felicitate I.

24

whose foreshore was heavily mined, while a horizontally beamed searchlight on Ile Vierge swept an arc over the whole operation area.

Seven sorties were made to that inhospitable spot.

It was on the night of 3 November 1943 that the first of five sorties expressly for the evacuation of escaping Allied airmen from the uninhabited islet of Ile Guennoc off the Finisterre coast took place. The first three were code-named 'Envious', and the last two 'Felicitate'. In addition to the 'bodies' there was a considerable amount of top-secret mail from all over occupied Europe to be collected and brought back to England. Two earlier sorties in March and April code-named 'Cook' had taken place in that area but those were for landing stores and an agent, and getting accustomed to the area.

Fifteen airmen were awaiting rescue on 3 November—but it was not until the early hours of Boxing Day, after four unsuccessful attempts, that the evacuation was successfully completed. By that time the fifteen had swelled to twenty-eight, and the suitcase of mail had increased to the extent that a horse and cart had to be used to transport it to the island across the mile of sand for a short time at low water.

If ever a series of sorties by the 15th MGB Flotilla reflected every aspect of Clandestine Sea Operations, surely 'Cook', 'Envious' and 'Felicitate' would be hard to beat for disappointments, bad liaison between the French and British secret organizations, filthy weather, and near disasters, all made up for in the end (from our point of view) by complete success.

But to start at the beginning and on the French side.

In the area around Brest and inland from L'Aber-Vrac'h there was, by early 1943, a most efficient network of Resistance workers dedicated to returning to England Allied airmen on the run in France—including many Americans. The chief of the group was Paul Hentic, alias 'Mao', his assistant was Pierre Jeanson, alias 'Sarol' and their radio operator, code named 'Jeannot'. With the aid of numerous local helpers, they collected, housed, fed, transported and finally conducted the escapers to either Ile Guennoc or Ile Tariec from where they would return to England. 'Mao', 'Sarol', 'Jeannot' and many others of this heroic team were caught by the Gestapo after the Christmas Day

25

Operation, tortured and met their deaths in concentration camps. The group was, I believe, denounced by a former member known as 'La Chatte' early in 1944 who, having double-crossed the Resistance, imagined that she could become a double agent working for the Germans and the British. The British counter-espionage was fully aware of her intended dual role; she was brought over to England by the 15th Flotilla and spent the rest of the war in Holloway Prison. In 1945 she was returned to France to stand trial as a collaborator, convicted and sentenced to death which was commuted to life imprisonment. After serving a few years she was freed for some unknown reason. However, terrified of reprisals from those of the group still living, she retreated to a convent where she remains to this day.

The method of repatriating escapers by 'Mao' and his group was fraught with dangers. Allied airmen from far afield were brought to Landerneau railway station in the care of an agent who had boarded the Paris-Brest Express at Rennes. On disembarking, they were taken over by members of the group, assisted by the station staff who were sympathetic to the Resistance. From there they were distributed to 'safe-houses' in Landerneau and surrounding villages or taken by car to Brest where underground board and lodging was available. Then began the nerve-racking wait for sea transport to England and the really tricky part of the operation.

The whole area around L'Aber-vrac'h was alive with willing helpers and in particular the villages of Kernilis, Plougerneau, Treglonou, Coar-meal, Landeda, and the market town of Lannilis; this coastal region was also well patrolled by the Germans. Help took the form of transport by vans, cars and even horse-drawn carts, meals and accommodation, and a rowing boat with oarsmen for the final six hundred metres of swirling water between Ile Tariec and Ile Guennoc when that was the chosen rendezvous.

Lannilis was the advance headquarters of the escape organizers and here, in an attic above Amedée Rolland's café in the main square where German soldiers were frequent customers, 'Mao', 'Sarol' and 'Jeannot' would crouch on the night of a sortie from England, tapping out messages to London and anxiously awaiting the replies which came as coded messages in French at the end of the BBC's overseas news bulletins.

Operation Envious: 3–4 November 1943

It was decided by DDOD(I) to send MGB 318 to the L'Aber Vrac'h area on the night of 3 November 1943, in response to a request by the local Resistance group, to collect agents and land boxes of stores, ammunition, radio sets, etc. The pin-point advised to MGB 318 was to be Ile Rosservor, another insignificant and uninhabited islet two miles westward of Ile Guennoc.

There was a misunderstanding between London and the Resistance Headquarters in Lannilis regarding the pin-point, the latter thinking that Ile Guennoc (not Ile Rosservor) was the chosen site and that the operation was to collect fifteen Allied escaping airmen and some highly important top-secret mail—which included details of the V1 and V2 launch sites. This misunderstanding was, to say the least of it, unfortunate for all concerned.

Thus it was at 16.47 on the night of 3 November, MGB 318 slipped from the Coastlines wharf at Falmouth en route for Ile Rosservor— while at the Brittany end during the afternoon of the 3rd, fifteen airmen with their guides had at low water crossed the sandy bar between the mainland at Presque-Sainte-Marguerite and Ile Tariec. This mile-long journey was fraught with dangers, for it was completely overlooked by three enemy coastal defence batteries, and mined above the high water line. Disguised as shellfish gatherers and with their hearts in their mouths they arrived without mishap at Ile Tariec, trying to appear unhurried and intent on gathering their harvest in buckets—knowing that German binoculars were trained on them. A rowing boat was waiting on Tariec to ferry the party across the swiftly flowing stream to Ile Guennoc, and there the fifteen airmen were left by their guides—who had to get back to the mainland before the rising tide covered the sand bar—to await the arrival of MGB 318.

Paul Hentic, in overall charge of the rescue, having deposited the airmen on Ile Guennoc, returned to Lannilis to await developments, and he with his assistant 'Sarol' and his radio operator 'Jeannot', installed themselves in their attic hideout in the café.

The arrangement with London was that at 18.00 hours 'Jeannot' would broadcast the following message: 'Les faux-cols de Georges Henri sont prêts chez la blanchisseuse' and that if the operation was 'on', London would repeat the message after the BBC's Overseas News bulletin at 19.15 hours. They were therefore delighted when, at the appointed time, the BBC's message, read by Bruce Belfridge, confirmed that the operation was to take place.

In fact, at 19.15 hours MGB 318 was already an hour and one minute *en route* from her departure position four miles south of the Lizard, heading South 5° East at a speed of 16 knots bound for Ile Rosservor. At that time, the weather was good: a south-west wind force 3-4, producing a slight to moderate sea and swell—enough to confuse the German surface radar detectors and enough to make me seasick. Best of all, the sky was overcast, which cut down the likelihood of phosphorescence—always a danger on starry nights. Commander Ted Davis was in overall charge of the operation, Charles Martin in command of 318, Tassy Uhr-Henry dinghy officer in charge of the landing party, Petty Officer Mould coxswain of the MGB, and I responsible for navigation. All our hopes were running high until 19.00 hours the centre engine started spluttering and a quarter of an hour later stopped from fuel starvation. From that moment onwards until we reached harbour the next morning, one of the crew had to pump the petrol by hand. By 20.00 hours the sudden appearance of very low cloud and drizzle greatly reduced visibility and two hours later it had become definitely misty.

At 22.25 hours, engines were silenced to pass over the German Coastal Convoy route twenty miles off the coast, but we kept up our speed as the landing of the heavy cases would take up precious time—and time was something of which there was never enough.

Twenty minutes later we had reached our first alter course position to counteract the coastal tide stream.

'South 10 East,' I called up the bridge voice pipe.

'South 10 East it is,' Charles replied, 'and we bloody well can't see a yard ahead.'

28

Very bad visibility was always a worry when the MGB was approaching the rock-infested Breton coast, but I'd done my homework thoroughly so there was no point worrying; anyway the QH was giving one position line which added to my confidence.

'How long on this course,' asked Ted, 'until we reduce speed at 23.14?'

'At 23.13,' I warned, 'reduce speed to 1000 r.p.m. in one minute and alter course to South 20 East'—a large alteration.

We were now on the final approach at 10 knots and relying to a large extent on the echo-sounder. At 23.35 it packed up, closely followed by the QH set. By midnight I had calculated we should have been within sight of Le Relee—a rock which I was using as a sea mark, being a mile from Rosservor. At 23.55 I was rewarded by a shout from the bridge that white breakers were 200 yards ahead on the port bow. 'Thank you,' I replied, 'that will be Le Relee. When it's abeam, stop and I'll have a shot at the echo-sounder.' At 23.59 we stopped and I managed to get intermittent soundings after tightening one of the leads.

'All right,' I called up, 'on we go. Slow ahead on wings course South 80 West for twelve minutes and we should be a quarter of a mile off Rosservor.'

At 8 knots, MGB 318 started nosing towards the land and I went up onto the bridge. Visibility was down to two hundred yards or less as the patchy mist swirled around the gunboat. At 00.10 the mist cleared for a second and an island became vaguely visible a quarter of a mile ahead—then the blanket came down again. We anchored and Tassy and his crew went in a dinghy to identify the island; they were back in under an hour, verifying that the island was indeed Rosservor—but no one was waiting. So back they went in two dinghies with the boxes which were duly landed and hidden in rocky crannies and behind stones. At 02.45 Tassy and the two rowing dinghies returned, and by 03.06, as the mist was clearing, we were *en route* for home.

Close to Le Relee an FH 830 position-finding buoy was dropped and a course North 11° East was set for the Lizard and speed increased—seventeen minutes later two enemy flack trawlers appeared dead ahead about a mile away. As the official report later recounted, 'the second trawler was well astern and a beautiful target for us, but as we were so close inshore, it was decided to pass the opportunity as it would undoubtedly look peculiar for an enemy vessel to come sauntering out of the rocks to attack, and so near our own rendezvous. We stopped engines and gave them the honour of crossing our bows, then we went gently ahead and altered course around the second trawler's stern. The failure of navigational aids was terrifying ...'

We arrived back at Falmouth at 10.00 in the morning after a disappointing night.

If we were disappointed, how can one gauge the frustration of the fifteen airmen awaiting rescue two miles away on Ile Guennoc. At midnight they had heard, and even thought they'd seen, an MGB in the misty morning westwards, and had frantically flashed torches in her direction, but to no avail.

On the morning of 4 November, 'Mao' and his group returned quickly to Lannilis and that night tried in vain to establish contact with London by radio. By 5 November it was obvious that the airmen had at least to be provided with food and water. This was done at considerable risk during the afternoon, in full view of the German look-outs and once more 'Mao' and his group became seaweed and shellfish gatherers. The stricken airmen—starving, freezing and sopping wet—fell on the food. But in spite of protests, they had to remain where they were in case a rendezvous could be arranged for the night of the 6th. Contact with London was not possible, and on 7 November 'Mao' decided that the fifteen airmen must be brought back to the mainland at all costs. That night they were evacuated from Ile Guennoc with all the symptoms of wild animals, starving and unshaven, and were distributed over the countryside to await another rescue attempt in place of the one that had gone so wrong.

Operation Envious II A—26–27 November 1943

Another rescue attempt by MGB could not be made until the beginning of the next non-moon period, which was the night of 26 November. Once again MGB 318 set off from Falmouth at about the same time as on 'Envious'. Ted Davis was in overall command, Charles Martin commanding MGB 318, P/O Mould coxswain, Tassy Uhr-Henry in charge of the dinghies, and I as navigator. We collected the SOE agent from a launch off the Helford River. The weather across the Channel was reasonable, though the long westerly swell made several of us extremely sick, including SOE's agent, whom we were to land on the Breton mainland after collecting the escaping airmen from Ile Guennoc. Surprisingly, 318's engines worked without a murmur, and we were able to maintain a speed of about 18 knots.

At 21.27 engines were silenced, and soon after, search-lights lit up the sky and the French coast glowed from numerous lights in the L'Aber-Vrac'h area—ours not to reason why. At 22.27, about twenty minutes offshore, we reduced to 12½ knots for the convoy route, then half an hour later to about 10 knots for the final approach. Being slightly too far to port, we found ourselves in an awkward position among the Grande Fourche Rocks and went into as quick a reverse as possible.

At 23.32 we saw the Petite Fourche Buoy looming ahead out of the drizzle which had started at about the time of our encounter with the rocks. Down the L'Aberbenoit Channel we crawled, anchored off Ile Guennoc at midnight and launched the dinghies. An hour and a quarter later they returned with the news that Ile Guennoc was deserted; a minute later a white Very light was fired from one of the islands, illuminating a mile or more of foreshore. We wasted no time in moving from such a conspicuous spot, up anchored and crept up the L'Aberbenoit Channel back to the buoy. Here we turned to port for Le Relee rock and our previous anchorage off Rosservor. Le Relee appeared dramatically and iceberg-like out of the mist a few yards away and we turned south-west to the Rosservor anchorage. At 02.22, 318 anchored and the seasick but otherwise cheerful agent was rowed ashore on the Ile du Bec. At 03.15 we were on our way back to Falmouth—at 06.00 the usual engine troubles began and the weather started to deteriorate, so it was not until midday that we arrived back in port after twenty hours at sea. At least the agent had been landed, but the non-appearance of the escapers on Ile Guennoc remained a mystery.

Operation Envious II B: 1–2 December 1943

From the French account, no arrangement had been made to collect the airmen on the night of the 26th—in fact 'Mao' and 'Sarol' were travelling down from Paris on that day to make arrangements for a new rescue bid by MGB 318 on 1 December. They were, as usual, met at Landerneau off the Paris-Brest train. Transport, arranged by the Lannilis policeman, 'Derrien', was waiting to take the airmen to safe houses. By 27 November, all was arranged locally and with DDOD(1) for the night of 1 December—land transport for the airmen and a flat-bottomed boat and boatman to ferry them the six hundred metres between Tariec and Ile Guennoc.

On the afternoon of the 1st, all fifteen airmen assembled at Landeda about two miles from Tariec; then, in small groups, some carrying long handled pitchforks, they moved off to the pin-point headed by 'Mouden', 'Mao', 'Person' and Rolland Coum. They had to cross a fairly wide minefield before reaching the shore; in addition to barbed wire covering the area, pickets and lookout posts seemed to be everywhere. Nevertheless, this ill-assorted group were guided past the obstacles and onto the beach. From now on the airmen and their guides had to become seaweed gatherers or shell collectors and this ordeal, under the scrutiny of the German lookouts, lasted until they reached Tariec a mile and a quarter across the sand. Later that afternoon, 'Mao' and 'Jeannot' were installed once more in Roland Amedée's attic in Lannilis, tapping out the message: *'Le Loing est une rivière rapide'*, at intervals of an hour. After the second transmission, London sent the eagerly awaited reply on the 21.15 GMT BBC News bulletin: *'Le Loing est une rivière rapide.'* 'Mao' and'Jeannot' clasped each other's hands: the operation was 'on' and MGB 318 had already left. They allowed themselves a thanksgiving drink in the bar below and 'Mao' set off for Tariec again to join the airmen, and to ensure that all would go according to plan. As the rendezvous had been fixed for Ile Guennoc, 'Mao' set off for Tariec in a single-seater canoe at about 00.30 to intercept the MGB and pass on the news that the airmen were on Tariec, but soon he was in bad trouble owing to the rising wind and heavy surf. After an hour of being lost, he suddenly saw a distant red light flashing through the spray. With supreme effort he paddled furiously towards it and finally, exhausted, landed on Tariec to find the gunboat's dinghies already there. The time was 02.22.

At 16.00 on the evening of 1 December, MGB 318 had slipped from the coastline wharf at Falmouth and, after passing the boom defence ship at the harbour mouth, set course westwards towards the Helford River. It had been decided by DDOD(1), in view of the number of escapers involved, to co-opt another gunboat, MGB 329 (CO Lieutenant Fanner) for one operation only, so we had company.

Off the Helford River we rendezvoused with an SOE launch and took on board stores, including sweets for the children and ammunition for the French. At 17.03 we took our departure as usual from the D3 buoy four miles off the South Lizard and headed for Brittany and Ile Guennoc. Ted Davis was in command of the operation, Charles Martin CO of 318, Michael Pollard First Lieutenant, Tassy Uhr-Henry in charge of the landing dinghies, and myself as navigator.

The wind, which on departure had been force 4, produced a moderate sea, but by the time we were half-way across the Channel it had increased to a south-westerly force 5. 318 was plunging into it and as usual the sea was dousing her from bow to stern; 329 was behaving in much the same way, and I was not by any means the only one being violently sick.

It was not until 23.45 that La Petite Fourche Buoy was seen. As we proceeded slowly down the L'Aberbenoit Channel, it was noticed with consternation that 329 was nowhere in sight; it was not the kind of night to spend searching for a gunboat with white water breaking around us on the half-submerged rocks which line the Channel. Fortunately 329 was spotted in the blackness of an exceptionally dark night making straight for the Grande Fourche Rocks—the radio telephone had to be brought into action and quickly too. At last, with 329 following astern, we reached the pin-point off Ile Guennoc, and at eight minutes past midnight we dropped anchor with 329 following suit. The wind and swell were now becoming awkward, our anchor started dragging and we were in imminent danger of getting tangled with our sister ship.

Finally, at 00.25 the three dinghies left for Ile Guennoc—Lieutenant Uhr-Henry in the first with two ratings, Sub Lieutenant Pollard in the second, also with two ratings, and the Coxswain of 329 and one seaman in the third in line ahead and each carrying crates of stores.

At 00.45 Lieutenant Henry reported on the walkie-talkie that, though he had combed Ile Guennoc, there was no sign of life but that he could see a flashing red light on Tariec. He was told to investigate and twenty-five minutes later announced that there were twenty escapers ready and waiting. He was told to unload the stores and get back to the MGB as fast as possible in view of the deteriorating weather.

In the rolling chartroom I noticed that the barometer was racing downwards, and at 02.00 a violent squall of wind and rain hit us. At the same time a radio message had been received from England saying: 'Weather deteriorating rapidly, gale force 6–7 approaching your area.' This message was of academic interest, for the wind had already increased to force 6 and was howling through the rigging; great waves rolling in from the Atlantic were smashing themselves onto the reefs and rocks around us; the sea was a mass of foam and our engines had to be started to take the strain off the anchor cable. It was a most awe-inspiring and frightening sight. MGB 329 was having her own troubles and at one ghastly moment she managed to foul our anchor cable with her propellers.

At 02.20 Lieutenant Henry reported that all three dinghies with twenty escapers were starting back to the mother ships. From that moment onwards, no further word was heard over the walkie-talkie and the sea was getting worse every minute.

At 03.35 our already tense nerves were jangled further by all 318's gun-buzzers blaring out in unison and the navigation lights switching themselves on, having short-circuited from inundations of sea water and pelting rain. The wires had to be cut to stop the noise and extinguish the lights.

At 04.18 it was decided that we could wait no longer as dawn was not all that distant, for not only would everyone get caught, but the pin-point would be compromised for ever if the Germans spotted us at our unlikely anchorage. With heavy hearts we up-anchored and began a slow turn northwards. At that moment, one of the dinghies was sighted astern. She was making no progress at all and heavy seas were breaking over her. We dropped astern towards the helpless boat and the reef which she had negotiated—a line was thrown but the wind hurled it back. Scrambling nets were lowered as the gunboat and dinghy bumped into each other. All available hands on 318 dragged the men out and finally pulled the sinking boat on board, while every second the reef got closer.

It could hardly have been classed as a success, yet it might have been worse—seven out of twenty escapers rescued, Lieutenant Henry and his two oarsmen safe. Thirteen escapers, two agents and five sailors left behind, and two dinghies wrecked.

At 04.50 MGB 318 started up the L'Aberbenoit Channel on the long slog to England, and, looking back at Tariec, a red lamp was seen flashing from the island indicating that those left behind were safe. Then followed a nightmarish return journey in the worst possible weather.

It was not until 05.30 with the sky starting to lighten in the east that we were clear of the French mainland; and then the MGB was caught in the full force of the wind and sea. In my log book I wrote: 'Wind west-south-west force 7, sea very rough, heavy and confused swell, sea covered with streaks of foam.' The movements of a small flat-bottomed over-top-hampered ship in such conditions almost defies description—suffice it to say that seasickness was the least of our worries. We altered our course to the east parallel with the French coast to avoid being rolled over by a beam sea.

By 09.30 and in full daylight we were still only thirty miles from the Breton coast and making good a mere 8 or 9 knots. Crisis was in the air for, among other hazards, neither MGB had enough fuel to carry on in that way for too long (i.e. making no headway homewards), and the rolling of the MGBs, which was estimated at the time to be in the region of 50°, was causing worry. Lashings parted and heavy objects started rocketing across the deck—the chart room became chaotic and I had to wedge myself against the chart table to remain

35

on two feet. The table was an indescribable mess of rusty water cascading down the voice pipe from the bridge, sick, and blood from the bashings of my head against every kind of projection. At such times, with pulpy charts slithering in every direction, parallel rulers careering madly across the table and onto the deck, pencils and notes flying through the air, navigation was to say the least a tricky problem.

At 10.00 the wind veered slightly so the opportunity was taken to alter course northwards and bash our way home. At that moment four unidentifiable fighters swept out of the mist and spray, creating further worries. Action stations were manned but the fighters didn't reappear.

To conserve fuel, one engine was cut and on we plodded, more like a semi-submerged submarine than an MGB, with personnel on the bridge hanging onto the side rails and their legs clear of the deck. From now on, starboard and port engines competed with each other for stopping.

It was not until 17.20 that 318 and 329 were secured alongside the jetty in Falmouth harbour. Twenty-five hours continuous for all on board both MGBs in extremely rough conditions without a break of any sort; sadness at having left two dinghies and their occupants behind; but at least we felt we had done our best with all odds against us—and undoubtedly we would have another shot at it.

'Mao' had arrived in Tariec soaked to the skin and completely exhausted from his superhuman canoeing efforts at precisely the same time as the three dinghies from the MGBs with their cargoes of food and equipment. But the return journey to the MGBs with twenty passengers was a very different undertaking. Even getting the escapers on board the dinghies was difficult enough, with the boats rolling and pitching against the reef-fringed island.

The crossing from Tariec to Ile Guennoc was dangerous at night, even for the local fishermen who knew the whereabouts of all the submerged rocks and were well acquainted with the fierce current which runs between them. For the dinghy crews on that stormy night the crossing was a nightmare. Only one (as has been told) reached the gunboat in the nick of time as its bung was knocked out on a rock and Tassy Uhr-Henry had to stuff his naval cap into the hole to stop it from sinking. Of the other two boats, one capsized, and the other was smashed against the rocks. Remarkably, there were no fatal casualties and all the passengers and dinghy crews managed to scramble and swim to Tariec, where, battered and bruised, they had to spend that night.

Thus on the morning of 2 December the score was seven escapers *en route* for England, leaving fifteen airmen and agents behind, plus the crews of the two ill-fated dinghies (four ratings and one officer). The situation with which 'Mao' had to deal was still unchanged: twenty passengers—five new sailors, two agents, thirteen original airmen—for England.

Once more the mile and a half crossing of the sand between Tariec and Saint Marguerite had to be done during the morning of the 2nd, once more the refugees became seaweed gatherers and again the German look-outs did not challenge.

As a temporary refuge, the party was taken to the farm of Monsieur Le Guen, appropriately enough a seaweed gatherer, near Landeda. 'Sarol' and 'Derrien', waiting in Lannilis, were told of the mission's failure. 'Mao' was on his way to Brest. To everyone's consternation the Germans had found one of the wrecked dinghies and had put up road blocks on all roads leading from Saint Marguerite: thus only 'Derrien', because he was a policeman, could reach Le Guen's farm. Eventually the refugees were guided across fields to Landeda, where Claude Tanguy's van was waiting to take the sailors to his home in Lannilis and the remainder on to Brest.

Operation Felicitate I: 23–24 December 1943

'Mao', never daunted, immediately began arranging another rendez-vous with London, and a new attempt was fixed for the night of 23–24 December. On the 23rd, Claude Tanguy, in his lorry, picked up 'Mao','Sarol', 'Person', the shipwrecked sailors, the airmen, and 'Jeannot' and 'Pierrot'—the radio operators of the group. They all got off at Bel Air in Landeda from where they were to be guided by Guillaume Le Guen, Louis and François Coun to Tariec.

So much secret correspondence had accumulated since Operation Envious on 3–4 November that it had to be carried on a horse drawn cart guided by Amedée Rolland. Thus thirty-two people, divided into three groups each led by a Resistance member, set off from Landeda for Ile Tariec on the evening of 23 December.

For the first mile or so, to the beach at Toul-An-Dour, the party kept to cart tracks and fields, the only incident *en route* being a barking dog at a nearby farmhouse.

From Toul-An-Dour across the mile and a half stretch of sand to Ile Tariec was, as usual, the most dangerous part of the journey. The first obstacle was a newly laid minefield in the sand above the high water mark which had to be crossed. Each mine consisted of a canister of explosive buried under the sand with its detonator, three metal prongs, showing an inch above the surface. One of the leaders had watched the Germans laying them, so he volunteered to lead the column, bent double, passing his hand gently over the sand. His name: Guillaume Le Guen. The men followed in a long line, each holding onto the shoulder of the man in front, and thus they passed in safety through the danger.

Once through and onto the sand the groups reformed, and for the next mile and a half once more became seaweed gatherers—again under the noses of the German look-outs who manned the three observation posts guarding that stretch of beach. It seems quite amazing that the seaweed gathering fooled the Germans, who were now particularly on the alert since the Envious II B's dinghies had been found smashed on the beach.

When the party of thirty-two reached Ile Tariec in safety,'Jeannot', 'Mao's radio operator, started sending out the message: *Les Troenes sont en Fleurs*; London replied in usual way, indicating that the operation was 'on'. The weather seemed reasonable and hopes were very high. At 23.00 [2] contact was made with MGB 318 and the message came back over the walkie-talkie that the dinghies were on their way.

MGB 318, under the command of Jan Mason, with Tassy as dinghy

2   23.00 hours Central European Time used by the French = 01.00 GMT (actually 01.25 in my log
    book, but dinghies were not reported as *en route* until 02.15)

officer and myself as navigator, had slipped from Falmouth harbour at 16.00 on the evening of 23 December (with Lieutenant Commander Ray Guest of the US Navy as observer). At 17.27 the gunboat was at Lizard and a course of South 8° East was set for La Petite Fourche Buoy. The journey across was comparatively uneventful, though the swell was greater than forecast (easterly wind force 3, confused sea, moderate south-westerly swell) and sea sickness was rampant.

By 20.45, visibility had become bad owing to a continuous drizzle and the QH position-finding equipment was again giving us trouble. Courses were altered several times and at 21.25 engines were silenced for crossing the coastal convoy route. At 00.40 La Petite Fourche Buoy was sighted and our course was altered to South 3° West while speed was reduced to 8 knots. Thus we proceeded once more down the L'Aberbenoit Channel with an increasing wind and breaking water on each side. At 00.50 we anchored off Guennoc, but a quarter of an hour later the wind had increased to force 5 and trouble once again seemed to be imminent.

At 01.25 contact via walkie-talkie was established with the shore party, which reported that a dinghy landing was possible, though tricky. Thus encouraged, MGB 318 moved in closer to Ile Guennoc and dropped anchor. A few minutes later the anchor's grass line broke and a new anchor with a stronger line was dropped; luckily it held. At 02.15 (00.15 French time) the two dinghies, with Tassy Uhr-Henry in the first with his crew and the second in tow, left for Ile Guennoc. Five minutes later, owing to bad weather, 318's second anchor was lost and from then onwards position had to be maintained with the wing engines.

At 04.20, with wind and sea increasing in strength every minute and anxiety on board increasing similarly, Tassy reported that he was returning but could make no headway against the sea and swell. He was ordered to sink the dinghy he had in tow.

I shall never forget the next quarter of an hour. We could just see the dinghy struggling to reach the MGB—great waves were breaking over her and our passenger Ray Guest was shouting at the walkie-talkie, 'Pull, Tassy—for God's sake, pull! Good lad, Tassy—you'll make it—pull ...!'(as though Tassy had the inclination to use the radio at such a horrific time!). Tassy and his crew pulled for their lives as wave after wave broke over the sinking dinghy. By 04.38, Tassy and his crew had made it and were hauled aboard, battered and exhausted. It had been a very close shave indeed.

MGB 318, after a very rough and at times dangerous Channel crossing, tied up at Falmouth at 13.15 after twenty-one hours of shocks and horrors. I noted in my logbook, 'The entire ship's company had been extremely seasick.' Some had passed out, others had been injured, though all were grateful to have made it back to Falmouth. Worst of all, we had again failed to bring out the escapers. Every single man on board was resolved that next time we would succeed.

And next time came very soon indeed—just one day later.

Operation Felicitate II—25–26 December 1943

Christmas Day was cheerless, grey and depressing. All of us on board 318 felt dispirited with the disappointment of the previous day. Moreover we were dog-tired. As was usual at Christmas, a make and mend and a splicing of the mainbrace was the order of the day; in short, a day's rest for all Coastal Force craft in Falmouth harbour.

So officers and crew aboard the gunboat set about counteracting the general gloom. After our Christmas lunch, turkey and plum pudding, we all turned in for the afternoon to sleep off our over-indulgence.

At three o'clock it happened: a telephone call from London to say that the operation was 'on' again that night as weather reports were good. But operating conditions within the stomachs of our ship's company were less than favourable and even the toughest constitution quailed at the prospect of at least twenty hours tossing and rolling. But there it was. Jan Mason began preparing the ship for sea and I set about working out the night's courses.

And so it was that at ten minutes to four in the fading light of a Christmas afternoon, MGB 318 slipped unobtrusively from her moorings along Coastlines Wharf in Falmouth Harbour, and on the last of the ebb-tide nosed slowly and silently downstream towards the open sea. As the little ship—the only one at Falmouth on the move that

40

day—heard the boom defence vessel at the harbour mouth and turned westwards into the wind towards her departure position off the Lizard, she must have looked a very lonely speck against the dark background of a white-flecked leaden sea.

The ship's radio was at full blast until the moment we actually set course for France—Vera Lynn's voice rose from the mess deck with 'Yours' and 'We'll Meet Again' bringing a lump to my throat as it always did: '... but I know we'll meet again some sunny day.' Off the Manacle Rocks all guns were tested with a shattering roar, sending sea birds panicking high into the sky. On board there was a great feeling of optimism—Christmas Day—surely nothing would go wrong this time. I had even strung Christmas decorations across 318's chartroom.

We stopped off at the Helford River to pick up another boat crew (supplied by SOE) and a twenty-foot surf boat to add to the two ten-footers which we carried on board. This we towed to France.

At 17.42, with a north-westerly force 3 wind behind us and a starless sky, we took our departure from D3 buoy, increased speed to 15½ knots and turned South 5° East for Brittany.

Meanwhile in Lannilis, on the morning of 24 December, 'Mao' had sent off another message to London, asking for a return of 318 on Christmas night; he was delighted to receive confirmation that the MGB would try again. That evening, all thirty-two escapers gathered for a celebration party at the house of Mme. Paillier in Lannilis and after plenty of wine and food had been consumed, the strains of 'La Marseillaise' and 'It's a Long, Long Way to Tipperary' filled the house. The revellers ignored the fact that the Germans occupied a building close by. It was Christmas after all, and perhaps—perhaps— by the next night they would be on the way to England.

On the morning of the 25th, the message: 'Les Troenes sont en Fleures' was sent to London from Lannilis and the reply came back: 'Joel aura un an au mois de juin.' So Operation Felicitate II was 'on'. The assembly point as before was Bel Air at Landeda, and all the groups had arrived there by 20.30 hours (22.30 GMT) without mishap. The night was so dark that the leader of each group softly whistled

41

the tune of 'La Madelon' to establish their identities. Doctor de la Marnière had arrived with some escapers housed further afield—by ambulance, being the most likely transport to get through the German road-blocks. Everything worked like clockwork, and the thirty-two people in two groups reached Ile Tariec again without attracting the attention of the German look-outs.

At 23.34 GMT in a calm sea the watchers on Tariec saw MGB 318 drop anchor a few hundred yards away and contact was made via the walkie-talkie.

MGB 318 had had a trouble-free crossing: the weather was ideal and she had maintained a speed of 15½ knots. At 21.12 engines were silenced for crossing the convoy route and courses were altered to offset the coastal tide stream. Apart from a searchlight piercing the darkness ahead, nothing untoward had happened. At 23.00 land was sighted, and at 23.10 La Petite Fourche Buoy, with which we had all become so familiar, lay dead ahead. As Navigating Officer, I was elated that my courses had been on target.

A minute later we had altered course down the L'Aberbenoit Channel at a steady 10 knots, and had reached our anchorage after fourteen minutes, very close indeed to the southern tip to Ile Guennoc.

At 23.30 contact was made by walkie-talkie with the shore party and the three dinghies were quickly on their way to the island. They did two return trips, and by 01.52 the operation was completed, with thirty-two escapers and the load of mail safely on board.

The return journey to England in the early hours of Boxing Day gave everyone on board 318 a tremendous feeling of achievement and satisfaction: after five attempts, a success at last. We were all so happy that no one really cared that at 06.00 all three of the MGB's engines began spluttering and an hour later stopped altogether—twenty-five miles from England. By 08.00 we were underway again, and at 09.45 stopped off at the Helford River to transfer our night's takings to the motor launch from SOE's Helford base. Congratulations were in the air; we even earned a good mark from General Eisenhower, for the mail we brought back included detailed information about the V1 and V2 rocket sites.

By 10.50 it was all over, and MGB 318 slid back to her moorings in Falmouth harbour, creating as little interest as she had done on leaving the previous night. But what a night it had been. As the official report put it, 'This operation will long be remembered by those on board, not (only) because it took place on Christmas Day, but because of the smooth way in which the internal organization of the ship ran. All officers and men fulfilled their duties in a highly efficient manner.'

So ended the L'Aber-vrac'h Saga: seven sorties, the first on 28 March and the last on Christmas Day, to one of the most treacherous areas with which the 15th Flotilla was involved. This was to be the last operation in the area.

But for the Resistance workers, with the end of our visits to Ile Guennoc and Tariec, a disastrous period had begun.

The gallant 'Mao' (Paul Hentic) and Guillaume Le Guen started planning another escape operation for mid-January 1944, but on 6 January 'Mao' and his radio operator 'Jeannot' were arrested by the Gestapo in Paris, tortured by the Masuy-Fallot group at the Gestapo HQ in Avenue Henri-Martin, and deported to Dachau where they died.[3] The same fate befell 'Sarol' a few weeks later. Dr de la Marnière and his family were also caught, but after imprisonment and torture were eventually released.

The farmer Joseph Mouden who had guided escapers across the beach was also arrested and subjected to ghastly tortures by 'Shad', the Gestapo Chief at Saint Brieuc, and died during deportation of the savage wounds inflicted by his interrogators.

So ended the activities of a heroic group who, in spite of crushing disappointments, had laboured for the repatriation of British and American airmen against almost overwhelming odds. What a reward for heroism—and what a terrible price was paid by that gallant Resistance group.

David Birkin, DSC, Légion d'Honneur

3   Ralph Patton informed me on 5 August 1993 that Paul Hentic did not die in a concentration camp. He is still living in the South of France. Ralph had received this information from Louis Coum in Caen the previous April.

To continue the 15th MGB Flotilla story and L'Aber-Vrac'h Saga, turn to page 233 ie., evader Harold Thompson story.

The Enemy's Gruesome Revenge

O a holiday visit to Norway I found in a cruise guide a précis of the following story aptly named 'The Enemy's Gruesome Revenge', translated by T. Angus from the Norwegian title: *Klar til Kamp.*

'The King of Froyshoen' (the stretch of water between Bremanger-landet and the mainland), Lieutenant Andresen was possessed of boundless energy and a unique optimism. In his head there was a steady swirl of new plans as to how the enemy could be inflicted with great disruption and loss.

There was one special idea which persisted and took shape. It was an English Engineer Officer who put the idea in his mind. In Portsmouth lay some small fast MTBs which were equipped with 2 x 18″ torpedoes and a powerful main motor giving a speed of 92 km. per hour, to 50 knots. But these 55′ craft could also glide soundlessly along under two small auxiliary motors. They needed only a seven man crew, and this had many advantages both in battle and when lying in hiding on the Norwegian coast.

Lieutenant Andresen formed a plan. The plan went through numerous military channels and ended up with the Admiralty, who approved of it. One day Lieutenant Andresen flew on a British commercial flight on his way to Portsmouth to collect his little 'battleship'. His crew were among the plane's passengers.

It didn't take long for Lieutenant Andresen to complete the hand-ing-over arrangements. The MTB was put in order, ready to undertake the long journey from Portsmouth to Shetland. Ordinarily, warships managed to reach their destinations by sea, but Lieutenant Andresen had to divert from this rule. His MTB was placed on a railway transporter and covered with camouflage. The vehicle was coupled to a goods train and Lieutenant Andresen and his men travelled with it.

44

They stood guard over the boat and took care that no one got to know what was under the camouflage. It was essential that the transport went as secretly as possible.

The journey took a long time, but eventually the MTB, under cover of darkness, was transported from the railway station in Inverness to the harbour there. One and a half days after, they were on their way north in the beautiful summer weather (here the story differs from the account in 'Lang Kysten'). Lieutenant Andresen wasn't one to stand still. Not long after MTB 348 had reached Lerwick, the boat set course for Norway.

On 9 June 1943 at 13.05 she cast off and took station astern of MTB 653, which was loaded with petrol cans to refuel MTB 345 on arrival off the Norwegian coast. The little MTB couldn't cross the North Sea twice with her own fuel capacity. She had to top up her tanks for the return run.

The MTBs steered out of the south harbour entrance, but soon set course eastwards. The fog was as thick as a hedge, and they couldn't see more than 100 metres. There was a light south-west wind, and occasional rolling seas gave them an extra push eastwards. The fog was thick all day, and it became dark early. It was with the greatest difficulty that MTB 345 managed to follow in the other's wake. The boat they couldn't see. At 01.00 the white bubbling wake disappeared. Lieutenant Andresen stopped and listened. Yes, ahead, on the starboard side they heard a faint motor noise. He steered towards the noise, stopped again, but could hear nothing. They had lost contact with MTB 653.

It was a long way back. Lieutenant Andresen thought for a moment, set course for Utvaer light, and increased speed to 25 knots. At midnight, speed was reduced to 8 knots, and the fog and darkness surrounded them like a black blanket. Lieutenant Andresen did some reckoning while they glided towards the Norwegian coast. Suddenly, at 02.30, they saw the top of Utvaer light only half a nautical mile to the north-east. The craft wasn't equipped with any mechanical or technical navigational equipment, so he had done well. They steered further between holms and skerries, right south of the light, and went

45

through Indrevaer. By 03.30 on 10 June, they moored in a sheltered little creek in Outer Solund. It had become dangerously light, but the little craft was soon camouflaged so completely that it blended in with the surrounding landscape.

The chaps jumped ashore and stretched their legs. It was wonderful to feel firm ground under their feet having been at their stations for fourteen hours. The cramped quarters didn't allow any movement.

Lieutenant Andresen began to get anxious. The remaining bunkers were far too little to enable them to return to Lerwick. They had no idea where MTB 653 was for the moment and it was impossible for anything to be done until petrol was obtained. Meanwhile, MTB 653 had also reached the Norwegian coast. The fog suddenly lightened about 04.00 on the morning of the 10th, but they didn't only have land ahead, they had land on both sides. It was now quite light, and Lieutenant Matland took no unnecessary risk; they would undoubtedly be spotted. They returned therefore to Lerwick. The petrol cans for MTB 345 still lay on deck. At midnight of 11 June Lieutenant Andresen cast off and steered northwards. It was lovely summer weather, with a shining clear sky. They passed west of Storoy. Holms and skerries swam in in the moonlight. It all reminded them of a coastal trip in peacetime. But in among the skerries went German patrol boats, scouting. They just had to hope for the best. At 02.10 they moored in a bight, but were disappointed that no MTB 653 could be seen. The arrangement was that they should meet here for bunkering. Lieutenant Andresen took it with a smile, and prepared to wait. It was the only thing to be done. 'Hey, turn out.' Lieutenant Andresen swung himself out of the cramped bunk right for'ard and clambered on deck as fast as possible. The watch pointed, smiling, 'There they come.' And there came MTB 653 gliding in the bight and up alongside. It was 01.20 on 12 June.

Andresen jumped aboard to Matland and clapped him over the shoulder. 'It was great that you came now, for I've got just enough petrol for my cigarette lighter.' Matland laughed and said he had to pass on lots of regards from Lerwick. They had left the day before to search again.

Lieutenant Matland didn't wait long. They had been observed as they came in. An hour and a half later he cast off and waved adieu to the chaps on MTB 345. He made sure that he was seen going out again before he left the coast and made off for Shetland.

MTB 345 stayed on the Norwegian coast right up to 23 June at 01.20. On arrival at Shetland, Andresen handed over seven closely written sheets containing much information which became of priceless use later. In Captain T. Horves' report to the English Admiral Wells, the Captain observed: 'Lieutenant Andresen and his crew showed unique endurance in staying on the Norwegian coast for twelve days in such a little craft as MTB 345.'

It was decided that the light nights made operations difficult. Lieutenant Andresen waited therefore before he set out on his next trip. On 25 July he was again under way. The course was set for Utvaer light. The weather was good, but far too clear. This time they were accompanied by MTB 620, with Lieutenant Prebensen as Captain. At midnight they saw Utvaer to the north-east and steered up to the shelter of some holms to get calmer water. The MTB chaps were ready for immediate action. Twice earlier in the day they'd been seen by enemy aircraft. In addition, a signal rocket had been fired from Holmengra. The MTBs came alongside each other and stopped. At 24.00 they began to manhandle the petrol cans aboard MTB 345. They took as many as was possible. The cans clattered as they kept hard at it. Twenty minutes later they saw that a three-engined German sea-plane, a Blohm and Voss 138, was approaching them from the south. MTB 620 cast loose, while Lieutenant Prebensen gave orders to fire at 1000 metres. The 'plane came on but soon had enough! Several direct hits set it on fire. A shell exploded in the starboard motor, and the 'plane swerved over past Utvaer, with a long black tail of smoke behind it. It disappeared behind Indrevag, but lost height every second. Lieutenant Prebensen went alongside MTB 345, but Lieutenant Andresen, who was the senior officer, ordered that MTB 620 should return as quickly as possible. Lieutenant Prebensen still had several cans on deck but order were orders, and he headed westwards at full speed.

The whole coastal area was now alarmed. But Lieutenant Andresen nevertheless managed to get in to the coast, thanks to the smallness of the ship, and the auxiliary motors, which were almost noiseless. MTB 620 met MTB 618 by arrangement some distance from the coast, and they went back together. They were observed by German 'planes who reported, certainly, that both MTBs had returned to base.

In the meantime, MTB 345 glided almost silently in towards Olderoy. There is no existing report from the vessel as to its brutal fate. But the MTB flotilla's contact man from Indreoya on Solund can tell what happened later.

Lieutenant Andresen wanted help to get hold of twenty-one cans which a brother of the contact man had hidden on a previous trip. The contact man got hold of his brother, who pointed out where the cans lay.

But Lieutenant Andresen wanted to obtain the petrol which should have been hidden on Aspoy. It was decided that he should go there on Monday evening after dark. At midnight the contact man, Andresen, and one of the crew, Hansen, began to search for the hidden petrol, without success. The contact man went to see the local policeman, who knew two persons who knew where the petrol was. At 21.00 on Saturday 27 July the three rowed over to Aspoy, where it transpired that the petrol cans lay sunken right beside MTB 345.

The petrol was quickly taken up, but great was Lieutenant Andresen's disappointment when the engineer told him that the petrol was the wrong sort and couldn't be used. They took it calmly and discussed the situation with the crew, who said that they had enough petrol to return to Shetland, but not enough to undertake any operations on the coast. About midnight a rowing boat passed just fifty metres from the MTB, but there was no sign that they had been seen.

The three men left Lieutenant Andresen and his men on Wednesday morning, and there ends the contact man's account.

On the morning of 28 July, it became light early. Over the skerries blew a light breeze, which later died away. Out on the island, the MTB chaps had enjoyed a good breakfast, while the lookout kept watch from a nearby height. The peaceful morning was suddenly broken by three German 'planes which flew towards the hiding place. The MTB crew immediately took all necessary precautions, and assumed that it was an ordinary German patrol. But to their alarm the enemy 'planes began to circle round the island. Now and then they swooped right over where the MTB lay hidden under its camouflage. They had been spotted. Lieutenant Andresen gave the order to get ready to fight, but it was too late. Several small German naval vessels came full speed towards the island and hemmed them in. Lieutenant Andresen saw that there was no way back. He gave the order for his men to arm themselves to the teeth, and to fight as long as was possible. The crew took up the most favourable positions on the land and waited with excitement on the enemy's next move.

Aboard the MTB a time bomb ticked away. It had been placed there to blow the MTB into the air. The silence was broken by the crackle of machine gun fire and shouts from German soldiers, who attacked from two different directions. The small MTB crew fought against the overwhelming odds, and there followed a short but fierce duel. The MTB chaps used their hand weapons very effectively and cold-blood-edly. They had been through a hard school, and were determined to sell their lives as dearly as possible. When the MTB chaps were captured and disarmed, sixteen Germans lay dead on the battlefield. Three of the MTB's crew were injured by hand grenade splinters, but only one was seriously injured. During the heat of the battle one of the crew managed to set the MTB afire but unfortunately the enemy managed to get there in time to extinguish the fire, and to remove the mine. MTB 345 was later towed to Askevold, where Admiral Von Schrader himself inspected the craft.

Lieutenant Andresen and his men, as dangerous prisoners, were taken to Bergen, where they were imprisoned in Bergenhus. They didn't get much peace. At 23.00 the same night they were taken out to be interrogated by the German Lieutenant Horst Paul Kent Walter Fanger (coincidentally 'fanger' in Norwegian means prisoners!). In his account he said:

> I had to see seven men, Lieutenant (ship's captain), second in command, radio operator, and four seamen. Apart from the radio

operator (who was English) all were Norwegian. The crew had a uniform-brown battle dress, jumpers and rubber boots. The uniforms bore the insignia of the Norwegian Navy. The crew had their pass books. Two men who were slightly injured were treated by the doctor. The third, G. B. Hansen, lay on a stretcher. The prisoners were brought in to me one by one. I talked first with the ship's commander, then the second in command and the English radio operator, and thereafter with the rest. The questions were about the MTB flotilla's operations on the Norwegian coast, types of craft, their artillery equipment and technical instruments for locating U-boats.

Later I asked for information about the British and Norwegian fleets, together with information about Britain in general. The prisoners were tired, bone-weary, and despondent, but in general their behaviour as soldiers was good. The result of the interrogations, which stopped about 03.00, were therefore of little value.

Meanwhile, there had been lively radio and telephone activity between Bergen and Oslo. The whole episode was eventually reported to Reichkommissar Terboven, who sent the following telegram to Hitler's HQ in Berlin.

The commander of the KDS (Gestapo) reports that seven commandos have been taken prisoner from a British MTB. I suggest that these people should not be treated as ordinary prisoners of war, but as saboteurs, and that the matter be treated by the KDS. I request further orders: signed Terboven.

It wasn't long before the following answering telegram arrived.

The Führer is satisfied with your proposal. Further orders regarding this matter have been sent to 'Wehrmacht Norge': signed Keitel.

This resulted in the Admiral of the west coast handing over the MTB crew to the Gestapo chief in Bergen, Obersturmbannführer and Kommandeur Hans Wilhelm Blomberg at 02.00 on 29 July. Admiral von Schrader gave as his reason for the handing over a telephone call from

General von Falkenhorst and an order from Hitler on 18 October 1942 in which Hitler had said that Commandos operated outside the Geneva Convention, and should therefore be shot out of hand. Any German officer disregarding this order would be court martialled.

This regulation spoke for itself. The fate of the MTB crew was sealed. HW Blombert telephoned Obergruppenführer Rediess in Oslo and asked for further order. The answer was that the MTB crew should be treated as 'Pirates', and shot at 0600 that same morning. As Blomberg didn't have a copy of Hitler's order, he hesitated to carry out the telephoned instructions. He requested written orders, which the German military chief in Oslo refused to give. At 08.00 the MTB chaps were placed single cells. Immediately before the crew's arrival at Ulven, prison camp commander Etma Hollenia ordered that each prisoner be confined, that all doors be closed and all windows covered. If anyone tried to go out or even to peep, they would immediately be shot. Hollenia set a heavily armed guard around the area. This order created a depressing and serious atmosphere among all the political prisoners in Ulven. They looked at each other but none knew what to think. Most probably there was one or more of them in great danger.

Three of the prisoners, Hakon Kvamme, naval captain Rosberg and Einar Midtun, were occupied in the camp kitchen. Through holes in the window blinds they had a fairly good view of the camp area. What they witnessed in the following day has been described by Kvamme. Some time later he managed to get permission to work on a farm in Softeland, about 6 km. from the camp. With great stealth Kvamme managed to pass on his report at Softeland. Not long afterwards the report was received by the British authorities.

In the camp commander's office it had become crowded. Nevertheless Hollenia felt it was an honour to have fifteen high ranking Gestapo men around him. In the half dark solitary cells, the MTB chaps sat and pondered their fate. They didn't know about Hitler's order. They reckoned therefore that they would be treated as ordinary prisoners of war, as evidenced by Lieutenant Andresen, who wrote the following on the cell wall: 'Taken as prisoner of war on 28 July 1943, Andresen.' It wasn't long before the Gestapo began their work. With white pillow cases put over their heads the MTB chaps were led in for interrogation, one at a time, and they got to feel the special Gestapo methods. The Germans especially showed their love towards Hansen, who was wounded. If the pain became too great they just gave him an injection. The MTB crew were led thus, back and forth the whole day, without food. But they gave away nothing of any significance.

Meanwhile the German chiefs in Oslo shouted louder and louder on the 'phone to the Gestapo chief Blomberg that the earlier order should be carried out. But he kept insisting that the order be in writing. At 1800 Blomberg received the following telegram:

> With reference to the proposal from Reichskommissar Ter-boven, the Führer had ordered that the crew of the British MTB who were captured by German forces, should not be treated as ordinary prisoners of war. Your orders are to hand them over to the KDS Bergen (Gestapo). Report when the execution has taken place.

Commander Blomberg ran immediately to Obersturmführer Erwin Lang and ordered him to carry out the received order at daybreak next day. At 04.00 on 30 July 1943 Lang led his execution squad of six men to the shooting range, which lay about one kilometre from the camp. After taking up position the squad got their last instructions. Fifteen minutes later the first of the MTB crew was brought to the place of execution in a Gestapo car. With bound eyes he was stood facing the execution squad. Six rifle shots broke the silence. A murder had been done.

The names of the executed were:

Lieutenant Alf Andresen, from Sandefjord; Quartermaster 2nd class Bernhard Kleppe, from Bergen; Seaman 1st class Jens Klipper from Sandesund; Stoker 2nd class Agnar Bigseth, from Hereid; Leading radio operator Ronny Hull from Blackpool, England. Seaman Jens B. Hansen, from Bergen; Seaman Kjell Hals, from Namsos.

The Gestapo did thorough work. Commander Blomberg ordered that all traces should be obliterated, so that there could be nothing to be used as evidence against them later. It was significant that they had a bad conscience.

As soon as the last of the crew had died, the bodies were laid side by side in their uniforms. Four of the MTB crew were laid in coffins, three were sewn in canvas and fastened to stretchers. They were all placed in a large goods wagon, which was covered, but open at the back. The Gestapo covered the bodies with branches. The vehicle set off, but the Gestapo stopped at Ulven. They threw themselves down on the grass, and, quite undisturbed by the event, basked in the warm summer sun. The breakfast, which Captain Rosberg had been ordered to bring, looked very tasty.

But in the camp commander's office lay 42 empty cartridge cases, 7 pairs of long white woollen socks, and 7 pairs of rubber boots. Hakon Kvamme later was ordered to wash the socks, but he cut off the name tape 'Hull' which he hid. This was of great value after the war, when material for evidence was being gathered.

At 09.00 the German wagon drew in to the Gestapo's garage in Kalmarshus in Bergen. On the evening of 30 July, two vehicles drove at great speed towards Gravdal, west of Bergen. One was a well known type of car, with Lang, Faldenmayer, Fischer and Clitsch as passengers, followed by a large goods wagon. On the quay at Gravdal they turned beside a small German craft, with one Tidemann as captain. With all haste, the seven dead were taken aboard under cover of dusk. The craft immediately glided on a course out Byfjord and southwards. Two hours later the vessel stopped north of Skorpoya in Korsfjorden. Lang set the others to work to carry out the orders given by Commander Blomberg. The coffins were opened and filled with stones. They fastened iron bars to the stretchers. One by one the bodies were sunk, and sparkling bubbles by the hundreds streamed up to the grey-green surface.

Thus was lost an officer who was full of initiative, and his splendid men, who must never be forgotten. The MTB flotilla received the news of the fate of the crew of MTB 345 with sadness. Under the cover of Hitler's desperate order they had been stamped out as saboteurs, but there could have been no doubt that they belonged to an Allied warship.

The enemy was to pay many-fold for the outrage.

A memorial was built to the crew of MTB 345 at Ulven army camp, south of Bergen.

The inscription at the top of the stone reads:

> This stone is raised to the memory of the crew of the Norwegian motor torpedo boat 345 who in battle were taken prisoner, and outside the law and without sentence executed by German criminals here at Ulven on 30 July 1943.

A service is held every year at this memorial site to honour the dead of both countries, two flag bearers parading the Norwegian flag and the White Ensign with a guard of honour.

Member No. 72 N. A. Caffey

Brief Encounter 'Legs Eleven'

On joining Coastal Forces, after a stint in the RNPS, I was issued with a white woollen frock and a pair of leather sea-boots. We commissioned HDML 1287 at a boatyard near Hampton Court on 23 June 1943; our destination was Glasgow via the East coast.

When we arrived in Aberdeen I discovered that both my sea-boots were left feet. As we were tied up near the stores, I took them over there to see if I could get a right-footed one. The Wren at the counter wasn't quite sure of the procedure in a case like this, and as we were discussing the matter a smashing looking Wren (officer I think) appeared on the scene and took charge of the situation. 'Follow me,' she said, and made her way to a ladder affixed to the wall which led to an upstairs room. This was not the run-of-the-mill ladder, but one of those you usually find in stables, an upright plank of wood with hand and footholds carved into it. She started to climb up, with me following.

Now, with the best will in the world and having to look where the next handhold was, I could not avoid getting glimpses of those elegant legs climbing above me. Anything above the knee was a rare sight to the males of our era. We arrived in the room above, and she seemed oblivious to the emotions she had unleashed in her follower. By this time I was madly in love with her.

After ferreting around, she found a pair of boots to suit me, and led the way back down again: a natural leader, my loved one. Handing me back to the Wren at the counter to do the paper work, she walked away into the blue, out of my life without so much as a backward glance.

Incidentally I never did get to wear those boots, as we went to the Far East and bare feet were the order of the day there. What happened to them, I forgot; perhaps I swopped them for a bottle of arrack.

Member No. 1858 Clyde C. Rothery, Ex PO Engineman

Tiddley Jack

Neat, fashionable, tidy. Tiddley Jack was the epitome of what he thought a sailor should look like. His cap was slightly concave on the crown, giving the impression that it had been used as a pillow on more than one occasion. The cap tally or ribbon: for security reasons ships' names were not displayed on cap tallies, usually just HMS, but HM Patrol Vessels, HM Minesweeper, HM Submarine, HM Destroyer etc. were allowed. The most prized tallies were those picked out in gold wire; later on in the war the only ones available were made with what seemed to be yellow cotton, and these were anathema to Tiddley Jack. Next the bow of the ribbon: regulations stated that this should be situated over the left ear, but not Tiddley Jack, he wanted his over his left eye and a Tiddley bow to boot. This was achieved by placing the ribbon round the cap and where it met it was cut, the two ends were then sewn together and the excess ribbon could then be fashioned into a Tiddley bow. The bow had to resemble a butterfly with swallow tails reaching up towards the crown. The bow was then sewn over the stitching where the two ends joined, giving the impression that the ribbon was all one, bow included.

Now the collar: the ideal one was a well-washed Pusser's issue which had reached Mediterranean blue stage. Unfortunately, sometimes when this stage had been reached the white tapes round the edge had started to fray, but this was no problem to the dedicated man as you could buy new tape at the slops and sew on a fresh set, a marathon of a sewing task. Med blue collars could be bought from naval tailors, Bernards or Flemings, but this was considered cheating by the purists. The new issue collar was a very deep blue, almost black, and attempts to wash it usually ended with the blue dye running into the white tapes. Some of the older hands would swop a sprog his collar with a cash adjustment. The collar then should have two creases in it.

Now for the Tiddley suit. Before there were naval tailors ashore and some rating had an account with them, after your first issue of clothes and gear, you were given a kit upkeep allowance and expected to maintain your kit. Tiddley Jack, when ordering his new suit, wanted the vee in his jumper to be U-shaped and more plunging. The jumper would be skin tight and would need the help of his oppo to get it off. The tapes to bind his silk would be about three longer than regulation stated. Trousers, the regulation ones, were 28″ at the bottom, but until he could afford a Tiddley suit he had most likely a gusset put in his issue ones making them sometimes as wide as 36″ and looking ridiculous. So 30 or 32 inch were the norm. The suits were always folded inside out, making the seams inverted. The trousers had horizontal creases in the legs about six inches apart; there were five of these, said to represent the five oceans, but actually it was how they happened to fold to make the smallest bundle for stowing away. A pair of glaze kid boots or shoes, Pusser's issue burberry, and a white silk scarf completed Tiddley Jack's ensemble. Pusser's issue gear was found to be of better quality than you could buy at the naval tailor's ashore.

Motor Torpedo Boat 769—63rd Motor Torpedo Boat Flotilla; normally based at Great Yarmouth. (Commanding Officer Lieutenant Bill Dye, RNVR.) Armament: Two six-pounders; one × 2 20mm.; two × 2 0.5"; two × 2 .303"; four 18" torpedo tubes. Has been fitted with a type 268 Radar Set: one of the first boats to receive this set.

Yellow Decks

In the December 1988 Newsletter, Bob Montgomery wondered, as we who took part wondered at the time, whether the yellow decks of RMLs 512 and 498 were responsible for their not coming under attack when rescuing a Beaufighter crew in broad daylight close off Texel while under surveillance by German aircraft.

Rescue MLs were given yellow decks to improve their recognition from the air so that they could be more easily located by searching aircraft and directed to a search area or, even, that should an aircraft in distress spot them, the crew might, with luck, ditch or bail out nearby and so improve their chances of being picked up. Since no distinction was made between friend and foe in the matter of air-sea rescue, it was hoped that the yellow decks might be regarded with the respect accorded to the Red Cross.

It was after the rescue, when we had time to think about it, that doubts began to develop that our faith in the protective qualities of yellow decks might not be entirely justified.

One reason was that, while based at Immingham, air-sea rescue was a secondary part of the 60th Flotilla's duties. Each night, except in the severest North Sea weather, boats from the flotilla, working in pairs, maintained an anti-E-boat patrol on the same Z position roughly midway between the Humber and Dutch coasts. As with all Z patrols, we were required to intercept and challenge any suspicious vessel entering the sector and, if necessary, engage while signalling an enemy report to Base.

We regularly exercised intercepting tactics and, though lightly equipped for the purpose compared with an MGB, we carried an Oerlikon, twin .5 and four .303 machine guns as well as six depth charges, and a close observer would have seen torpedo-tube mountings. So, unlike the fast rescue boats of the RAF which were armed purely for self-defence, RMLs were acting as vessels of war when not on a rescue mission and, certainly, that was how we saw ourselves.

Another reason for our doubts was that we felt it was highly likely that German intelligence had a fairly accurate picture of our Z dispositions, particularly that allotted to the 60th because it was never changed. Its being the nearest to the rescue area on this occasion might have led the Germans to suspect that this accounted for our early morning arrival on their doorstep.

There were, therefore, at least two good reasons why the colour of the decks may have had a smaller part in saving from attack than we had first believed. Had the enemy decided that it was a poorly applied cosmetic to disguise our potential in other directions, I believe that they could have claimed justification for ending our careers there and then. In the event we were not even challenged.

A third reason for my not placing too much store by humanitarian convention in wartime is my own, having early in 1940, on passage in a minesweeping drifter, passed the East Dudgeon Lightship the day before it was destroyed and many of the crew lost through enemy action. The following year I was watchkeeping in the Lantern Room of Lowestoft lighthouse (with the light operating!) when it was strafed by a night intruder—no casualties this time. These were two quite inoffensive targets, as helpful as aids to navigation to E-boats lurking offshore as to ships in convoy. But this was no protection.

Thus, while accepting that the yellow deck theory may well be the correct explanation for our safe return, I doubt whether those who were there will ever be totally convinced, especially since, in due course, we were instructed to paint over the yellow paint with grey!

Member No. 1500 Don Mackintosh

Jock Lamont was the Oldest!!

The query as to the oldest member of Coastal Forces serving during the war prompts me to claim this privilege on behalf of A/B Thomas (Jock) Lamont, whom I knew when serving in MGB 312.

Jock joined the Navy as a boy seaman in 1899, and did his early training on sailing ships. From then on, until he was demobbed in 1948 at the age of sixty-four, his life was centred around the sea and ships, alternating between L/S and A/B, depending on the official view of his conduct!

He won the DSM with the Naval Brigade at Gallipoli, and was awarded a bar to it after the Normandy landings.

My first meeting with Jock was late one Saturday afternoon in August 1943, when, as a very green telegraphist straight from training, I found my way to Haslar and thence to MGB 312. Half the crew, including the cook, had gone ashore, but Jock, on learning that I had had nothing to eat since breakfast, disappeared into the galley and produced the most marvellous fry-up.

He was a mine of information about anything related to ships, Naval or other; he was an artist in rope and canvas; he was the only man I ever knew who could make a decent smoking plug from Pusser's leaf tobacco: and if my memory serves me right he was recruited by the then skipper of MGB 312, from a shore job tiddleying up HMS *Dolphin*.

When 312 paid off, I believe he stayed on board as C & M party but his Naval career didn't end there because the last news I had of Jock is contained in a cutting from the *Manchester Evening Chronicle*, dated 6 March 1948. It shows a picture of him, kitbag on shoulder, leaving MTB 2016 for demob. The gist of the write-up is that Jock Lamont, oldest sailor in the Navy, was being demobbed that day. He started his career in sail and ended it in one of the fastest ships afloat.

Not only, then, can MGB 312 claim the oldest sailor in Coastal Forces, but also Coastal Forces can claim the oldest sailor in the Royal Navy.

Incidently, the skipper of MGB 312 (and SO 1st Coastal Force Flotilla) was Lieutenant Commander John Coste, DSC and Bar. His predecessor was Lieutenant Commander A. R. H. Nye, DSC.

Member No. 1540 Oswald (Shiner) Wright

Did you know Jock prior to '43?

I was very interested in the item by Shiner Wright about Jock Lamont. At *Hornet* in 1946 we understood Jock Lamont to be aged fifty-six, and were surprised that someone his age could be serving aboard an MTB; for after all Coastal Forces was a 'young man's game'. However, as Shiner Wright has revealed, Jock was then actually sixty-two, and we would have been shattered had we known that.

In 1946 I was on MTB 2017 when our flotilla was operating from Dutch and German ports and we eventually ended up in the Baltic. MTB 2016 was the SO's boat, and it was a very tiddly craft, especially the ropework, due in no small measure to the presence of Jock aboard. A few months after our return to *Hornet* many of us were demobbed and I always assumed this included Jock so I was really amazed to learn that he continued aboard 2016 until 1948 at the age of sixty-four.

What intrigues me is not only how he managed to serve in the Royal Navy to such an age, that in itself is remarkable, but to continue as an active crew member in Coastal Forces must be really unique in the history of the Royal Navy. Perhaps as a result of his long service Jock 'knew the ropes' in more senses than one, and was able to exert influence in the right quarters. It certainly is remarkable that someone his age was able to continue as an active crew member of an MTB when many three-badge ratings younger than him served out their final years as 'barrack stanchions'.

As Shiner Wright says, Jock must have been the oldest rating in the Royal Navy and Coastal Forces, and it would be interesting if some research could be done to trace his record in the latter, e.g. how many different craft did he serve on, and how long had he been in Coastal Forces before Shiner Wright met up with him aboard MGB 312 in August 1943?

Jock was a grand type, respected by everyone, and I am sure that many others will appreciate Shiner Wright's account of the career of this grand old 'Sea Dog'.

Member No. 1924 H. Brown

Introduction to
Operation 'Aquarius': MTB 718

Four Norwegian agents, Jan Larssen, Arnold Hovland, Jens Johannsen and Svere Vinningland, had been waiting in a cave facing seaward on the Island of Skarvoy near Egersund, south-west Norway. MTB 718 was four hours late in arriving at the pin-point, having been challenged by the escort of a nine-ship German convoy, illuminated by enemy star-shell and searched for by a Dornier. The agents had mistaken a passing E-boat for a British MTB and hailed it, but fortunately they had not been heard. At 0400 hours, the four Norwegians had given up hope of rescue and had started to climb up the hill to return by boat to their mainland hide-out, when one of them turned round and was amazed to see 718 only ten yards off the beach. He says that was the best moment of his life!

Some of 718's crew met Larssen and Hovland in Norway in 1981 and in England in 1982 and are in regular contact still.

Charles W. Milner, DSM

The story is continued by John S Townend, Navigating Officer of MTB 718 …

After we had successfully collected the four agents from the rocks off Egersund, my job, as ship's navigator, was to accompany them below to the wardroom. I poured four half-pint tumblers half full of Scotch and handed one to each agent—they all grinned hugely and in no time had 'taken their medicine'—they then ate some sandwiches which had been prepared and were ready for bed.

While the two in the wardroom were getting turned-in, I topped up their 'medicine' and handed them their glasses. Armed with the other two glasses I crossed to the Captain's cabin and knocked on the door.

It was opened by a very large agent and as I handed him the glasses, my eyes almost popped out of my head. On the top bunk was a growing pile of armaments, the like of which this young sailor had never seen before! Balanced precariously on top was the smallest automatic I'd ever seen. Without thinking, I reached forward and lifted it up. The large agent grinned. 'You like?' he said.

I replied that I'd never seen such a weapon.

'You like?' he repeated. 'You haf!'

I immediately replaced it amongst the hand grenades, knives and other armaments, being embarrassed and wondering what my CO would say if he knew. At that, the large agent grabbed me in a ferocious grip; he pressed the small gun into my hand with some boxes of ammo and insisted, 'You like—you haf.'

I thanked him and retreated hurriedly, stuffing the present into the pockets of my sea gear. I carried that gun on every operation from then on and still have it today—my only souvenir.

Member No. 642 John S. Townend, VRD

The Rescue

We had put in a lot of sea time and it showed. Upper deck paintwork had suffered and a repaint, particularly of the deck itself, was a matter of urgency. So, at the first stand down for routine engine maintenance, we found a berth where we would be spared the passage of people to and from the boats moored outboard, and out came the paint and the brushes.

The drill, you'll remember, was to paint the deck all over except for a strip between mess deck and wardroom on the quay side of the boat to allow for shipboard life to continue for all practical purposes. The unpainted part would be treated later.

Amongst us, at the time was an enthusiastic but dangerously wet-behind-the-ears young chap who, out of discretion, we will call Ordinary Seaman Eyesplice. But keen? You only had to tell him once to do a job and he did it. Then you had to get him to do it again—right!

But he never lost heart and was popular with one and all, probably because he represented light relief and it is probable that his shipmates covered up for more of his errors that ever came to notice!

When the painting chores were allocated, OD Eyesplice was given the fo'c'sle where there was lots of open space and he would be out of the way. Meantime, those who were not painting ship got on with their duties. The CO decided to make himself scarce and went into town for a haircut and Number One busied himself in the wheelhouse on chart corrections.

Number One was thus engaged when the Cox'n came to ask permission to draw the ration for 'Up Spirits' and he and Number One set off aft to open up the rum locker. However, as they reached the bridge, they found a small crowd of sailors gathered abreast the boat's bow and in a state of great merriment. The cause for their mirth was, I am sorry to say, the hapless OD Eyesplice.

You or I, charged with painting the fo'c'sle, would have started right up in the bows, and worked aft towards the wheelhouse. Not so Eyesplice. Left to himself, he had started at the wheelhouse and worked steadily towards the bow and, so concentrated on the task in hand, it was with considerable surprise that he found his feet over-hanging the bow and that he was marooned on a small island between the jack staff and the anchor winch, surrounded by a sea of grey paint and with a drop to the drink behind him!

'Don't you dare move,' yelled the Cox'n, 'We don't need you treading all over the paint. We'll find some way of getting you off.'

By now it was nearing the peak of the tide and the boat rode high. Also, Mr Eyesplice was in a position about ten feet out from the quay. Number One who, being navigator, knew all about angles and the shortest distance between two points, estimated that we would need a ladder about twenty feet long to bridge the chasm and the other painters were despatched to find one which, in time, they did.

However, the ladder was heavy and as all the manoeuvring had to be managed from the quayside—it not being possible for anyone to get onto the deck to handle the other end—closing the gap proved impossible.

'How would it be,' suggested Eyesplice, trying to be helpful, 'If you hauled on the headrope and eased off aft to bring the bow in so that I could drop down.'

'Thank you, Eyesplice, no,' said Number One, 'You may notice there's still a fair current passing and there's no way we'd get the stern out into it without engines.' In any event, he had no wish to be caught out by the Skipper on his return hazarding the boat in a dodgy bit of seamanship.

The spectators of the drama had, meantime, suspected that the solution when it came was likely to require their involvement and, noting that 'Stand Easy' was soon to be piped, had gone their ways. How wise they were!

The answer to the problem, when it came, meant that Number One had to ask the CO of the boat lying ahead of us for permission to warp ahead so that our bows overhung their stern, so allowing the unhappy

67

Eyesplice to clamber down. Hauling a 100 ton ML against a stiff tide is hard work and not without harm to naval personnel or property.

What it cost OD Eyesplice in 'sippers' and duty frees is not revealed. It seemed unkind to ask and, anyway, it was probably not the first time!

Member No. 1500 Don Mackintosh

Enemy Shipping Casualties in Minefields laid by Motor Launches of Dover Command

Their Lordships have noted that some 17 enemy ships have been sunk or damaged in the minefield laid during the last 15 months by the minelaying motor launches working from Dover.

This represents a casualty rate of one ship for approximately every 80 mines laid, which, having regard to the nature of the area, the comparative scarcity of suitable targets and the indirect effects achieved, their Lordships consider a very satisfactory record.

This recognition of the fine work carried out by the minelaying motor launches is well deserved and is to be promulgated to all concerned.

(Admiralty letter M/OD 2140/42 of 30/10/42) (Dover 663A)

H. D. Pridham-Wippel, Vice Admiral.

Luck, Bluff or What?

On a night early in June 1942, RMLs 512 (Lieutenant S. Davies, RANVR) and 498 (Lieutenant D. Harding, RNVR) from the 60th Flotilla at Immingham were on station ninety miles east of the Humber. The weather was warm and calm and a haze gave visibility of about two miles.

Shortly before midnight came a signal from NOIC Humber to the effect that during the afternoon contact had been lost with a Beaufighter in a given position and at 1600 another plane had reported a dinghy, possibly with survivors, in that area. RMLs 512 and 498 were to proceed at first light to carry out a search.

The position was four miles west of Texel Island, one of the Friesian group off the Dutch coast. Four miles from the enemy coast on a June morning!

498, having also decoded the signal, had come alongside and the two skippers conferred on what, with or without a 'pick-up', promised to be an interesting mission!

There were many imponderables to consider. How accurate was the sighting position? Already the dinghy had been adrift for many hours and many more would elapse before we could begin a search. What would the drift be by then? Our last fix had been hours ago when we passed the Outer Dowsing beacon. How accurate was our present DR position for setting course for the search area? Even with the best estimation, luck would play a big part, never mind that we would be sitting on the enemy's doorstep in broad daylight!

We were cheered to have a further signal from NOIC to say that we would have air cover. We signalled that we would leave station at 0500 with ETA at the search point as 0900.

Still, the weather stayed pleasant, though the haze, if it persisted, would be a mixed blessing—screening us from the enemy but making it harder to find the dinghy, assuming we got anywhere near it and that the Germans or local fisherman had not got there first.

So there were good reasons for not being surprised when, arriving at the search area by our reckoning, no dinghy was there to greet us.

As unit senior officer, Sid Davies decided to alter course to south, reduce speed and to place 498 out to starboard to broaden the search front.

The boats had been at Action Stations since 0800 and now the atmosphere on board was tense. We were certainly hidden from the shore, some four miles to port, but with the continuing haze, at any moment we could blunder into an enemy patrol or minesweeper at nearly point blank range.

However we were not to wait long for things to happen. After a matter of minutes on the new course came the cry from the after gun position, 'Aircraft astern!', and out from the mist swept three Hudson fighter bombers. Our air cover, and right on time! But, if they were, they missed us and kept on course until a minute later they were lost in the haze again. From the direction of their departure came the sound of machine-guns.

Minutes later and again the shout, this time from a bridge lookout, 'Aircraft Red Two Oh. Low on the water!' Through the glasses it was plain to see, though almost at the limit of visibility, a Blohm and Voss flying boat, with German markings of course. And there where it was about to come down was a dinghy!

We flashed 'DINGHY' across to 498 and altered towards it. At this point the German pilot seemed to change his mind, for he regained height and turned away towards the land and disappeared into the haze. We got close in on the dinghy and as we got nearer we heard a cheerful 'Good morning' in accents unmistakably English. There were two of them, in RAF uniform but without caps or tunics. (It turned out later that they had expected to be home for tea and so had not bothered too much with full flying kit!)

Quickly we hauled them aboard, scarce believing our luck, while 498 collected the dinghy.

During the pick-up, I had been vaguely aware of aircraft noises in the background but, assuming that our air cover had returned, I carried on with the rescue. With the airmen safely inboard I could now see that I was mistaken. We had air cover all right, but it consisted of four ME210s, and they were circling us at little more than mast height at a distance of not more than a hundred yards. Their aircrews were clearly visible!

They seemed to be unsure of our identity. Our ensigns hung limp in the still air and perhaps they were as poor at ship recognition as most of us were at aircraft recognition. Anyway, could anything but friendly boats be hove to so close inshore on that coastline on a sunny summer's morning?

498 was within hailing distance and Lieutenant Davies called over to Lieutenant Harding to hold fire and not to shoot unless we were attacked. Doug Harding replied with something very, very rude!

Sid Davies knew that, had it come to a shoot out, the RMLs might have done some damage, but would be sitting ducks themselves against the combined firepower of the four Germans. It was essential to play for time and hope that we would soon get the promised air cover.

So we held our fire and, instead, waved in the most friendly manner we could while the enemy planes continued to circle. Two or three times one of them would dive low over us as though to force us into some action that would reveal our true identity, and it says much for our young and fairly novice crews that they kept their nerve.

All the same, we could not stay here forever hoping that the Germans would go away; there were plenty more where these ones came from. We had to make a move, but in which direction? East and south was the enemy coast, and a course directly west would be a give-away. So we went north, still at half speed as though we had every right to be in those parts and were in no hurry to leave. For a while our full escort came with us, but then three of them turned away and we saw them no more.

But one hung on and we quite expected to find a reserve team joining him at any time. None arrived. On the other hand, we were no nearer getting our passengers home. Surely our chum up there would have to go at some time to refuel and give us the chance to lose ourselves from prying eyes in the mist?

Then, after nearly half an hour, we sighted a white shape indistinctly ahead which, on closer acquaintance, resolved into a Danish fishing boat. We approached cautiously in case it was some sort of decoy or off-shore radio or radar station but it was exactly what it seemed, an innocent fishing trawler. We came close and made signs that we wished to come alongside. As though waiting for this moment our remaining escort made a final circuit and went away. The time was 1030.

There is not much more to tell. The Danes gave us a generous fry from their catch, and we parted from them with gestures of great goodwill and set course for home at last.

Even now we could not believe we had got away with it and so we stayed at Action Stations until well past noon. As we opened the distance from the Dutch coast, the wind freshened and the visibility improved so that it was extreme by the early afternoon.

Late in the evening we entered the Humber Estuary and so back to Base. A national newspaper got hold of the story and, with a touch of imagination, had us going in with guns blazing to snatch our quarry from under the Germans' noses!

Yes, we did what we were sent to do. But not a shot was exchanged in the process. Was it luck, bluff, a Divine Hand or what sometimes takes the full bitterness from warfare, an unexpected chivalry? All I hope is that those German airmen who paid us such close attention were not court-martialled when the full situation came out. Whether they intended it or not, that day saved our lives.

Member No. 1500 Don Mackintosh

Mediterranean Clandestine Operation

My short period of time in the Coastal Forces was served with the African Coastal Flotilla, a clandestine outfit carrying out operations in the area of Ligurie, Genoa and other such places along the Italian coast, being attached to the PT Boat Squadron 22 at Gulfe Juan in the South of France. The Squadron 22 boats used to cover us on any landings which we made but also worked with our Coastal Force boats on operations.

We in MGB 177 also did a couple of operations with the CF boats, one of which I would like to tell you about. We were at the time working out of Leghorn and the piece that follows is a copy of an article from the book *At Close Quarters, PT Boats in the United States Navy*, by Captain Robert J. Bulkley Jr., USNR Retired.

On the night of 17/18 December 1944, a striking force of the trawlers *Minuet*, *Hornpipe*, *Twostep* and *Ailsa Craig* rendezvoused with the control group, Commander Allan in PT302 with MTB 419, the northern escort group, Lieutenant E. Good, RNVR in MTB 306 with MTBs 377 and PT 309. Ahead of the main body ranged the northern scouting group, Lieutenant Eugene G. Wilson, USNR in PT 304 with PT 313 and MTB 422, and the southern scouting group, Lieutenant-Commander Dressling in PT 310 with MTBs 378 and 375. The 17th Squadron, South African Air Force was to have sent a flight of bombers to illuminate the enemy by starting brush fires ashore with incendiary bombs, but because of low visibility was unable to take part in the operation.

Dressling's scouting group picked up a south-bound F-lighter convoy, only to lose it when it moved close to the beach. Later it picked up a north-bound convoy of F-lighters and a coaster escorted by an R-boat, and shadowed it for three quarters of an hour, giving constant reports of its position to Commander Allan's group. When the convoy came within range of the trawlers, Commander Allan ordered Dressling's group to retire to seaward. Two of the trawlers illuminated the convoy with star shell and the other three immediately opened fire with their 4-inch guns. The F-lighters fought back savagely with their 88mm. guns, but the trawlers had the advantage of surprise and scored many hits, whereas the best the F-lighters could do was to spray one of the trawlers with shell fragments, slightly damaging its bridge and wounding one officer. By the time the F-lighters began to get the range, Commander Allan ordered MTB 420 to lay smoke to cover the retirement of the trawlers. Commander Allan assessed the damage to the enemy as two F-lighters and one R-boat sunk, but again German records do not confirm this.

This was one of the attacks which MGB 177 took part in and our boat is not mentioned, possibly because she belonged to a clandestine group. Possibly we were there because we carried Radar, being an ex-PT boat, and also to make the numbers up, but to me it was a time for hitting back as I had spent the previous four years on the receiving end as I had been the Coxswain of an A/S trawler, the *Northern Gem*, on both the Atlantic and the Russian convoys.

You can imagine what I felt at being in a fast MGB after four years on a 12- to 14-knot trawler, attacking a German convoy instead of being attacked. The fact that we could hit back at last was exhilarating to say the least.

Since I joined the CFV Association I have met one man at least who was on one of the boats on this attack, and last met him in Leghorn, Italy, at Christmas 1944; quite a few lamps were swinging in the bar. Crew members of the MTBs 306, 377, 375, 378 and 422 may remember this one as well as I do. Wishing all the members well.

Member No. 1771 Sid Kerslake, Ex Coxswain MGB 177

Inner Thoughts
AGM Hayling Island 1988

We all stood—as the standards passed by:
Time serving Matelots, with a tear in their eye.
A Thousand Faces—
A Thousand Ships—
A Thousand Prayers, on a Thousand Lips,
A Thousand Memories of a Thousand Days,
A Thousand Deaths—in a Thousand Ways.

Each with his memory,
Each in his soul
Searching for peace,
That ultimate goal.

The good fight was fought,
Matters not who lost or who won:
But we all paid respect,
To some poor mother's son.

We will remember ... how could we forget?
The good times,
The bad times,
It's all vivid yet,
When history is written,
As surely it must,
We'll count that Great Victory,
In Ashes and Dust.

Yet out of this evil,
One thing's to the fore,
The mates that we served with
Are our mates evermore.

Lex (1988)

75

Extract from Corsairs at Large

Farewell to 'All-the-Sixes'

The Fourth of July—American Independence Day—1944 found Lowestoft bristling with activity. The 'Shorts' (72 ft. MTBs) had returned from an action off Holland in which they had sunk a trawler, and orders were for our 58th Flotilla to prepare for a sweep.

At 7 p.m. we cast off and formed up outside the harbour with our boat MTB 687 at the head, then 684, 729, 666, 683, and 723 as 'Tail-End Charlie'. The 729 was manned by the original crew of the 681, which had caught fire and sunk in our first action. They had been rekitted, sent home on seven days survivor's leave, commissioned the 728 and re-joined the flotilla with her. Thus had MTBs become 'consumable stores'.

Perfect conditions favoured us as we sped eastwards towards the Dutch coast. I watched the 683 break formation and head back to Lowestoft with engine trouble, then made my usual agreement with the 1st Coxswain whereby he took the wheel for the outward trip and I took it for the homeward run.

At midnight all the watch below were shaken and a few minutes later the pipe 'Hands to Action Stations' echoed throughout the ship. Wrapping myself as warmly as possible in my duffel coat I reported to the bridge that the mess deck was cleared and all hands were closed up to action stations.

It was my first night in my new capacity as Navigator's Yeoman, my task being to report and log all buoys, bearings, lights etc., and to watch the course of the torpedoes and report their effects. I was soon at work logging two white flashes on our starboard beam from a Dutch lighthouse—a clear indication we were in enemy waters. Half an hour later a fixed red light was reported ahead and Gemmell pronounced it to be Ijmuiden harbour entrance. Three white flares bursting over the

76

sea some miles to the south of us were believed to be an enemy force carrying out a night shoot.

One o'clock found us about eight miles off Ijmuiden and cruising around on two engines. All was quiet and tense with the murkiness of the night disturbed only by a bright green flashing at five second intervals from a nearby buoy.

For the next two hours we cruised around waiting to ambush an unwary Nazi convoy. It was adventurous to be on such missions and comparable with the pirates of the Spanish Main—truly we were 'Corsairs at Large'.

Without warning, searchlights from the shore commenced to sweep the darkness around us. Being mounted high on the cliffs they had the effect of being much nearer at hand, but were obviously uncertain of our presence and began to sweep the sea all around us. One trained directly on us and dazzled us by its glare, causing us to think we had been detected. Patiently we stood around our brightly-lit deck awaiting a barrage from the shore batteries while the searchlight remained fixed on our bearing for nearly half a minute, but it then joined the other two in aimlessly sweeping up and down the coast again.

At 2.10 a.m. flares were fired to seawards of us by an enemy patrol approaching the coast and our Radar reported three ships closing us on the port beam. Gemmell was unwilling to attack them from inshore as it would bring us between two lines of enemy fire—from the shore batteries to starboard and the enemy patrol to port. Instead, we led the flotilla out to sea to carry out the attack from seawards.

Five minutes later the battle was started by a brief order from Jimmy Fisher yelling, 'Rockets commence, commence, commence.' Hardly had he uttered the words than the air was reeking with the fumes and gunpowder smoke from the rockets speeding off to illuminate the hitherto unseen target. Unfortunately most of our rockets were failures and fell into the sea without bursting, but our misfortune was compensated for by the stupidity of the enemy in opening fire with small-calibre guns in an attempt to shoot down the three that did burst. Tell-tale green and white streaks of his tracers disclosed an accurate bearing of his position—the precise object of our rockets.

77

We held our fire and crept in for the kill.

Panic broke out in the enemy ships and they commenced to battle wildly among themselves. Apparently they had mistaken the fire of one of their own ships shooting at our flares and thought it to be our fire attacking them. For three or four minutes they bombarded each other.

Those few minutes proved long enough for Gemmell to manoeuvre the flotilla into position and we were close in by the time they realised their mistake and ceased fire.

They soon spotted us and opened fire.

Red, white and green tracers raced across our bows in the thickest concentration of 'Flak' that we had yet encountered. Red tongues of flame appeared astern of us as our own ships joined in the battle. Overhead, well-directed enemy flares burst to illuminate our decks as light as day.

Defiantly we steamed slowly into the Nazi barrage through another menace from white-hot cinders cascading down on our decks from the burnt-out enemy flares.

At 2.22 a.m. our torpedoes were fired and as gracefully as two trained sea-lions they plunged into the sea to be lost in their own spray. I managed to take a hasty bearing of their track from the white wake that rose to the surface. The barrage was too intense for me to follow them all the way, as the enemy was putting over the heaviest fire we had yet experienced. New to us were the anti-personnel shells bursting simultaneously in lines of black puffs of smoke overhead. Heavy shells were dropping dangerously nearby to send up clouds of black smoke mingled with the green phosphorescence of the sea.

A bright flash ahead lit up a trawler to indicate the first of our 'fish' had struck home. Abruptly the streaks from her tracer-firing guns ceased and she disappeared below the surface in a matter of seconds. Hardly had she gone than another trawler fell victim to our torpedoes and disappeared just as quickly. Two fleeting glances were all we saw of them. Three heavily armed enemy ships remained to fight for their lives. Desperately they fought to send shells of all calibres crashing home among the MTBs faithfully following us astern.

We drew away from the fire and led the flotilla out of range and hove to. On either side the MTBs closed us and a hasty check revealed that five MTBs went into the attack, but only four came out.

The 666, Lieutenant-Commander Buller's boat, was missing.

Over the radio-telephone system Buller called up Gemmell. His plight was desperate, yet he spoke so casually and seemed as unconcerned as though he was telephoning a friend ashore.

On the bridge of our 687 we listened to him reporting in his usual matter-of-fact tone, 'I am in a bad way with all engines disabled. I have lost some men over the side and am preparing to abandon ship having destroyed the CBs [Confidential Books]. I have one of the blighters snooping around my stern while another is steaming up my starboard side.'

Evidently the Nazis were not aware that we had left one of our number in their midst. Our lookouts reported that they had last seen the 'Sixes' (666) almost stopped and listing heavily to port with black smoke belching from her bows.

Gemmell picked up the microphone in a determined tone—'Hold on, we're coming in. I'll draw their fire while Archie [723] and Aspic [684] will come alongside you to take off your crew.'

'Aspic, Roger, Out,' and 'Archie, Roger, Out,' were the brief acknowledgements by radio-telephone from the COs of the ships detailed.

We swung hard a-starboard and headed back into the fire. Obediently, each ship turned and took station astern of us. The enemy intensified his fire and the battle raged more furiously than ever. Smithy came clambering over the cat-walk with blood streaming from his right eye. In his broad Scottish accent he yelled something about a 'Starrer-shell' and pointed to his eye. His words were drowned by the incessant rattle of our .5 guns but I managed to bundle him into the charthouse, where Flash Gordon was ready with the first aid box. Leaving Smithy to his care, I took up his action station as number two of the starboard .5 but the turret was silent as the fire had been coming over the port side since we had circled.

Even when the flares had burned out the whole battle area was lit by the tracers of colours. I went aft to assist the 6-pounder crew, but they required neither help nor inspiration. Almost knee-deep in empty shell-cases the lads had formed a human chain to pass the shells from the ammunition lockers below decks; the upper deck ready-use boxes had been long since emptied. Amidships, the Oerlikon gunners were hitting back with equal ferocity and Jock Orr was being shaken almost out of his skin as he clung grimly to the twin guns. He had discarded his steel helmet, and the spattering tongues of flame from his guns reflected his determined expression and tousled head in an eerie reddish glow.

Further din broke out for'd as though someone was mending his boots on an empty oil drum. It was the pom-pom-pom-pom of our pom-pom striving to make itself heard above the rest of the barrage. By this time we were fighting a close-range battle and the enemy shells had a screeching whine about them as they whizzed overhead. All around us the sea was a mass of black patches of spouts caused by near misses.

Overhead the anti-personnel shells were leaving a trail of black puffs in the flare-lit sky. About twenty heavy calibre guns were concentrated on us in addition to small arms fire. It seemed apparent to all that we could not hope to survive much longer in face of such devastating fire. Reluctantly Gemmell realised it was impossible to rescue our comrades on the doomed 666 and even to save ourselves was now a serious problem. He grasped the microphone and called the flotilla, or rather what was left of it as only 723 and 729 were remaining faithfully in our wake astern.

'Hello Jackals, Hello Jackals,' he called into the microphone in a disappointed tone. 'It's too much, too much. Follow me. Follow me.'

Our engines roared and a buzzer on the bridge sounded twice as the engine room crew acknowledged orders for full speed ahead. The ship shuddered with the vibration and we swung round to place our stern towards the enemy. Even under such trying conditions there was not the slightest trace of confusion and 723 and 729 followed us around with the perfect formation station keeping of a flotilla exercising under the critical eye of an Admiral. Our only gun to bear was the aft

6-pounder, but it maintained its fire to the unceasing clattering of empty shell-cases falling from the breach to the shell-littered deck.

The enemy continued to bombard us with flares and heavy guns as we sped to sanctuary beyond their range. I was just about to credit the miracle of escaping unscathed as I watched the flotilla stern when 723 received a direct hit on the bridge. A shower of red sparks burst amidships; she reeled, slowed down and swung off course, but regained station a few seconds later.

Gemmell yelled into his microphone, 'Hello, Archie. Are you OK?'

A dazed voice faintly replied, 'No. We have received a direct hit on the bridge and have three seriously wounded and one slightly.'

By 3.30 a.m. we were safely out of range of the enemy guns, though the flares were still bursting around us as they tried to seek us out. As we sped towards England I carried out a hasty inspection of the ship. We had suffered no casualties beyond Smithy, who had been injured in the eye whilst assisting Tam Trainer to remove a flare-rocket from the locker. It was wedged in the locker and Smithy stepped down to peer into the locker while Tam tugged frantically to free it. By sheer force Tam freed it while Smithy was gazing into the locker, and one of the metal fins struck Smithy in the eye. We had survived the action very well. One shell had penetrated the starboard .5 turret without detonating the ammunition when it exploded inside the locker. Another had struck the starboard signal locker and finally embedded itself in the engine room hatch.

At 4 a.m., weary and dirty, the lads fell out from action stations, but I took the wheel as we made good speed through a becalmed sea and by dawn we were well clear of the coast.

Two hours later a speck was sighted on the horizon ahead. It was a high-speed RAF launch speeding to meet us with medical assistance. As it approached us Gemmell waved it down the line to 723 and held up his hand to indicate the third boat. At the same moment 723 flashed us: 'Lieutenant McDougall has died.'

Thus in one action we had lost two of my former Commanding Officers and I recalled Lieutenant McDougall standing on the deck of the blazing 686 a few months previously in Lerwick.

On that November morning we were firm in the belief that he wanted to go down with her and, ironically enough, he had been killed in action on the 723, manned by the survivors of the 686.

Gemmell ordered the 723 to break formation and proceed to Lowestoft with all possible speed and she passed us sending up clouds of spray in her life and death dash to land her wounded. As she passed her white ensign was dipped to half mast for her fallen Commanding Officer.

I had plenty of food for thought on the way to Lowestoft. I had only been transferred from the ill-fated 666 a few weeks before and she had gone with all hands, Stanton, the bearded Mechanic; Old Bill from the Bahamas, a bewhiskered old prospector who had sought gold all over the world; Yando, a lad still in his early teens; the bearded Cox'n. They had all gone in one stroke, and with them, former shipmates of the 723 and 666.

At 7 a.m. Lowestoft was sighted dead ahead and we entered to find 723 alongside the fuel jetty with ambulances waiting to take off the wounded. Medical Officers were giving a blood transfusion to her badly-wounded First Lieutenant, Lieutenant Goldsmith, while 684 had moved alongside her to take off a .5 gunner who was too badly wounded to be carried across the decks.

Another action had been fought and we set about the task of preparing the 687 for the next operation.

Footnote:

This extract is from a manuscript I prepared over forty years ago. It is authentic and word for word as written at the time. No attempt has been made at subsequent editing as the original was written immediately after the action of 4 July 1944.

One fact striking me as odd today is the mention of searchlights on the cliffs of Holland, a flat country, but this effect was probably due to our being close inshore and the searchlight batteries mounted on the highest points of the sand dunes, probably in the form of searchlight towers.

Randall Tomlinson

The Final Chapter of the 'Sixes'

MTB 666 was under heavy fire from two heavily armed trawlers, one on each side of us. They were using quite a lot of their new anti-personnel shells. We had been hit several times. All engines had stopped, there was a fire in the engine room, and we were getting an increasing list to port. Our guns were out of action owing to lack of power from the engine room.

After what appeared to be ages, but must have been only minutes, the trawlers ceased firing, but they held their stations. When two of our flotilla tried to reach us to give us aid, the German trawlers left to meet them and presumably to join in the fray. The respite must have given our skipper Lieutenant Commander D. N. Buller time to ascertain casualties and damage. With at least fourteen men requiring hospital treatment, some very urgent, and a boat that could not defend itself, appeared to be sinking and was on fire, the order 'abandon ship' was given.

It seemed like a lifetime in the water before we were picked up by a German armed trawler. It was cold, I will never forget. They did what they could for us. They had a lot of their own wounded to attend to. It was while on board the German trawler that I saw Lieutenant Clive MacIntyre, RN; he with Lieutenant James Linley, RNVR came on board the 'sixes' just for a trip on a 'safe boat'. I'm afraid we let them down especially as I understand that Lieutenant MacIntyre had just been passed fit for sea after being ill and was going on leave as soon as he got back.

At that moment he was lying on a top bunk in the seaman's mess with a hole the size of a saucer in his back. What beat me was that he was still as cheerful as if he had a cut finger. He was just the same in hospital. At times he had us in fits of laughter. By the time we reached Ijmuiden it was daylight.

Those who were able to walk were taken away, I believe to an empty school room. The remainder of us were put into the back of lorries with straw to lie on, a most uncomfortable journey to hospital. The German hospital staff looked after us reasonably well. It was the guards that I did not care for. They were from the Herman Göring Regiment.

We heard, how I can't remember, that the 'sixes' had been towed into Ijmuiden harbour and had blown up while the German top brass were inspecting her. CPO Les Stanton, motor mac, said 'that the scuttling charges had been set but both had failed to fire.' Poor old Les was badly crippled and was immediately repatriated. Frank Heath and Jock Macky, both from the engine-room, died within a few days.

We left the hospital after approximately four weeks and were taken to an interrogation camp in Germany for another six weeks, then to the main POW camp where we were reunited with the rest of the crew and there we stayed.

Member No. 112 Stan Cross, MTB 666

Motor Gun Boat 315—12th Motor Gun Boat Flotilla. Normally based at Great Yarmouth (Commanding Officer Lieutenant Perter Mason, RNVR). Photograph taken 1941/1942. Armament: 1 x 2-pounder pom-pom for'ard; two x 2 0.5' Vicker's amidships. One Holman projector amidships; one 2-pounder Rolls aft; four depth charges, two port, two starboard aft.

The 'Lucky Lady' Again

It was the winter of 1941, and it had been another successful trip; we had left base early the previous evening, and apart from the odd blips on our radar screen and the occasional drone of aircraft engines in the distance, we had enjoyed a comparatively peaceful journey to the Dutch coast. We had landed our friends.

Every so often I revolved my 0.5 machine gun turret, scanning the sea and air for anything unusual. The gentle brightness of the moon made one want to sing, and I did; fortunately for the rest of the crew my voice was drowned by the noise of our three engines.

Out of the corner of my eye, behind me, I saw the long lean shape of our 1st Lieutenant (Bob Goodfellow) hurrying aft, not a cause for concern as he often visited the engine room when at sea. As the minutes ticked by I realised that I had not seen him return. Then a second shape left the bridge for aft, and minutes later the 1st Lieutenant was seen to return to the bridge. Somehow a feeling of tension reigned, it cannot be explained in any other terms. Something was wrong, but what? I could not even guess.

A tap on my shoulder revealed our Skipper, Lieutenant Peter Loasby, RN, also SO 12th MGB Flotilla. He then explained what was happening. The Stewart Turner auxiliary engine had broken down, which meant that water was pouring into the bilges and we were sinking fast. Ordinarily this was not a cause for concern as it often happened, and skilled motor mechanics or stokers quickly repaired them, but this time it was more serious and not only was the flooding slowing our speed but we were perilously near to sinking.

Peter Loasby detailed all available 'hands' aft; just the cox'n and he were to remain upon the bridge. AB Vic Copeland was to stay at his starboard turret, and I was to remain at my port turret, both acting as main lookouts. The rest of the crew, excepting the MM and the

86

Killick stoker, who were working feverishly upon the Stewart Turner, formed a bucket chain, physically passing buckets of water from the bilges into the North Sea, and so for approximately seventy-five miles the lads baled out, bucket by bucket, gallon by gallon, until at long last the engine functioned again. Ironically we were almost within sight of Great Yarmouth when the 'all clear' was given, and a very tired and relieved crew of MGB 320 sailed back into base.

The lucky lady again!

Member No. 120 Jack Davies

Motor Launch 1145—141st Motor Launch Flotilla Mediterranean. Armament: Two single 20 mm. Oerlikons; two × 2 .303" Vickers on the bridge.

Lord Allan of Kilmahew, DSO, OBE

Anyone who served in Coastal Forces in the Mediterranean remembers the name of Bobby Allan and I expect you have notices and reminiscences from abler pens than mine, but I thought I would write a line to you to set down something of Bobby's great record. A few weeks ago Mark Arnold Forster rang me to tell me that Bobby had died suddenly in Australia on a visit there, and I then read about his fine post-war career as a politician and a statesman. This caused me to think back and review his remarkable wartime with us in Coastal Forces.

Bobby was a peacetime RNVR officer from the Clyde division and he joined MTBs in the spring of 1940. I was then commanding MTB 102 and rejoiced in the resounding title of Senior Officer of the Training Flotilla at HMS *Hornet*—actually the Training Flotilla consisted only of my boat and MTB 100 and we had very little idea of what we were doing. Nevertheless we 'trained' Bobby Allan and, incidentally, Mark Arnold Forster and a number of other super people.

Bobby went on to command MTB 100 and then to the Mediterranean where he commanded various Elco boats and a flotilla during the dreary years of retreat and failure in 1941–2.

In November 1942, after the North African landings, he was appointed to command the Coastal Force Base at Bone, which he did with great success. This was the first appointment of an experienced, serving MTB officer to command a Coastal Force Base and it was also the first appointment of an RNVR officer to such a command—he made sure that it worked.

In May 1943 I arrived in Bone with my 24th MTB Flotilla, shipped out from England, and was delighted to renew my friendship with Bobby—indeed, he gave me a bed in his room at the strange little beachside hotel which was our mess.

At this time our Mediterranean offensive was preparing and we all knew that some invasion was imminent. Bobby was given the job of creating, developing and commanding the first lorry-borne Mobile Advanced Coastal Force Base, which was set up and used for the invasion of Sicily in July 1943, where the base was initially at Augusta.

For this job Bobby was made an Acting Commander at the age of twenty-eight. This was a remarkable achievement and he was probably the youngest Commander in the Navy at the time.

Throughout 1943–4 he served with his advanced base in Sicily, Italy, Sardinia and Corsica and made possible the extensive operations of the MTBs which would otherwise have been greatly limited by the long distances from the main bases.

During this period he devised, created and commanded the combined units of MTBs, US Navy PT boats (used also as Control Ships because of their superior PPI radar sets) and Royal Marine Landing Craft (Gun) with 4.7-inch guns. He christened these units Battle Squadrons, and did great service with them against the enemy's night time coastal traffic on the west coast of Italy. The Battle Squadrons operated largely from Bastia.

Late in 1944 Bobby was appointed Senior Officer of the Inshore Squadron, and this was a considerable final Naval compliment to him as a quite outstanding RNVR officer, for he relieved a celebrated RN Captain, Norman Dickinson, who was promoted to be Senior Naval Officer, Adriatic.

For all Mediterranean Coastal Force officers and men Bobby Allan's name was a byword. He was a fine leader, strikingly good looking, light-hearted but determined and brave and, above all, knowing his stuff—he was both loved and respected and will be sadly missed.

Knowing him from those days, it is no surprise to note that he went on to great success as a politician and statesman in the years since the war, and was justly made a life peer as Lord Allan of Kilmahew.

Commander C. W. S. Dreyer, DSO, DSC

Motor Torpedo Boat 102, Vosper's Private Venture Motor Torpedo Boat.

MTB 102 and our Return to Dunkirk

For months now I have been boring everyone who would listen about MTB 102 and our return to Dunkirk for the Fiftieth Anniversary. Now it's happened and I can shut up 'till we do the Diamond one'!

Of course 102 was not the only MTB there in 1940—our only claim to fame is that she still exists in running order and, within reason, so do I. In fact, from my memory there were 67 and 68 (55-foot Thornycroft CMBs built in 1939 for the Finnish Navy and taken over by the Admiralty); 107 (a 40-foot experimental Thornycroft CMB with one engine, no astern gear and a half-mile turning circle); MA/SB 8 and 9, and probably one or two others.

In 1940 MTB 102 was mainly used as a Despatch Boat between Dover and Dunkirk and around the beaches and harbour. In the generally fairly disordered conditions it was important for the Flag Officer, Dover, Vice Admiral Bertram Ramsay, to be able to get messages to the Naval Officer in Charge, Dunkirk, Captain William Tennant and the Flag Officer, Afloat, Dunkirk, Rear Admiral William Wake-Walker and to get their answers.

We made altogether half a dozen trips over, perhaps seven, in the course of which we carried Admiral Wake-Walker several times. On our first meeting with him, when we took him and his staff and two wounded sailors off the old flotilla leader, HMS *Keith*, which had just been bombed off the beaches, my torpedo man, Leading Seaman Peter Dawkins, made an Admiral's flag for him out of a pusser's dish cloth and some red paint. We flew that flag always whenever we carried him again (and it is now a cherished relic in a glass frame since Captain Christopher Wake-Walker presented it to 102 some years ago—I gave it to the Admiral as a memento of his time with us in 1940).

On the last night we made a quick trip over and back and brought off Captain Tennant, a general, a group captain and someone else. I have always thought and reported that the general was Alexander, but I now know that it wasn't. (Oddly enough, when we came to do the invasion of Sicily in July 1943, when Alexander was the Army Commander and I was SO of the 24th MTB Flotilla, I suggested to the Captain Coastal Forces (Med) that, since I had brought General Alexander off from Dunkirk, it would be fitting if I popped him back into Sicily. CCF was delighted with the idea and took it to the C in C, but the message came back that, though the general very much liked the plan, sadly he must be in the HQ ship so that he could have all the signals and reports.)

On the last night, 3–4 June 1940, we took Admiral Wake-Walker over and acted as the Control Ship in Dunkirk Harbour, calling in the destroyers and the passenger ferries onto the east pier from which they took off the French rearguard.

Later that summer I left 102 and commissioned MTB 30 to join the 4th Flotilla at Felixstowe and then, in the autumn, I left MTBs for some eighteen months.

In 1973, long after I had been invalided out of the Navy and started working for Vosper, MTB 102 was bought by the Norwich Sea Scouts as their Training Ship. Since then, with a lot of loving care, hard work and devotion from the Scouts and their leaders, some good luck and the great generosity of the Perkins Diesel Co. (who gave two new 8-cylinder engines and gearboxes in 1985), 102 is transformed and looks very much as she did fifty years ago, although she has no torpedo tubes. She can go some 15 knots happily, compared to her youthful 45. She does a marvellous job doing sea training for the Scouts every weekend of spring, summer and autumn.

MTB 102 is a member of the Association of Dunkirk Little Ships and we returned this year as part of their convoy. In 1940 some five hundred ill-assorted yachts, pleasure cruisers, fishing boats, harbour launches, Thomas barges, etc. etc., went over to Dunkirk to help rescue the Army. Some took men from the beaches to the ships offshore; some took men directly home; some were sunk and many were damaged; many crews were killed and wounded. The little ships did not bring off the majority of the Army—the destroyers and cross-Channel ferries did that: but they did perform an absolutely invaluable task in doing the ferrying jobs and they did indeed bring off many soldiers.

For this Jubilee occasion I arranged with the Scouts to bring two important guests as well as my twelve-year-old Sea Scout grandson from the Torridge Group in North Devon. Firstly we had Lord Cameron, a retired Scottish Appeal Court judge. He commanded MTB 107 in 1940 and she, taking off the blockship's crew at 04.00 on 4 June, was the last British warship to leave Dunkirk. He is now ninety. He was a midshipman at the end of the 1st World War and joined up in September 1939 and came to us in MTBs early in 1940. He was a Scottish KC, aged forty then and we called him 'Grandpa', but he was a much loved and respected member of our team. Secondly we had Captain Christopher Wake-Walker, whose father we had carried several times in the operation.

I had hoped that my friend Peter Dawkins (Ch.PO Peter Dawkins DSM), who belongs to our association and who probably spent longer in CF than anybody else, might be able to come too. Sadly, he had a bad motor-bike crash some years ago and his legs aren't too good, so his doctor told him not to—a great shame.

Our trip over with the Little Ships convoy was somewhat lacking in charm. On Thursday 24 May 1990 we slipped from Wellington Dock in Dover and had a wonderful and touching send-off from the considerable crowds. It was blowing about Force 4 from the north-east, so our trip over towards Calais was not too bad. When we turned east for the Dunkirk Channel, however, the wind backed to east-north-east and increased to Force 5, at least, and got much colder. We had a dreary passage at about 5½ knots with some 1½ knots of tide against us. I was worried that the wind was increasing, it was decidedly chilly and some of the Little Ships were only thirty feet! However, we made it at last.

All Dunkirk hotels were fully booked when I started arranging this family do before Christmas, and the nearest hotel I could find was about thirty miles away in Belgium. So my family and the others with us, who had all come in cars by ferry to Calais, met us in Dunkirk and we eventually found our hotel at about three o'clock in the morning.

We all had a lovely time in Belgium and took the opportunity to visit Waterloo and Ypres, which I've always longed to do. I had not before realised that the Belgians do a wonderful little ceremony at the Menin Gate memorial at Ypres every night. At eight o'clock the traffic through the gate is stopped and buglers play 'The Last Post' and then 'Reveille'; it's quite something.

On Sunday 27 May they had the Remembrance Ceremony at Dunkirk. The boats slipped from their berths at the Town Quay and made their way out through the basins and locks and formed up in a circle about half a mile from shore, just east of the eastern harbour breakwater where the great long sands begin.

They steamed slowly round in a circle and an RAF helicopter came and lowered a wreath into the middle and some of the boats dropped wreaths, too. Then a Hurricane, Spitfire and Lancaster flew in formation low over the boats, turned and flew back and on to England. The Red Arrows made a brief visit.

I watched this from the beach near the Memorial where hundreds and thousands of Army Dunkirk veterans were watching too. It was very impressive—though, sadly, this part of the beach and dunes from about a mile east of Dunkirk is pretty commercialised and a bit like Blackpool.

We came home by ferry on Monday and 102 made her way directly home to Yarmouth and her berth up the river—some of her crew had to work on Tuesday.

It was a truly memorable voyage and, God willing, MTB 102 and I will do it again in 2000 for the Diamond Jubilee. We'll certainly try.

Commander Christopher W. Dreyer, DSO, DSC, RN (Rtd)

SGB 4 - GREY FOX. Note the single 2pdr Pom-Pom on the bow, in place of the more usual single Oerlikon. In addition, 1-3 inch aft, another 2pdr for'd, single Oerlikons aft the funnel and on the transom, 2 twin 0.5 inch Vickers (abreast the wheelhouse), 2 twin 0.303 inch Vickers (on pedestals abreast the bridge) and 2-21 inch TT.

The Mining of MGB 2002 in the Skagerrak, Four Days after VE Day

As many of our readers will already know, the 15th MGB Flotilla consisted of the following boats: MGB 2002 (ex 502), MGB 2003 (ex 503), MGB 718, MGB 318 and MA/SB 36.

This Flotilla was primarily engaged on secret operations to enemy-held territory and if you have read C. Hampshire's book *The Secret Navy*, you will understand what these types of operations entailed.

MGB 2002 sailed from Aberdeen at 0800 hours on 11 May 1945 on a mission to Gothenberg in Sweden.

In addition to her crew of twenty-five, four additional RN and Merchant Navy personnel were embarked. E.T.A. Gothenberg was 2000 hours on 12 May.

At approximately 0345 hours on that morning, MGB 2002 struck a floating mine. About two-thirds of the boat was blown to pieces, the bows, messdeck, midships galley, PO's mess and bridge were gone; all that remained was the engine room, ward room and tiller flat.

There were only two survivors, PO Motor Thomas H. Sheehan and Able Seaman Norman T. J. Hine, DSM.

One of the crew of MGB 2003 received the following letter dated 28 May 1945 from Tommy Sheehan, who was in Christiansand Hospital, Norway.

This letter is quoted verbatim with the approval of the writer. Any alteration would detract from the narrative and pathos of the situation.

'Hi ya kid

How you going pal; alright I hope, as it don't leave me so good at present. I am lying on my back in a Norway hospital waiting for an operation, you see Bert, I am going to have three of my toes taken off

(Frost Bite). gangrene has set in. Yes pal, we have had a rough time Norman Hine and myself; it has been a proper nightmare son.

The boat was mined about 3.45 am I was very lucky, I relieved Hearn at 3.30 and he went up forward along with Jock. I was on watch with Bristow when all of a sudden 'Wipe' Bigger Bang than that. Bristow runs up the hatch, don't worry I was behind him. See how much damage, when I looks, all forward didn't exist, it was blown to smithereens, so you can guess what happened to Jock, and Charlie, also Andy can't you, including Jim Gordon, Coddy, Olly. Anyway Taff Bartlett he had half a face and arm hanging off; Jenny Wren he was alright; Norman, Hugh Coppins and Bristow and a couple of Merchant Navy Officers.

She was sinking very fast Bert, and we couldn't cut away the SN1, it was well lashed down. The dinghy has a great hole in it. We were properly in — street, the time came when he had to abandon. When I dived in I had no life belt, come to think of it none of them did. I managed to hang on to Carley Float which had been blown apart; along with me was Bristow. Well kid, you can imagine how long it lasted with our weight. All of a sudden Bristow said he thought he saw another Carley Float drifting well out. Well, Bert, I took off my jacket I still had on and swam for it against the tide and believe me pal what a swim; yes, it was one and intact as well but I was dead beat. Anyway I managed to get back to Bristow and he climbed aboard and Bert, the cries of someone was terrible, it proper shook me up and we couldn't see them because of the swell.

We paddled around to find anyone, when old Norman popped out from somewhere hanging onto a hammock and an SN6 standard. We pulls him aboard and we started off again, and pal the sights that we saw was something terrible. I felt like spewing and breaking my heart crying. We saw one bloke in the water tank he must have got wedged inside and couldn't get out and suffocated and drowned. I don't know who it was but the tide was carrying the water tank away very fast, and we could just see him bobbing up and down. Anyway Bert, everything went very quiet and we couldn't hear anyone else about; we kept shouting 'is there anyone about' but no answer, and then the tide started to carry us away. We kept with the wreckage the best we could thinking that we would be picked up but we never saw a thing; in fact, I think I can go as far as saying that nothing was sent out to look for us—we were like God left by the Jews.

Well Bert, we drifted about on that raft for 7½ days without food and very little water and what water we did have was stale and a horrible taste. it was that canned water Bert. Anyway it lasted for about four days and then we had none at all, and Bristow started to get panicky. I kept cooling him down by saying think of your Mrs and children, we shall be picked up by someone in a minute. No, it was no good, pal, down went his mouth into the oggin, more mouthfuls than that, you ought to have seen him Bert, he kept drinking mouthfuls of salt water until he went completely stark raving mad. Oh! what a sight, I couldn't hit him as I was weak as a kitten and my hands were soft and tender with the water, if I had have hit I should have broken my wrists.

You can imagine what his ending was Bert, poor old Fred. That left Norman and I, and I might tell you I started losing hope a couple of times, but old Norman soon talked me round soon as he mentioned my old kid.

A very bad incident happened one of the days Bert, about 8 planes passed over us and we waved and shouted but after two of them flashed us up nothing came of it. Was we wild. Another day we were within stones throw of some fishing boats and the tide absolutely carried us away from them, and we finished up losing our paddles. We were eventually picked up by a Norwegian merchant ship who were very good to us and fetched us here. Norman was unconscious and I was laying there talking to the water, so you can see what state we were in. Oh! by the way Bert, Norman has got to have all his toes off, he likewise is waiting for the operation.

Well kid, how's Myra, remember me to her, also your mother and family, also all the boys abroad, especially old Tubby. Tell Ken about Jim and Coddy, Bert, will you let me know if there is any more survivors please. God knows what is going to happen to me when I come back. Do you want another Motor Mechanic (Ha Ha) I know how to grease water pumps ahem don't you forget to write Bert, won't you and don't hang it about kid, let's know all the news and whether

Coppins survived. Remember me to Bill Shaw and tell him the lighter he made for the Mrs is at the bottom of the oggin with my No. 1 suit and everything else. We haven't got a stitch of clothing. Well pal, nurse is waiting to wash my bum so I will love you, leave you. All for now, Cheerio kid, your old pal,

Tommy

P.S. Say Bert, would you ask old Turner to write and tell the boys to make sure there's some corned dog in your Carley rafts—we almost starved to death.

Norman

The two survivors were picked up at 2200 hours on 15 May (actually 3½ days after being mined) by the Norwegian MV *Uranus* approximately six miles north-west of the Lista Light and were taken to Christiansand Hospital suffering from exposure.

Tom Sheehan had both his legs amputated and Norman Hine lost all his toes.

Editor

Motor Gun Boat 502. All this class were renumbered by adding 1500 to read in this case 2002. Senior Officer's Boat, 15th MGB Flotilla. Designed and built by Camper & Nicolson; completed February 1941. Sank 12 May 1945 after striking a mine off south-west Norway whilst on passage from Aberdeen to Gothenberg, with only two survivors. Machinery: three Paxman diesel engines, 1,000 h.p. each. Armament: 2-pounder pom-pom in power turret for'ard. 2 × 2 5" machine guns in power turrets each side of bridge. One × 2 Oerlikon power turret amidships; one × 6 pounder hand-operated aft; two × 2 0.303" machine-guns; four depth charges.

'Sidelight on the Silent Service'
Small Ships—Big Results

Copy of an article published in the
British Forces newspaper *Union Jack* No. 383,
dated Friday 16 March 1945.

The men who fight in small craft off the coast of Italy are making holes in German shipping.

The greater part of that 45-mile stretch of enemy-held coast between Spezia and Genoa is amply protected by guns of six-inch calibre and downwards, some of which are mobile and can be moved as necessary along the coastwise road between Sestri Levante and the north.

There are minefields off-shore, and the Germans are well provided with location devices for spotting approaching ships, and can illuminate whole areas of sea with flights of star shell.

It is at night, up and down and close inshore along the coast, with the tall ridges of the Apennines black against the lighter darkness of the sky, that creep the enemy convoys carrying stores and munitions for the German army in Northern Italy.

It is here too, that a small force of British MTBs and American PTs, manned for the most part by young men who hardly thought of being seamen before the war, have ravaged these enemy convoys in no small measure.

Between May 1 1944, and January 8 of this year, they sank 28 enemy vessels, probably sank 11 more and damaged at least seven.

The majority of these 'kills' were moderately fast, well-armed 'F' lighters, though included in the total were merchant vessels, torpedo-boats and corvettes. Judging from the satisfactory explosions after being hit by torpedoes or set ablaze by gunfire, a number of these craft have been carrying petrol or ammunition. The operations of this Flotilla, whose base I visited the other day, are controlled by Commander R. A. Allan, DSO, OBE, RNVR, who is also the holder of the French Legion of Honour.

His experience of light coast craft is unrivalled.

I noticed that several of the craft bore one or two miniature Nazi flags on the fore part of the bridge, these being awarded to those definitely responsible for a 'kill'.

I was on board some of the boats just returned from an operation, 'the same old thing', as one of the commanding officers put it.

I asked him what happened.

'We were about a couple of miles off the coast,' he said. 'It was about 1030 when we located an enemy convoy. So far as we could see, there were four or five "F" lighters. We went in to attack and they opened fire. So did the shore batteries and pretty well accurately, with their star-shells bursting overhead.

'I managed to let drive a couple of torpedoes, and 30 seconds later the third ship in their line went up in a lovely column of smoke and fire. It was a pity that we couldn't have bagged more, but things were too hot, and we had to disengage, worse luck.

'We'll have better luck next time.'

I could understand his regret, but MTBs are wooden-built and not much thicker than stout cardboard.

The crew were busy stripping and cleaning their guns and generally preparing for the next expedition. One of the gunners had been a lorry driver in civil life, another a baker's assistant.

'Would you like to leave MTBs and go to a cruiser or a destroyer?' I asked a lad hardly out of his teens, with tired-looking, red-rimmed eyes and a struggling fringe of flaxen beard.

'God forbid, sir,' said he, meaning it, 'I like the pirate's life.' Yes, he had to admit life was uncomfortable at times, but he'd got over it by now. It was kill or cure for newcomers when MTBs started their antics in even a moderate sea.

Lieutenant A. H. Moore, RNVR, the Senior Officer of the Flotilla, was an accountant in civil life and hails from Barrow-in-Furness.

Of the other commanding officers, R. H. Slemeck, who lives near Dorchester, and N. L. Ilett, of Winchmore Hill, were both Oxford undergraduates. E. S. Good, of Hull and R. Aitchison, of Woodford Green, were the only two in the RNVR before the war. G. R. Masters came from the Argentine.

The others, I was told, G. H. Bullwinkle, of Beckenham; G. P. H. James, of Edmonton, and Leslie Hewitt, of Wigan, were still at school when the war started. The average age of the officers and men of the Light Coastal Forces lies somewhere in the early twenties.

Some of those I spoke to showed signs of strain after their many hazardous operations, which was little to be wondered at.

They have their periods of rest in harbour, but sleepless nights of nosing through the minefields off the enemy coast and under his batteries, with eyes peering through the darkness and nerves tense, are bound to have their effect. One can never relax on patrol. There is always the strain of suspense and physical discomfort. In winter it can be rough and bitterly cold in the Gulf of Genoa.

Their battles, when they come, come suddenly—fierce, high speed scurries in the midst of a welter of smoke and shell-splashes, and the varicoloured streams of tracer criss-crossing, in the darkness.

The least hesitation, the slightest error of judgement, may end in disaster. The courage and determination of these young men of ours who man the coastal craft in this and every other area need not be extolled by me.

The proof of their gallantry lies in their records. Amateurs they may have been when the war started; but now, hardened and experienced after more than five years of war, they are prime seamen and masters in the art and instinct of offensive inshore fighting.

Good luck to them, wherever they be—and good hunting.

Submitted by Arthur J. Scardifield, Cornwall Branch

To the Memory of 'The Greatest Raid of All': the Raid on St Nazaire

On 28 March 1942, Coastal Forces in home waters carried out this daring raid, and succeeded in their objective, but at a terrific cost.

Their mission was to destroy the entrance lock to the only dock on the Atlantic coast large enough to take the largest battleships of the German Fleet, and to destroy all boat pens and harbour facilities. Their objective was approximately twelve miles inside the Loire from the French coast, and very heavily defended. The force comprised: the old destroyer *Campbeltown* with the forward part filled with high explosive and delayed action fuses, and intended to ram and completely destroy the lock gate. MGB 314, MTB 74 and MLs 156, 160, 177, 192, 262, 268, 270, 298, 306, 307, 341, 443, 446, 447, 457. Unfortunately 341 developed engine trouble and had to turn back. There was also a large party of commandos distributed in the boats.

Of the total force which went in: 1 destroyer (with a skeleton crew), 1 MGB, 1 MTB, 14 MLs, with a total complement of 62 officers and 291 ratings, 3 MLs returned to UK under their own power, 1 MGB (314), and 2 MLs, 246 and 270, were contacted and towed part way, by HMS *Cleveland* (Commander, G. B. Sayer) but had to be sunk owing to weather and threatened enemy action. Of the number who went in, 28 officers and 140 ratings returned. And of the total decorations and awards published for this operation, to Naval personnel came (immediate) two VCs, three DSCs and four DSMs. There were also, after hostilities ceased, and prisoners of war returned home, a VC, several CGMs, and DSMs, one of whom was our National Chairman Bill Lovegrove, ChMM of MTB 74, who was awarded the Conspicuous Gallantry Medal.

The special citation for the St Nazaire awards stated, 'That they are in recognition of those others, unnamed, who did not return'. Some of us will never forget, for others, the years may dim the memory, so let me close with the lines of the Toc H prayer:

Age shall not weary them, nor the years oppress,
As the sun goes down in the evening, and in the morning,
We will remember them.

Amen

John Dorey, DSM

Two of our comrades who gave their lives at the St Nazaire raid now lie at peace in Falmouth cemetery.

The full epitaph reads:

W. A. SAVAGE V.C.
ABLE SEAMAN C/JX 173910
H.M.M.G.B.314
28th MARCH 1942 AGE 29

T. G. PARKER
MOTOR MECHANIC
H.M. MOTOR LAUNCH 447
28th MARCH 1942 AGE 20

LEST WE FORGET

These, too, were Expendable

One evening during April 1943, as the battle for Tunisia was thundering into its last phase, a signal to British naval headquarters at Sousse from Sir Andrew Cunningham, Commander in Chief of Naval forces in the Mediterranean, ordered three motor torpedo boats to 'carry out a slow inshore patrol of the Cape Bon peninsula in daylight', and to 'open the sea lanes in that area'.

It sounded crazy. MTBs operated at night. They were not expected to commit daylight suicide under Nazi shore batteries and swarms of Me109s.

But there was good reason for the order. Allied troops were ready to open the final offensive, and it was essential for General Eisenhower to know whether the Afrika Korps was going to stage a Dunkirk. Reconnaissance planes could get no accurate information about the superbly camouflaged landing stages which could be used for an evacuation, or the coastal gun positions which would protect them. There was no alternative but to send small boats to almost certain destruction.

All night the crews of MTBs 639, 633 and 637 laboured with old pieces of bunting and red, white and black paint to produce Nazi battle ensigns. The time-honoured naval ruse of a false flag was their only hope. At that, even the optimistic leader of the expedition, twenty-six-year-old Lieutenant Stewart Gould, thought it a slim one. 'Rum show, chaps,' was his tense comment to his two commanders—twenty-eight-year-old Lieutenant Henry Butler and thirty-five-year-old Lieutenant George Russell. Nazi spotters, he feared, would surely recognise the unmistakable lines of a British MTB.

The three tiny ships slipped out of the harbour and arrived off the German shore line exactly at daybreak. Just half a mile away, the lookout saw a powerful coast-defence battery. But the Germans on the beach only waved. On the MTBs the British white ensigns remained furled at the yard-arms, ready to be broken out the moment the ships went into action. Their swastikas whipped smartly in the wind.

The ships cruised slowly past Hammamet, past Nabeul, examining each little cove. Still the Nazis waved from the beaches, while the MTB commanders charted every camouflaged gun position and tent hidden in the bushes.

They were nearing Kelibia Point, the place from which the Axis would probably launch their evacuation, and Gould had been told to find out about the capacity of the piers that were being constructed. Powerful guns frowned down on him, any one of which could have blasted his ship into eternity with one shell. But for half an hour he and his consorts cruised around, when the officers filled their notebooks, and Nazi soldiers, not more than a few hundred feet away, worked feverishly on the piers.

Round the point was the principal anchorage for German warships and supply vessels. Gould decided to have a look. During half an hour, Gould and his officers spotted a gun emplacement, radars, storage depots, ships, ammunition dumps and troop concentrations.

Only a few hundred yards away, German and Italian officers kept looking at them through field glasses. There was a bad moment when the big guns of a nearby battery began to swing in their direction. But the Nazi gunners were only testing their traverses. The grim muzzles swung past. German prisoners later revealed that everyone had thought the MTBs were German E-boats cleverly disguised to resemble British vessels.

Gould, his map-making finished, calmly weighed anchor and moved deeper into enemy territory. Every few minutes an enemy plane would streak over them. But the Messerschmitts, never suspecting that Allied ships would snoop round Axis harbours in broad daylight, didn't even bother to take a good look.

By 9.30 Gould was sixty miles behind the enemy's lines. He had found out everything that Admiral Cunningham wanted to know. But there was still the matter of 'opening the sea lanes', that the orders called for. He was deciding how to begin, when he spied two Italian mine-sweepers in a small cove. A German convoy escort ship lay nearby. Directly behind them, on shore, was an important-looking factory.

Gould signalled for battle. On three diminutive masts, the swastika disappeared and the cross of St George whipped out. For twenty minutes, at 300-yard range, the MTBs raked the sweepers and the escort vessel with two-pounders, pom-poms and machine guns. Those shells that missed the ships crashed into the factory behind. The Axis crews, too startled to resist, scampered overboard.

The sweepers quickly went to the bottom. By the time the larger boat had been set ablaze, Nazi pilots were running to their cockpits at nearby aerodromes. But Gould was on his way before they got going.

He went back the way he had come, shooting at everything that looked interesting. The two-pounder shells made little impression on the coastal airfields, though their moral effect was devastating. The German command thought that a large-scale raid was brewing and hastily ordered troops to the shore and more planes into the air.

And then, after shooting down an observation plane that would probably have caused trouble, Gould ran into something important. Scattered along the beach were a number of huge German transport planes, remnants of the hundred-plane Axis air convoy which US Warhawks had sent plunging into the Mediterranean in the now famous 'Palm Sunday massacre'. Some had crashed but quite a few were intact. Within easy range, Gould's gunners destroyed every one.

Gould could have gone home then with honour, but just as they came abeam of Kelibia point, MTB 639 made a signal: 'Intend to close and bombard.' Butler in the 633 and Smith in the 637 stared as their leader's ship began to swing. 'Lord Lumme,' said one of the helmsmen, in an awed voice, 'We're going to be bloody 'eroes.' He was right.

About a mile offshore was a sizeable enemy merchant ship, guarded by two destroyers, an umbrella of fighter planes and six-inch coastal batteries.

With the signal 'Full speed ahead', Gould began one of the most brazen attacks in naval history. He had worked out the tactics for such a situation with Butler and Smith the night before.

Gould's 639 headed for the destroyers, to draw their fire while 633 and 637 manoeuvred into position to torpedo the freighter. It took

109

twelve minutes to do that, and in those twelve minutes all hell broke loose.

A bare second after Gould had opened fire on the leading destroyer, with his comparatively ridiculous popguns, the Nazi warships began to blast with four-inch salvos. The six-inch shore batteries also opened up. A moment later anti-aircraft guns, their barrels depressed to sea level, joined in. Fighter planes dived in groups of twos and threes to pump cannon shells and machine-gun bullets into the outrageous little ships.

The incredible happened. 'Get the destroyer's bridge,' yelled Gould to his gunners over the din of bullets and shrapnel beating against the armour-plate of his diminutive bridge. And within a few minutes the destroyer began to withdraw, seriously damaged. Dodging water-spouts that threatened every few seconds to engulf it, 639 laid a smoke-screen between the second destroyer and the other two MTBs, while they got ready for their deadly business. Less than a thousand yards from the Nazi merchantmen, Butler sent his two tin fish plunging into the water. A moment later Smith's torpedoes were under way. There was a deafening explosion and the Nazi ship literally jumped out of the water—in bits.

'Withdraw,' came the signal from 639. But Butler and Smith hesitated, for 639 was afire. On its bridge lay Gould, his right side sprayed with machine-gun bullets from face to knee. A few feet away his second in command was dead, killed instantly by a shell burst. His first lieutenant, John Hayden, was running the ship, with a bullet in his back.

Six-inch shells churned the sea as Butler and Smith came alongside their stricken flagship to take off Gould and his crew. ''Alf a mo','' roared the 639's coxswain, 'There's a midshipman below wot's got it.' And while the rescue ships patiently waited in the inferno round them the coxswain fought his way through smoke and flame and back again. ''Ere 'e is,' he yelled triumphantly. The midshipman—half his left hand blown off and his jaw shattered by bullets—managed a smile. 'What about a spot of morphia, chaps?' he asked.

As the last of 639's survivors were brought aboard the other two MTBs, forty Axis fighters struck. But they were cheated again.

Dodging and weaving, their decks loaded with dead and wounded, Butler and Smith made for Sousse. Even the wounded cheered when one of the gunners sent a Focke-Wulf flaming into the sea. Then a squadron of American Warhawks roared over and cleared the sky of enemy planes.

'Pretty good show,' said Gould, shortly before he died an hour later.

George Palmer

George Palmer wrote of naval combat from first hand experience. Assigned by the United Press to cover the British Mediterranean fleet, Mr Palmer sailed for fifteen months in numerous Malta convoys—and was lucky enough to come through with only one torpedoing. In the commando raid on Tobruk, then three hundred miles behind the enemy lines, the small boat he was aboard was dive-bombed for twelve hours. He also covered the naval bombardment of Italian shore installations.

Normandy Incident

On the morning of 24 July 1944, ML 204 of the 13th Flotilla lay in the beach head anchorage off the Normandy Coast.

Having had a very noisy night with the Luftwaffe dropping mines and bombs around the anchorage, I had taken a couple of hours kip in my usual resting place, between the Hall-Scotts, on a cushion. With only two of us running the engine room, it saved dodging up and down between there and the mess deck.

A sudden violent explosion shook the ship and my first thoughts were the tanks of the Monitor Roberts firing her giant rifles. On peering through the scuttle, I was greeted with the awful sight of a large transport, the MV *Derry Cunihy* on fire with her back broken abaft the bridge and the after section, containing the troops, sinking fast. She had started to get underway to get nearer the beaches to unload her cargo, the 43rd Recce Regiment, when she exploded an oyster mine. We started up and were soon coming alongside the ship. Looking into the after section, I could see soldiers, still undressed, frantically trying to escape. The seamen started to use the deck-hose, vainly trying to stem the flames.

An already dangerous situation, as we were fully fuelled, was made worse by ammunition from burning armoured cars and trucks flying all over the place. We began taking aboard survivors, many of them wounded and burned; this taxed our first-aid cabinet and eventually we had to chop up the battery box lids for splints. Our troubles were multiplied when a large salvage vessel attempted to come alongside us and in so doing, savaged us severely. Away went our port rubbing strake, rails and depth charges, fortunately set to safe, and the radar aerials.

Being completely overloaded, we pulled slowly away to look for the nearest hospital ship. Away near Le Havre, the Germans must have spotted our 'Jimmy', the late Arthur Franklin, who was dressed in

112

bright blue pyjamas, cap and rubber sea-boots. 'Woof Woof Woof' and the attendant water spouts from the bit shells were far too near for comfort; the throttles were opened wide with disastrous results; the main engine fuses blew and we were a sitting duck.

Our luck held, the engines restarted and the Germans missed but as we got under way, the 'Jimmy' ran along the upper deck to the bridge, and slipped up in the mixture of oil and blood which covered the deck, causing him to slide in the filth. This moment of high comedy earned the 'Jimmy' the nickname of 'Bluebottle'. I would add that he was rather rotund.

The Regiment involved were virtually wiped out before they even saw the enemy and the after section of the ship became a steel war grave for nearly two hundred men. In his book *Caen—Anvil of Victory*, Alexander McKee calls this incident 'Death of a Regiment' and at the end of the chapter the Revd J. E. Gethyn-Jones, MBE, an Army Padre, praised the actions of the crew of a large Motor Gunboat for being the first on the spot and performing such magnificent rescue work.

Once more, Coastal Forces had done their stuff.

Len Bridge, London Branch

Chariots of Fire ... Navy Style

Leaving Fairmile Engineering in April 1943, as a L/MM I was drafted to MTB 206 to gain some practical experience, after which time I returned to HMS *Attack*, and from there I was drafted to pick up a D type MGB 675 from Robertson's Boatyard at Loch Long on the Clyde. I had seen D-Boats before, but not like this one. It had a derrick fitted just forward of the six-pounder gun at the stern.

After completing acceptance trials we set sail for an undisclosed destination, a loch somewhere in Scotland. It did not take long to find out why the derrick was fitted to MGB 675. It was for lifting Chariots and one-man mini-subs. Things went well with the lifting until we tried to lift a mini-sub, but the extra weight was too much, and the guy broke. This caused the tube of the derrick to bend over at right angles, so back it went to Robertson's Yard. This time they removed the six-pounder from the stern and fitted two steel plates to the deck head port and starboard sides, then they fitted two davits both sides. We then sailed back to the loch and started over again; this time all went well. It was hard work lifting the Chariots, but once on board we went on trials. The ship we were to practise on was a Submarine Depot ship HMS *Bonadventure*. In order to get close enough without being spotted we diverted the exhaust through the dumb flow silencers and fitted coconut mats over the exhaust outlet to stop the water spray from being seen.

It was in September 1943, whilst watching a film on the *Bonadventure*, that a signal was read out to all on board. It was from Winston Churchill, wishing the crews of the six Ex Craft and the subs towing them to Norway to attack the *Tirpitz*, God's speed and the best of luck.

Later in September, with two Chariots on board, we set sail for Lerwick in the Shetlands, going via the Caledonian Canal and Scapa Flow. About the middle of October 1943, we loaded the upper deck with extra petrol in five-gallon cans to enable us to get to our destination, which was a fjord about fifteen miles from Bergen. It was late evening when the boat with all the extra crew, which included Marine Commandos, crews for the Chariots, and their dressers, pulled away from Lerwick, together with a number of Norwegian MTBs acting as escorts. The weather was not too good; it was blowing a gale. The escort boats asked permission to return to Lerwick, but permission was refused. However when the dawn came as we neared the coast of Norway, the escorts had disappeared and we were on our own.

We slipped into a small fjord, struck the mast, and tied up to the cliffs with grappling irons, and the boat was covered with camouflage netting. The commandos went ashore to have a look around, then came back and reported a German radio station close by. Around about midday a small fishing boat came alongside and told us we had been spotted by a Quisling boat, and it would report that we were here. The nets were pulled down, the mast reset, and we pulled away.

We must have been sailing for a couple of hours or more when we spotted a Dornier plane. Nothing happened for some time and the Skipper decided to turn about and try again. This proved to be the wrong decision for at approximately 1600 hours six German fighter planes, four ME 109s and two F/Wolf's, started to attack; it lasted until 1900 hours. By this time the gun crews had shot two down and one probable. The task now was to get back to Lerwick on the one engine that was still working, and have all the wounded attended to. It was a daunting task as the compass had been shot away and with the Skipper using the stars by night and the sextant by day it took seventy-two hours to reach land, and that was the Port of Dunbar. So instead of sailing two hundred miles we had done approximately four hundred miles. After all the wounded were taken to hospital and the boat cleaned up we sailed to Rosyth Dockyard and had the Chariots removed.

All the crew were fitted out with new uniforms and blankets to replace the gear damaged by enemy action. We then sailed down to Aberdeen to have repairs carried out and the damaged engines changed. The crew were given survivor's leave, but recalled after seven days. By this time other boats started to arrive at Aberdeen and a L/MM off one of the boats invited me on board to have a look at the steel plate fitted over the aft cabins. I remember him saying to me: 'Not bad, having armoured plating.' I just smiled to myself because I knew what it was for, it was for carrying the davits.

The hurried refit completed, we sailed once again for Lerwick, but on arrival the boat was found to be leaking like a sieve. It was decided by the C/Chief that 675 would sail back down to Falmouth and be paid off. So once again we sailed back to Scapa Flow, through the Caledonian Canal to Fort William then on to Larne in Northern Ireland and down to Falmouth. The crew then went on leave. By this time it was December 1943, and by January 1944 I was in Malta.

Member No. 1866, Thomas M. Robinson

MTB Rams U-Boat
by Wing-Commander E. G. Oakley-Beuttler

It takes all sorts to make up the average RNVR crew of a Motor Torpedo Boat—yachtsmen, clerks, gardeners, writers and so on—but although most of their training has been done during the war period, the result is the pick of the Wavy Navy. This particular MTB is a Vosper-built ship. The details of the drama speak for themselves.

117

Wonderful Spirit of Camaraderie—
Christmas 1943

There was a special treat for me on Christmas morning in the form of a plate of porridge for breakfast. After a leisurely toilet I went with the crew to a nice little service conducted by a Naval chaplain. The festivities then began on the messdeck. Our CO, Samuel Stewart, had turned up by this time and I found him struggling into the coxswain's second best uniform, whilst the wardroom steward, who is the youngest member of the ship's company, was struggling into Sam's stiff collar and tie. In less than no time I was a matelot again for the first time in eighteen months, a seaman gunner, whilst the motor mechanic was transformed into Jimmy-the-One.

And last but not least, Petty Officer Coxswain Gardiner had been demoted to the rank of ordinary seaman and was promptly put in the rattle for insolent behaviour and awarded 366 days' cells. Next on the list was Seaman Gunner Lovegrove who was summarily weighed off for being improperly dressed, i.e. for wearing a medal to which he was not entitled. Finally Jimmy-the-One was to be heard tearing the 'coxswain' off a strip for not running the ship properly. Meanwhile the 'Captain' lounged at his ease with a fat cigar, airily granting all-night leave to the entire ship's company for the next fortnight to come.

Then of course we all got down to the really serious business of eating and drinking. 'Ordinary Seaman' Gardiner and myself were detailed off by the 'Coxswain' as cooks of the mess and waited on the crew and washed up the dishes. Friend Eldridge improved even his past record and the turkey was only excelled by the superb pudding. You should have seen him. He had on a pair of frayed overall trousers, a black and white striped football jersey and a pink hood, no, bonnet, tied under his chin with a huge bow, and sweat was pouring down his face.

118

The crew were really terrific. They loved the reversal of roles and the wit was superb in its spontaneity and yet at the same time no advantage was taken of the situation. The slightest lapse of that nature would have spoiled the whole thing. After dinner came the coffee and biscuits, cigarettes and speeches, and each bloke in turn was expected to sing, dance, spin a yarn or say a poem. He was given ten seconds to think of something before going in the rattle. This hilarity went on until just before three when Sam and I went aft to hear the King's speech.

An hour later another party started aboard in the wardroom with the WRNS we were with the previous night. They were quite nice and didn't stay long. When they pushed off, Sam did too, and John and I went ashore to see what was cooking. We found a comparatively select and quiet pub and were just settling down to a quiet pint when who should walk in but the coxswain and Smith, our pet copper-boxer, and that fairly fixed the evening's programme, if you see what I mean ...

Member No. 2036, Frank Lovegrove

The Old Camber at Gib

For those of you in the 9th based at Gib, or the HDs likewise, you will be sorry to learn that our old camber is now what I would call a third rate marina. The army did have it as a sailing centre until a few years ago and the standard was quite good. Equally, all the navy buildings—the dentist and the like—from the chamber to the dockyard gate some hundreds of yards along the road, are, or were, derelict when I saw it last in 1988.

Won't be long before some developer pushes in,

Member No. 2104 Alan F. Buckland

119

'The Fighting 9th'

The 9th's torpedoes were those from old US (First World War) destroyers—none were on view during our 'T star' course and they received only casual mention. I am not sure whether I should have been thankful or sorry that 170 had no opportunity to use her 'tin-fish' as their performance could (to put it mildly) be erratic. Within two weeks of my joining CFB Gib an exercise 'run' of the 9th's torpedoes (with blowing heads, of course) was carried out. I was in ML 173 and Captain D's Torpedo Officer in 176. Off Europa, 176 fired her two torpedoes. The first ran on the surface and disappeared heading for the Spanish shore! The second had a gyro failure, ran in circles and passed under us (just!) in 173 but fortunately, at the end of its run, surfaced and was recovered by 176. Of the two we fired in 173 one ran true and was picked up by an HDML, our second initially failed to leave the tube owing to a mis-fire. We rectified this and fired again and the 'fish', I think, then ran true. 176's 'surface runner', despite protracted search, we never recovered—it had defected to the Axis powers! Which involved me in reports in quintuplicate (no photostats in those days!), murmurs about Courts of Enquiry or worse, personal payment for the loss, etc.—so no dinner and not much sleep that night! According to Richard Hough in *War at Sea—1939/45* US torpedoes in World War II were apparently just as unreliable, which gives me some retrospective comfort!

Member No. 1852 Alan F. Dakin

Officers' Mess

Shortly after joining the newly formed 60th Flotilla at Immingham Dock, RML 512 was ordered across the Humber to Hull to collect new Confidential Books. We left Immingham after breakfast but, though the distance to Hull by water is no more than a dozen miles, the trip took about an hour owing to the strong ebb.

Amongst our number was a certain Ordinary Seaman New. That was not his real name, but for this story, it is appropriate as an alias because he had been an Ordinary Seaman for all of eight weeks prior to which he had been at school. Mind you, not many aboard 512 were that much better experienced. I had been wearing a Sub-Lieutenant's wavy stripe for no longer than Ordinary Seaman New had been in square rig.

While we were locking out of the dock, OD New came to ask if we were going to be long in Hull. I told him I thought not more than an hour or so and that, at any rate, we would not be entering the dock but tying up at the river wall.

'Do you think it would be all right,' he asked, 'if I went ashore to see my uncle? He works in the port.'

I said I didn't see why not provided he was back within the hour ready for the return to Immingham. But I'd need to clear it first with the CO.

The CO raised no objection except to tell me to lay it on a bit about the penalties for missing ship. OD New expressed appreciation and, soon after tying up at Hull, he appeared on deck in Number One rig to request permission to go ashore. And away he went.

In completing our errand it was my job, as First Lieutenant, to do the leg-work. So, having arranged with Cox'n for useful occupations to keep everyone busy whilst alongside, I reported to the CO and then made my own way ashore in fulfilment of orders.

Threading my way through the wharves *en route* to Base Offices, I rounded the corner of a warehouse and beheld Ordinary Seaman New standing rigidly at attention. Confronting him was a four-ring Captain RN.

Disregarding the newness and waviness of my single wavy stripe and the fact that my greenness had yet to transfer itself to my cap badge which still shone like spun gold, I stepped forward to take upon my shoulders whatever 'bottle' our young crewman was being handed. I pulled up just short of the principals in the drama, saluted and was about to say, 'Is something wrong?' or similar, but Ordinary Seaman New got in first.

'Sir,' he addressed me, 'This is my uncle.'

Dealing with such encounters was not in the King Alfred curriculum, and I was left momentarily wondering how to follow up a line like that. I was saved the need by the said uncle thanking me cordially for allowing his nephew the short time ashore for them to meet, by which time I had my response ready.

'I wonder, Sir,' I said, 'if you would like to come aboard to meet our CO and see the boat.'

The Captain replied that he would like that very much if we could delay our departure until after noon when he would have some time free. Saluting, I left uncle and nephew in conversation, finished what I went to the Base offices to do and rushed back to the boat to warn the Skipper that we were likely to have a distinguished visitor shortly.

'Well,' said he, 'as you've done it, you'd better get up top and see that we've got a boat worth looking at.'

Cox'n and crew had done a splendid job, cleaning ship, so that, give or take, 512 would probably have passed muster at Saturday rounds. However, just to add the final touch, I instructed that the upper deck be given a hose down so that our visitor would find it shining up at him on arrival.

Now if you do not know the Humber, as I did not at that time, it is a kind of sluice that sweeps tons of Yorkshire and what is now Humberside outwards to be deposited on Spurn Point at the river mouth and washes it all back again with the flood. The effect is to produce a stream of liquidised mud which, when pumped over a vessel's deck, quickly covers it with a brown sludge which dries out to suggest that the vessel has sailed through a sand storm. What is worse, in trying to wash it away more of the deposit is added!

And so it was that, when the four-ring uncle hove in sight on the dock wall, he looked down on what, for all the world, looked like a part of the beach at Cleethorpes which had come adrift and been swept upstream.

'Someone should have warned you about the river,' he said as he clambered aboard. The Skipper then took over and, having toured the boat and been complimented on having a smart ship, forgetting the temporarily sad state of the upper deck, took the visitor to the ward-room, the sun being now well over the yardarm—a factor that may have had some bearing on his time of arrival—and we all relaxed.

'Your healths, gentlemen,' said our visitor as he raised his glass. 'A bit tactless to say "mud in your eye", eh?'

Member No. 1500 Don Mackintosh

Comrades

The Senior Officer of the Umpteenth ML Flotilla had been enter-tained ashore and returned to the Base late one night, brimming with, among other things, good humour and a kindly feeling towards all men, thoughts of the enemy having been temporarily set aside.

He halted and allowed the sentry at the gate to recognise him and bade a warm good night to him and the Petty Officer and the Guard before making his way along the quay to where his boat was berthed. He even commiserated with the duty Quartermaster on the tediousness of the task of tending mooring ropes as the tide rose or fell and wished him a trouble-free watch with no air raid warnings to disturb the peace.

Then he stepped aboard his boat, the innermost in a trot of three, and arrived at last at the wardroom hatch where, to his surprise, not to say concern, he found a recumbent figure propped against the doorway with legs stretched out on the deck and having every sign of enjoying a sleep in the open air. In fact, it was not possible for the SO to reach the comfort of his bunk without in some way shifting the sleeper in order to get the hatch open.

Now, the SO had not wasted his time in officer training and he knew that under certain circumstances, a friendly tap on the shoulder may be interpreted as an assault upon the person and that when that person is a slumbering matelot the repercussions could be unpredictable, including the possibility that a somewhat harder tap might come back, and nobody wants to provoke that sort of thing between a sailor man and a superior officer.

So, the SO retreated and went to consult the Quartermaster, now once more in his solitary vigil on the quayside. The Quartermaster accepted the SO's request to join him in an inspection of the sleeping sailor.

'Do you recognise him?' the SO asked.

124

'Yes, Sir,' came the reply, 'he's from ML [and gave the number of the outermost boat on the trot].'

'Then,' said the SO, 'Please ask the Cox'n of that boat to come along and get this chap to his bunk.'

The recumbent body stirred, raised itself to a position very nearly that of attention and straightened the cap from flat-aback to the regulation angle. 'I am the Cox'n,' he said. He saluted gravely and, with a dignified step and some help from guard rails and stanchions, made his way from the SO's boat, across the next one and at last reached his own boat. The Quartermaster followed him to ensure that no ill befell while the SO watched from a distance.

As the Cox'n reached his own mess-deck hatch, he turned, came once more to attention with the help from the hatchcover and again saluted.

'Goodnight, Sir,' he called across.

'Goodnight, Cox'n,' the SO replied. Then 'Goodnight, again, Quartermaster and thank you.'

'Goodnight, Sir.'

There was no air raid warning. Even the enemy was apparently feeling well disposed that night!

Member No. 1500 Don Mackintosh

Secret—Report HMMTB 218
Dover. 3/4 December 1941

Sir,

I have the honour to submit the following report on the proceedings of HMMTB 218 on the night of the 3/4 December 1941. MTB 218, under command, proceeded out of harbour at 1938 in company with MTB 219 (SO) and 221. Movements of the Senior Officer were followed until 2030 at position 320 degrees Gris Nez 1 mile, when orders were received to spread out and act independently. MTB 218 proceeded abeam to port of SO keeping visual contact and on a northerly course away from Gris Nez. Visibility was about 1,200 yards and at 2035 enemy was sighted ahead. MTB 218 was right in her course and by manoeuvring to starboard and round to port contact with the other MTBs was made and a firing position attained from inshore. At 2037 I fired both torpedoes with 10 knots deflection and at a range of 600 yards, but regret no hits were seen, and the torpedo tracks could not be observed.

After firing I proceeded on main engines as the boat had already been hit by enemy fire. Course altered to port as the other MTBs who had fired before me were to starboard. This necessarily brought us close to the enemy and some well aimed fire from our 0.5" turret was directed at him. This did not stop him from returning a heavy fire and hits were scored on the boat. Disengaging courses were set in south-westerly direction and at 2047 when a mile clear of the enemy the boat was stopped to examine the damage. At the time of firing the torpedoes the boat was holed by a 4" shell bursting below the waterline amidships and on the starboard side. Lockers were immediately blown in the crew's mess side beside the W/T compartment which was quickly flooded putting the W/T set out of action both for receiving and transmitting. Water was entering fast and the speed of the boat was greatly reduced owing to the increased displacement.

Other hits were received in the mess deck forward and the engine-room by explosive cannon shellfire. One AP shell entered the wheelhouse through the plating and burst, slightly injuring the First Lieutenant. Another incendiary entered the magazine and was brought to rest in a case of ammunition. One of these short circuited the electrical system so that the bridge compass light was faulty and navigational lights and stern lights were illuminated. This may have accounted for some very well aimed fire that accompanied us for some distance after the attack. The lights eventually had to be broken. At 2050 all SPs were jettisoned as there seemed considerable risk of the boat sinking or becoming waterlogged in enemy waters. The W/T operator meanwhile had bunged the hole in the ship's bottom with blankets and pillows which he kept in place by standing on them. The main entry of water was undoubtedly stopped by this. At 2053, course was set for home. Already there was four feet of water in the Wardroom, W/T and after mess deck bilges. A friendly MTB was passed at this time, but it was thought that she might not have completed her attack, and a signal was not made to her. An hour later, at 2155, the situation was becoming serious as the bow of the ship was below the level of the sea. All heavy gear had been moved from the forecastle and the forepeak; anchors and carley float had been removed to the stern, the depth charges released overboard. A hole in the petrol compartment–W/T bulkhead had been made to allow water to flood the petrol compartment where another suction pump could be brought into action as the connections for the main pumping system in the crew's mess and after mess decks had been shot away. The watertight door in the mess deck bulkhead was leaking badly so that the forward mess decks were also full of water and more was coming through a shell hole which was now under water level.

At this time the boat was turned about to go astern and courses altered to allow for the tidal change which was expected at 2300. About six knots could be made astern though steering was very difficult. The bow rose a few inches out of the water. Reverse gears of the three engines designed only for short periods of running had to be continually adjusted and speed was further reduced. Much time was lost in stopping engines to adjust these gears.

AT 0015 Sand Head buoy was sighted and closed and course set for the land. During this period water had only risen about six inches as the buoyancy in the forepeak was holding up the bow. The telegraphist was withdrawn as the water was above his shoulders and he was suffering from extreme cold. Land was made at Hope Bay and course altered towards Dover. Three Very lights (red) were fired whilst under South Foreland lighthouse, and the harbour was entered at 1255. At Ferry Dock Extension a trailer fire pump was ready. The water was then one foot above the wheelhouse deck amidships. The fore peak and after peak bulkheads held well as these were the only two compartments in the boat that were not seriously flooded. One of the splinter mattresses round the bridge received a direct hit from a cannon shell which exploded internally. Very few fragments penetrated the bridge. The action of the whole crew was excellent throughout and much good work was put in by the engine room personnel in keeping the engines and pumping machinery working in an efficient manner.

I desire particularly to commend the following:

P. PHILLIPS, Ldg. Tel. D/SSX14570. This is the eighth action at Dover in which this rating has taken part in MTB 218. He has on every occasion carried out his duties with efficiency and speed. On this occasion he was in the W/T compartment, and, although considerably dazed by the flash and shock of a shell bursting a few feet from him, he immediately realised that the set was out of action, and was able to wade to the hole, and cover it with blankets and pillows and keep them in place by standing on them. He remained in an awkward position until the water level had reached his shoulders, and he was suffering from extreme cold and exhaustion. He eventually had to be ordered away from his position after remaining there for two and a half hours and had to be lifted up onto the deck.

M. SAUNDERS, PO (Cox'n) P/JX 140425. PO Saunders has served in HMMTB 218 as Coxswain in eight actions against the enemy at Dover. He has always conducted himself calmly and coolly under enemy fire, setting a good example to the remainder of the crew. He was at the wheel for the entire trip and steered the ship astern with the aid of an electric torch, under extreme difficulties.

A. D. HOBBS, Acting Stoker PO, P/KX 84258. A/S PO Hobbs has been in every action in which the ship has been engaged. On this occasion, although not in charge of the engine-room, he was mainly responsible for the continuous repairs and adjustments to the reverse gears which enabled the ship to run for four and a half hours astern.

Midshipman M. T. BALL, RNR. This officer showed the utmost coolness and resource throughout. He was a great assistance to me and a fine example to the crew.

I have the honour to be, Sir, Your Obedient Servant,

(Signed) H. P. GRANLUND, DSC, Lieutenant, RNVR

This is an excellent example of the report a Commanding Officer had to write after an action. This report is one of the earliest MTB successers.

Big Eats—1944 Price

On revising from a text book that I had away at sea with me during the war I discovered a NAAFI account that I had used as a bookmark; it reads:

NAVY, ARMY & AIR FORCE INSTITUTES. S102468.

5th May 1944.

M.T.B. 687

2 lb Sausages	*@ 1/ 0½d.*	*2s.*	*1d.*
3 bottles Sauce	*@ 11d.*	*2s.*	*9d.*
36 Eggs	*@ 2d.*	*6s.*	*0d.*
6 lb Bacon	*@ 2/ 4d.*	*14s.*	*4d.*
		£1 5s.	*2d.*
	Less 5%	*1s.*	*3d.*
		£1 3s.	*11d.*
1 Box Nutty		*12s.*	*0d.*
		£1 15s.	*11d.*

A bit late now to claim overcharge of 4*d.* on the bacon. The sauce I presume was Allie Slopers with the instructions on the bottles reading: 'Take plenty of it with anything and everything.'

Member No. 474 Randall Tomlinson, DSM

Rescue Motor Launch 548 photograph taken 14th July 1943 at Skale Fjord Faeroes, note the sick bay abaft the funnel also the dome on the wheelhouse is the Radio Direction Finder.

Pages from the Diary of MTB 85

After the return from Komiza on 1 February 1944, an engine inspection revealed a defective port exhaust pipe and MTB 85 was declared unfit for operations. Just before midnight on 2 February, 85 sailed with HMS *Prodigal*, an KCT and MTB 297 to Manfredonia for repairs.

Soon after arriving at Manfredonia, a check-up by the base Engineering Officer revealed that the repairs were beyond the local facilities, and MTB 85 was sent down to Brindisi via Bari, where she secured alongside the badly damaged HMS Vienna, which had been towed down from Bari.

The stay at Brindisi lasted until 22 February 1944, during which time the starboard engine was replaced, a new port auxiliary engine was fitted, the port exhaust pipe repaired, an Italian 20mm. Breda gun installed, and the paint brushes worked overtime on the hull and upper deck. Also, our coxswain, Micky Watt, passed his Petty Officer's exam at Taranto.

On 22 February MTBs 85 and 297 left Brindisi for Manfredonia and on the way the replaced starboard engine broke down. The following day, when the defect had been repaired, she left Manfredonia for Vis with 297, but again the starboard engine broke down and she had to return to Manfredonia on her own.

The following day, after the engine had been repaired, Lieutenant P. Hyslop, our skipper, fell sick and was transferred to the sick bay ashore. He was replaced for a short time by Lieutenant H. Du Boulay, RNVR. At dusk MTB 85 crept out of Manfredonia bound for Vis, where she tied up alongside MTB 243 on arrival, and remained on immediate notice.

During the next few nights, when weather permitted, MTBs 85 and 297 carried out patrols between the mainland and the Dalmatian Islands, looking for German supply vessels. On 28 February Commander Wellman, RN visited Vis and inspected the boat and its crew,

132

and on the same day Peter Hyslop returned from sick bay to resume his command. On 3 March whilst on patrol at dusk in the Drevnick Channel with MTB 297, the two vessels were bombed by an unidentified aircraft, but no damage or casualties were sustained.

On 10 March 1944, MTB 85 accompanied MGB 674 on a night patrol in the Neratva Channel between Hvar and Korcula, again looking for German vessels supplying their garrisons in the islands. Lieutenant R. Davidson, RNVR, skipper of 674, was the SO. At 23.16 a ship was sighted, then challenged, but did not answer or stop. A shot was fired across her bows by 674; but this action failed to stop her, and she opened up with small arms fire in the direction of the two MTBs. The more heavily armed Dogboat soon silenced all resistance with a fusillade of 4-pounder, 20mm. and .5 ammunition. A boarding party from MTB 85 jumped aboard the large schooner, and promptly rounded up twenty-seven German prisoners and took them back aboard the Vosper MTB. Fresh outbreaks of small arms fire broke out after 85 had pulled away, and 674 had also tried to get alongside.

Lieutenant Davidson gave the order to sink the vessel by gunfire, and with excellent gunnery the gun crews complied with his request. When 674 and 85 returned to Komiza the twenty-seven prisoners were collected and interrogated by the military intelligence, and from the information they supplied it was obvious that this had been a highly successful operation.

The 150-ton schooner had approximately seventy-five German troops and supplies, ammunition etc., aboard from the enemy garrison on Hvar Island, and her interception and destruction must have been a severe blow to the Germans. Our losses had been nil.

At this period there was much activity by Coastal Force boats amongst the islands and on the following night of 11 March, Lieutenant P. Hyslop, DSC, RNVR as SO took 85, 84 and 243 for a dusk-to-dawn patrol off Murter Island, north of the Yugoslav port of Sibenik. Passing Blitvenika and on to Cavlin Island, they cruised around on silent engines looking for enemy shipping. These tactics were rewarded at 22.55 when a large enemy vessel was detected hugging the coast, and when she disappeared into a small cove, Hyslop in 85

133

followed in, instructing the two other MTBs to wait outside. When in position two torpedoes were fired at the quarry, but unfortunately both exploded when they made contact with the shore. Having survived the torpedo run the German vessel opened fire with heavy armament, hitting 85 on the port torpedo tube, and down the port side of the hull, forcing the Vosper to leave the cove with the enemy in pursuit. The SO by R/T ordered 84 and 243 to make a torpedo attack on their own and told them to rendezvous with 85 off Cavlin Island on completion of their mission.

Contact by W/T and R/T was then lost between the boats, and the badly damaged MTB 85 proceeded on her own back to Komiza, where she arrived at 05.20 in increasingly bad weather. MTBs 84 and 243 followed over an hour later. Both had managed to get in position to fire torpedoes but both 243's tinfish failed to fire, and 84's port torpedo as well. Only 84's starboard missile hissed out of its tube and narrowly missed its target.

From the individual skipper's report, the heavily armed enemy vessel was deemed to be of the destroyer/large torpedo boat class, and was obviously making her way into Sibenik harbour. The inspection of 85's damage called for major repairs, involving a new port torpedo tube, and patching up the holes in the hull on the port side. Fortunately there were no casualties amongst the crew.

MTB 85 was ordered to Brindisi for the work to be carried out, but very bad weather at sea delayed her departure until 15 March. On the 12th and 13th two early morning Luftwaffe raids on Komiza harbour failed to add further damage to her hull or superstructure.

At 23.30 on 15 March 1944 she arrived back at Brindisi, secured alongside HMS *Vienna*, and awaited the engineers' and shipwrights' inspection.

Bert Cooper

Unknown 'B' Class Motor Launch, fitted with long range tanks. Armament: one 3-pounder for'ard; one Holman Projector; one twin Lewis aft.

Joyous Reunion of War Heroes

Magnus M. Shearer JP, one of the long standing members of CFVA (No. 428), found a most satisfying job in his position as HM Lord Lieutenant of Shetland to officially welcome a return to Shetland of the crew and veterans of the former United States subchaser *Hitra*, loaned along with the sister ships *Hessa* and *Vigra* to the Norwegian Navy in 1943.

Here is a shortened version of the reports in the *Shetland Times*, Friday 12 June 1987 and *Shetland Life*, Number 81, July 1987.

Scalloway, Shetland had a joyous reunion with some of Norway's war heroes, when eighteen veterans of the 'Shetland Bus' guerilla operation returned to their home port.

There was a rapturous welcome for the recently restored submarine-chaser *Hitra*, forty-two years after she left for the victory celebrations in newly-liberated Bergen.

Escorted by four Norwegian motor torpedo boats, *Hitra*, after a moderately rough trip from Bergen, was greeted by several hundred people on the pier, along with the Lerwick Pipe Band and HMS *Shetland*.

On board *Hitra* was her wartime captain, Commander Ingvald Eidsheim, who was in command for 43 of her 45 hazardous missions between 1943 and 1945. Other veterans sailed to Shetland as guests of the Royal Norwegian Navy aboard the MTBs.

Among the official welcoming party were the author, David Howarth, whose book immortalised the 'Shetland Bus' heroes; The Lord Lieutenant, Mr Magnus Shearer; the Norwegian honorary consul, Mrs Nancy Sinclair; and members of the Scalloway's *Hitra* Welcome committee.

The veterans drove to Lerwick where they visited the graves of Norwegian Servicemen and after the civic reception were taken to Kergord, the secret war-time headquarters of the spy and sabotage

136

operation. Thence to Lunna, to lay wreaths on the graves of their fallen comrades in the ancient Kirkyard there.

The star of the show was, of course, the *Hitra*, restored so lovingly at a cost of five million Norwegian kroner (about £450,000). She was derelict when discovered by chance among some skerries in Sweden five years ago.

Admiral Helle, the chairman of the *Hitra* restoration committee, proposing a toast to his host said, 'I hope that *Hitra* will become a living symbol of friendship between Shetland and Norway.'

Commander Eidsheim, commenting on the handling of the *Hitra* on her voyage to the Shetlands: 'Maybe she was a bit light in the water,' he said, 'but then in the war we were carrying plenty of heavy ammunition in the magazine!'

All of the crew had stories to tell. One man was reminded that the last time he'd been in Lerwick the Sheriff had fined him £5 for leaving his lights on his bicycle during the blackout.

'HITRA' a remarkable story ...

The story of the 'Shetland Bus' is one of the most dramatic to emerge from the Second World War. It goes back to 1940 when German forces occupied Norway, resulting in a stream of refugees heading west, most of whom landed in Shetland. On 10 June 1940, Norway surrendered and almost immediately Norwegians began training with units of the British armed forces.

In the summer of 1941 a secret base was set up at Lunna on the north-east coast of the Shetland Mainland and during the winter that followed many successful missions were carried out, using small fishing cutters. They landed agents, radio sets, arms and ammunition and returned with refugees.

There had been losses of men and boats in that first winter at Lunna and these steadily increased after operations started at Scalloway. Five ships were either captured, sunk by enemy action or lost in bad weather with the loss of thirty men. It was even suggested that, in view of the heavy losses, the base should be closed and the remaining seamen transferred to the regular Norwegian Navy but the response of the men was emphatic—'Give us better boats and we will carry on the fight.'

A solution was found when the US Navy provided three fast sub-chasers with a cruising speed of 17 knots and a top speed of 22 knots. They were so well armed that German aircraft kept their distance. From November 1943 until the end of the war they carried on the same kind of operations that the fishing boats had done but they emerged virtually unscathed.

The importance of the Scalloway base was shown quite clearly by David Howarth in *The Shetland Bus*—nearly 400 tons of ammunition supplied to the resistance movement, sixty radio transmitters in Norway provided the Allied High Command with information on everything the Germans did in Norway and, as a sideline, 350 refugees, most of whom were in trouble with the Gestapo, were brought back to Shetland. Throughout the invasion of Europe troops were held in Norway. The base in Shetland of a hundred men was an essential link in a chain which bound down 284,000 German soldiers.

After the war the three sub-chasers joined the regular Norwegian Navy and eventually they were sold so that when interest revived in this remarkable wartime story their whereabouts were unknown. Then one day in 1982, during a detailed search of the coastline of Sweden, looking for an intruding Russian submarine, the *Hitra* was rediscovered lying derelict, half submerged among some skerries. She was taken to Norway and restored at a cost of 5 million kroner (about £450,000).

She is now used for educational purposes, travelling up and down the coast of Norway telling young people about this remarkable wartime story.

It is most poignant to read of the effort, money and organisation that have been lavished on the restoration of *Hitra* by the Norwegian authorities and people by the generous donations, even a small branch of the Shetland Norway Friendship Society in Yell donated £50. The Norwegians raised £450,000 whilst we are struggling to raise £50,000 to keep MTB 102 afloat.

138

The Arakan Coast 1945
with ML 854

The second part of the 36th Flotilla consisted of MLs 854 (section leader), 847 and 855. They were at Tek Naf, the Burma advanced base, on Christmas Day 1944, having lost 830 in a cyclone *en route* from Cape Town.

The Arakan is broken country netted with small rivers and narrow tidal *chaungs* navigable up to thirty miles. It was an unknown quantity and it was incumbent on the COPPs assisted by the MLs to seek out landing areas. The Royal Indian Navy sloop *Narbada* commanded by Captain Knott played an important part in these clandestine operations during early 1945.

On 1 January 1945, two Combined Operation Pilotage Party members (COPP for short) boarded 854 to reconnoitre Akyab island prior to a seaborne assault. During this night operation, the COPPs and the ML came under small arms fire and the unopposed landing on Akyab followed two days later.

After Akyab, 854 rendezvoused with the *Narbada* some miles off Myabon peninsula; representatives of the three services boarded the ML which set off to reconnoitre a proposed landing. ML 854 proceeded stern first up the estuary behind the enemy lines, observing obstacles placed to prevent such an assault. As soon as the craft started to retrace its steps it came under heavy shell, machine gun and rifle fire which ripped through the superstructure causing minor casualties, but as the Japs used armour-piercing shells they passed through the wooden craft without exploding.

Further reconnaissance was necessary; the first mission took four COPPs under cover of darkness to the proposed beach head. Two canoes were slipped 200 yards from the landing area. ML 854 sought cover under trees on the opposite side of the estuary, the anchor lowered on a grass line for silence and for a quick getaway in an emergency.

On the night prior to the landings, eight COPPs were taken to the area to destroy the obstacles with delayed charges before the Commandos hit the beach. It was an anxious wait for the crew of 854 whilst the COPPs fulfilled their dangerous task under the noses of the Japanese. The COPPs withdrew on 854 at dawn and saw their charges explode as the Commandos neared the beaches. Three days later whilst still at the beach head the crew discovered that the COPP members not called upon to venture ashore had left their explosives between the upper deck lockers—they were immediately ditched overboard.

With a draft of six foot the MLs were called upon to penetrate the uncharted *chaungs* to seek out and destroy the retreating Japanese. Such penetrations took the launches at night behind the enemy lines and were not usually successful. The launches would come under machine gun fire as they made their dangerous journeys inland. Silence was essential and engine revolutions kept to a minimum. Once under fire it would be full ahead to get out of range of the small arms fire. This would be followed by the eerie jungle sounds from monkeys and other wild birds and beasts. On reaching the destination, it would be a case of waiting with the anchor on a rope and a crew member standing by with a sharp knife to hack through the line, abandoning the anchor in an emergency in order to make a quick getaway. Invariably, after a short wait, shells would come over, landing very close as the machine gunners previously encountered would have advised their more heavily armed comrades. Thence back to base, past the machine gun nests with head down to rejoin the other craft. Such operations occurred regularly but it was time to push further inland.

ML 854 was again called upon for an unusual mission. This further push saw one of the fiercest battles in the Burma campaign. The site chosen to further cut off the Japanese was near the village of Kangaw some twenty miles inland from Myebon. During a lull in the fighting on that peninsula, ML 854 was summoned alongside RIN *Narbada* in the early evening. Captain Knott and other specialists came aboard. It was an operation similar to that carried out at Myebon—to survey and reconnoitre the proposed landing area many miles inland; ML 854 was accompanied by another ML, a Bym and two LCSs each carrying six Royal Marine Commandos. With the craft darkened and the crew suitably clad, the party set off. Within thirty minutes the Bym became stuck on a mud bank leaving one LCS to render assistance; the remaining raiders continued inland. Soon the other ML suffered a similar fate and was left to fend for herself. The journey through the narrow and treacherous *chaungs* with jungle wildlife noises took about three hours. Once more silence was essential; it was unlikely the Japanese would have anticipated such an inland waterway operation. At last the craft stopped with the *chaung* no wider than forty yards. The coxswain and Captain Knott ventured ashore to the *chaung* mud bank; this was the chosen landing area. The mission accomplished and with the crew still tense, 854 set out of the swamps and snipers' paradise for Myebon, picking up the stranded vessels on the way. Reaching the estuary just before daybreak, the crew relaxed until one of the MLs in the estuary, unaware of the operation, opened fire on the returning raiders.

The landing at Kangaw was organised in a matter of days. The initial few miles followed a route different from that taken by 854 because of the mud banks and rocks. Only small amphibious craft could be used in the jungle rivers where concealment among the tidal creeks and mangrove swamps was so essential. MLs, LCAs, LCSs and other small craft of all descriptions made up the attacking force. As the force moved inland 854's radar mast was snapped off by a Japanese communication wire across the *chaung* and during this time RAF fighters strafed each side of the *chaung*. The commandos were put ashore and slowly moved inland through the mangrove swamp. Kangaw village commanded the coastal road and, realising the importance of this attack, the Japanese launched suicidal attacks on the bridge head. The fierce fighting, much of it hand to hand, continued for about four weeks. As the morning mist lifted from the *chaung*, the launches were shelled, mortared and sniped at, wire guard rails would 'ping' as they were cut by mortar and shrapnel. The crew slackened

141

them off completely to eliminate this source of danger. Only one member of 854 suffered superficial injuries and remained on board.

Strange personnel came and departed from the launch: an Army intelligence officer and his two sergeants with the apparatus to intercept Japanese wireless messages. The Burmese agent was taken further inland on ML 854 with an Army commando to reconnoitre a village where the Japs were reported to be in hiding.

The launches at Kangaw were eventually relieved and sent to Ramree Island for a short rest. Here the crew were told that their CO, who had taken them so capably and calmly through the various *chaung* operations, including those of a clandestine nature, was to leave. They were very pleased to learn that he and the quartermaster were awarded the DSC and DSM respectively for their part in these operations.

With a new Skipper, ML 854 was relegated down the line and returned to the *chaungs* to work with the remainder of the flotilla. These activities included actual and decoy landings, shore bombardments, seeking out retreating Japanese and cutting off supplies but 854 no longer took a lead part in the campaign. MLs 854, 855 and 847 withdrew from the Arakan before Rangoon fell.

At Trincomalee, ML 854 began to ship water from damage incurred during their operations in the *chaungs* and was ordered to Mandapan for repairs. Returning to Trincomalee, the crew began to disperse. As well as fighting the Japanese, the Naval Force in Burma had to contend with many tropical diseases in addition to the more common forms of dysentery and malaria.

In the *Ceylon Review* of April 1945, Mr J. G. H. Gritten, the official Naval reporter, wrote:

> The narrow *chaungs* that gash Burma coast are the hunting grounds of our Motor Launches. It's small but deadly warfare, in which the fighting spirit and comradeship of the little ships gets full play.

The Central Office of Information stated in their Official Burma Campaign 1946:

> In these operations the Arakan Coastal Forces and the Bengal Auxiliary distinguished themselves. The Burmese Navy proved

142

to be as handy sailors as their comrades of the Royal Navy and Royal Indian Navy. The war in the *chaungs* called not only for daring in action but for unceasing care in the maintenance of vessels. It is an exacting job to keep your craft true after three months cruising through a swamp and the men of Combined Operations in the Arakan won their battle because they were better than the enemy at everything. He was outfought, outwitted, and outworked. As the Japanese retreated in this dark noisome fastness of mud and mangrove they found their waterways blocked by Coastal Forces. They were prey to flies, mosquitoes, scorpions and the most horrible crocodiles, and without food and water the Japanese died in hundreds.

Member No. 1389 W. Duncan Hill, Merthyr Tydfil

Coastal Forces and the
Bruneval Raid
27/28 February 1942

The 8th Army was in retreat in Libya, the Germans had advanced five hundred miles into Russia and were within sight of Moscow, the Japanese had destroyed the bulk of the American Pacific fleet at Pearl Harbour. All this on top of the retreat from Dunkirk.

There was however, one particular bright spot in this unhappy picture, and that was the defeat of the Luftwaffe by the RAF in the Battle of Britain. That victory came about through three factors: the airmen, their aircraft and radar.

Radar, an abbreviation of radiolocation or Radio Directional Finding (RDF), had been researched at Swanage in Dorset.

It is a commonly held belief, even to this day, that Britain held exclusively the secrets of radiolocation throughout the war years. This was not so, as the Bruneval raid exposed.

Suspicion had been aroused as early as 1940, when a British destroyer, HMS *Delight*, had been dive-bombed and sunk when sixty miles off the French coast in very murky weather and without having done anything to reveal her position. A further indication became apparent as the bombing campaign by the RAF over Germany suffered heavier losses by night fighters through their increasing ability to intercept and destroy.

Following the sinking of *Delight*, an RAF photographic unit took photographs of the whole of the Normandy coastline without revealing anything of importance. It was not until nearly twelve months had passed that information from Colonel Remy of the French underground plus a tip off from a well-wisher in the US embassy in Paris disclosed an unusual arrangement erected in a field outside the village of Bruneval near Le Havre.

In consequence, further photographs were taken at low altitude. What was revealed, appeared to be a large electric fire bowl in a field near to what was known to be a hotel, and also a flak battery nearby which had not been there before.

The reader must remember that at this stage in the war, British radar did not consist of large reflective moveable discs, but static lattice-work pylons up to 340 ft. high, criss-crossing the UK in groups of six or eight and passed off as radio aerials.

It was decided that the only way the German threat could be counter-acted would be to remove it completely by some kind of cloak and dagger operation and hand it over to Swanage where it could be dissected and hopefully some means found to minimise its effectiveness.

In consequence of the importance attached to this proposal Lord Mount-batten, who had recently been appointed chief of Combined Operations, submitted a plan with Churchill's backing to the combined Chiefs of Staff for a raid to be made which would involve all three services and, from the Army point of view, would bring into action for the first time the Parachute Regiment which had only recently been formed.

The plan was for twelve Whitley bombers, C Company of the Parachute Regiment, with the 1st Parachute Field Squadron of the Royal Engineers plus a small specialist group led by Flight Sergeant Cox, an RAF radar expert, to dismantle the apparatus and convey it on a trolley which would be dropped by parachute. A former Belgian liner, HMS *Prins Albert,* which had been converted to a special service landing ship and carried Assault Landing Craft would proceed to a point in mid-Channel escorted by five Motor Gun Boats of the 14th Flotilla which consisted of MGB 316, Lieutenant Commander W. G. Everitt, RN, S/O, which also carried Commander F. N. Cooke, RAN, Force Com-mander. MGB 317 (Lieutenant J. H. Coste, RNVR), MGB 312 (Lieutenant A. R. H. Nye, RNVR), MGB 315 (Lieutenant P. Mason, RNVR), and MGB 326 (Lieutenant F. D. Russell Roberts, RNVR).

The *Prins Albert* would lower eight landing craft and then return to Spithead and then the landing craft would proceed toward Bruneval, escorted by the gunboats who would wait offshore until the raiding party returned and then tow the loaded landing craft back to link up with *Prins Albert* once again. All, that is, except 312, who would load the Warzburg apparatus, as it became known, and return to the UK as fast as three supercharged Hall Scotts would allow.

In addition, however, 312 would carry Mr D. H. Priest, a backroom boy from Swanage, escorted by four commandos as a back up team to Flight Sergeant Cox if they experienced any difficulty. Mr Priest, it would appear, was regarded as too valuable a property to be dropped by parachute; he would also be dressed in RAF uniform, for obvious reasons.

To emphasise the importance attached to the proposed raid, Churchill sent Brendon Bracken, the Minister for Information, to *Hornet* to brief the officers of the gunboats concerned, and also to be made aware that as long as MGB 312 got back with the Wurzburg apparatus, the raid would be regarded as a success.

In company with the *Prins Albert* and the 8th LCA Flotilla under Lieutenant P. R. Mackinnon, RNVR (six Assault Craft and two Support Craft armed with Aerlikons), exercises took place in Weymouth Bay. The landing itself was practised in Worbarrow Bay, twelve miles east of Weymouth, where the coastline and shore silhouette bears a very close resemblance to Bruneval.

The outward run went without incident; the aircraft arrived on time and could be seen as they arrived over the dropping zone (the moonlight was quite brilliant) and were met with a steady stream of tracer. All that remained to do now from the point of view of the gunboat and landing craft crews was to sit back and watch the tracer and occasional flare going on ashore.

We know at this stage that the raid was expected to take about two hours and that anything over this time might cause difficulty, for two reasons: 1. Because of the retreating tide, the landing craft might become embedded in the beach; 2. It was known that there were German heavy reinforcements stationed about two hours' drive away.

After a while, the inactivity was disturbed by a message which came from the S/O, Lieutenant Commander Bill Everitt on 316, to say that on 317 Lieutenant John Coste, who had the seaward position with lookouts stationed down aft, had observed two destroyers accompanied by two E-Boats approaching from the eastward and that all engine room staffs were to be prepared for an emergency start. Fortunately, the German flotilla sailed past and turned into Le Havre without showing any concern. It would appear, however, that the paratroops landed without the German garrison being aware, apart from a company of twenty men who were dropped out of position and had to jog-trot through the lanes to link up with the main force.

The raid went according to plan, although there were some killed and several wounded. At the appropriate time, the landing craft steamed for the shore to give covering fire and embark the paratroops with their prize. As the landing craft did not return at the scheduled time, the S/O MGBs took the flotilla shoreward to shorten the time and passage out. As the tide was on the ebb, it would appear there had been some difficulty in getting the landing craft refloated after waiting for some paratroops who had become detached from the main force. Soon, however, the link was made, the radar equipment was transferred to 312 which made off at speed, and the four remaining gunboats took two landing craft each in tow and headed back to link up with the *Prins Albert* at Spithead: only just in time, however; the lights of the German reinforcements could be seen on the cliffs as the force departed.

On the return journey, Mr Priest was overheard to say to Sergeant Cox that after examining the apparatus, he was inclined to think that the Germans had been making the stuff at least as long as we had if not longer.

The return to *Hornet* was quite spectacular, with the jetties lined with naval personnel, newspaper and newsreel cameramen.

Within a short space of time after the raid, a large concentration of German paratroops were deposited in Normandy in an area directly opposite Swanage, with the obvious intention of retrieving the loot. Within a week, the whole research unit was removed to Malvern near Worcester, where it remains today.

There was a combination of three reasons why the German flotilla ignored the happenings around Bruneval. 1. A diversionary air raid

147

was taking place over Le Havre at the same time. 2. No tracer was being used by the invading force, only by the Germans, and so the impression to an observer could be of an exercise. 3. The gunboats were painted a red oxide colour known as Mountbatten pink which blended with the loam of the land on that and many other occasions. In retrospect, it is, I think, a fair deduction to make, that if the Bruneval raid had not been successful, the losses in the RAF night bombing campaign through radar detection, without an antidote, could not have been sustained.

Member No. 356 C. G. Neville

'No, we don't have jaunties in MTBs ... Does it show?'

The Action of the Three Ds

In early March 1943, Ken Gemmell took units of three Ds on a longish run above the north Dutch coast, past Borkum towards Heligoland, where soon after midnight we found an east to west convoy with their usual couple of merchant ships with twelve escorts. Not unusually, we were down to two units, 624 and 622, when we went in and came out alone. The last we saw of 622 was coming through the inner escorts, spitting fire. Later we heard there were few survivors; we were fortunate to have got away with three injured.

A sequel to this action came to my notice in March 1985 when a Remembrance Stone was found to Lofty Snowdon, 622's navigator, in Hathersage Churchyard near the grave of the legendary Little John of Robin Hood fame, set in a beauty spot near Sheffield. It is well worth a visit. The stone reads: 'In memory of Sub Lieutenant Nevil Snowdon RNVR, killed in action, 9th March 1942, Aged 21 years.'

Since finding the stone a few shipmates have with the help of the local British Legion laid a wreath during their Remembrance Day Service.

Having looked through our Newsletters for what seems years, I was rewarded in the Summer edition to find that Harry Leader, DSM, of 622 has joined the Association. Naturally I rang him immediately to find that he is one of the few survivors and we hope to meet soon for a good natter. Thanks to our Newsletter and whoever advertised the fact of our existence.

It is a fact that the Newsletter is the only contact for many of our members and a reminder of that part of our lives of which we are most proud. After all, those of us who were in Coastal Forces early in the war are now nearing seventy, whereas the members who served towards the end of the war and up to 1957 are now in their sixties and still fit enough to attend social functions in their area.

149

So, with the ever growing number of overseas shipmates and those who cannot through age and ill health attend meetings and functions, the Newsletter becomes more and more important as a reminder of the past. Personally I am more interested in reading about the past than the present activities.

Frank Coombes, DSM

Conspicuous Gallantry Medals awarded to Coastal Forces in the 1939–45 War

The following list was received direct from the Secretary to the Admiralty by member no. 175, Henry G. Franklin:

9 September 1941	A/B J. D. Lanfear	MGB 43
March 1942	CM/M W. M. Lovegrove	MTB 74
March 1942	A/B J. Booth	MGB 8
July 1942	M/M2 L. C. T. Adams	ML 139
July 1942	A/B G. A. Sandford	ML 139
August 1942	A/B J. R. Barnes	MGB 77
August 1942	Stoker R. J. Spinks	MTB 201
September 1942	PO G. Plenderleith	MGB 335

Able Seaman William Savage VC

Every one of our members will have received a letter telling them that the National Maritime Museum has achieved buying William Savage's Victoria Cross, which his wife sadly decided she must sell. The cost amounted to £55,000, including the buyer's premium.

On Monday 2 July I went to the Museum to unveil the medal for them in a small informal ceremony with Mr Richard Ormond, the Director, and Doctor Roger Knight, the Chief Curator. They are all thrilled to have it.

We all owe a great debt to Admiral of the Fleet Lord Lewin, who is Chairman of the Board of Trustees of the Museum, because he was largely instrumental in arranging the purchase. I have assured Admiral Lewin that we will do our utmost to raise a contribution towards the cost, and I know that Douglas Hunt has circulated his list of MTB and MGB officers. Mickey Wynn (Lord Newborough) CO of MTB 74 is alerting the St Nazaire Association, and Sir Derrick Holden-Brown has written to the Canadian D-boat COs (some of whom are our members) seeking their help, too.

The Museum has nobly stretched its funds by this purchase and I think we ought to try to help them for that reason. Furthermore I have made the point to them that, if we make a fair contribution to the sum paid, we earn the right to an interest in the medal and to borrow it on specific occasions, if we should want to do so.

If every member gives a bit and every branch manages to have a 'do' of some sort we ought to be able to raise a respectable sum without hurting ourselves too much. Although I was always clear that the Coastal Forces Veterans Association is not in the business of owning things, I must say that Savage's VC has always been rather close to my heart, not only for its citation for all our other shipmates but because his volunteer loading number on the 2-pounder pom-pom

151

of MGB 314 was my own rather special gunner, Able Seaman A. R. C. Stephens, DSM, from MTB 102. So it is a triumph that we've got it safe.

Commander Christopher W. Dreyer, DSO, DSC, RN (Rtd).

Victoria Cross
Able Seaman W. A. Savage—
HMMGB314

Citation in the *London Gazette*, 21 May 1942 reads:

For great gallantry, skill and devotion to duty as gun-layer of the pom-pom in a Motor Gun Boat in the St Nazaire Raid. Completely exposed, and under heavy fire, he engaged positions ashore with cool and steady accuracy.

On the way out of the harbour he kept up the same vigorous and accurate fire against the attacking ships, until he was killed at his gun.

This Victoria Cross is awarded in recognition not only of the gallantry and devotion to duty of Able Seaman Savage, but Launches, Motor Gun Boats and Torpedo Boats, who gallantly carried out their duty in entirely exposed positions against enemy fire at very close range.

Extracts from 'Karstensen's War'
by Tom Angus

First published in *Shetland Life* in March 1985

Oddvin Karstensen lives on the tiny island of Fanoy, which lies 'way out in the Atlantic west of Floro. I first met this jovial gentleman when I was teaching up in Unst in 1967, and the purse netter *Sunoy* came into Baltasound. We have been friends ever since, and have lived in each other's homes.

I wanted to know about my friend, though, and his story told to me across the kitchen table one sunny morning, with the cries of young seagulls, and the occasional chug of a fishing boat passing a few yards in front of the house is, I believe, worth recording. It is the story of an ordinary Norwegian caught up in the trauma of war, and of personal reaction to frightful influences.

Oddvin was called up to his military service just before the outbreak of war and set off for Voss, a town halfway between Bergen and Oslo, to do his square bashing. German military might, however, changed all that and Oddvin soon found himself back home.

German patrol boats constantly prowled the area between Floro and the off-lying islets demanding passes of fishing boats. German troops landed on the isles and inspected properties, looking for anything suspicious. Bribes of chocolate and cigarettes were used as a bribe to win over the residents, especially the younger people. Once, Oddvin refused an offer of a tin of tobacco from a German officer, saying he didn't smoke. A few days later the same officer, seeing young Karstensen enjoying a fag, asked peevishly why Oddvin had lied about smoking, whereupon the bold lad explained that it was German tobacco he didn't smoke!

Oddvin's father was the island's telephone exchange operator and he agreed to operate a clandestine radio transmitter. The transmitter arrived at the island of Alden, some thirty kilometres south of Fanoy. Oddvin fetched it, alone and in the dark, in a small open motor boat. The transmitter ran off a 12 volt battery which was charged during the day aboard a fishing boat as it went to and from the fishing grounds. Dismantled after each time it was used, the various parts of the transmitter were hidden in and around the house, unscrewed bed-knobs holding the valves. Karstensen (senior) audaciously used the telephone line as an aerial.

Information regarding the movements of German convoys was sent out from Fanoy until the autumn of 1941 when the operation was taken over by two agents based on the island of Skorpa, some three kilometres away. The transmitter had been in the Karstensens' house for about a year but their connection with the communications system still carried on, as Oddvin took food and samples, 80 kg. at a time, to the agents, over terrain that would scare a Foula man.

Towards the end of 1942 the Karstensen house became a rendezvous for refugees taking the Shetland bus to safety. The original Karstensen home was built on a peaked rock, upon which rested the floor joists. Running from gable to gable, the rock occupied much of the space under the floor, which meant that the Karstensen cellar was comparatively small, extending to only half the width of the house. By now hardened in their attitude towards the Norwegians, German soldiers smashed the wooden lining in the Karstensens' cellar and discovered the solid rock face. The rock sloped at an angle of 45° under the kitchen floor. Oddvin cut a hole in the floor of a cupboard next to the sink to form a trap-door leading to a narrow, uneven space, some 1½ metres by 10 metres. In this small space hid the refugees—agents, allied airmen, fleeing families—while awaiting the boats from Shetland. At one time there were twenty-seven people hiding in this small space.

In May 1944 it became the Karstensens' turn to flee from capture. At 8 p.m. on Whitsun Eve, a transmitted message told them that the Germans were headed their way, and that they had to leave there and then. The family, consisting of the mother, father, four sons and two daughters, hurried aboard a small motor boat and a rowing boat. With the rowing boat in tow, the motor boat headed for the west side of the isle to rendezvous with an MTB from Shetland. Because of mist the boat was late arriving, and it was 4 a.m. before the Karstensens heard the unmistakable rumble of an MTB's motors. The MTB had been piloted through the numerous reefs and passages by Lars Hovden, a local man. The family hurried aboard their rescuers' craft, sinking the motor boat by hacking a hole in the bottom with an axe. The rowing boat they cast adrift, and in fact after the war picked it up from the nearby island of Kalvag to where it had drifted.

The MTB had a fast trip across to Lerwick. Oddvin said they had morning coffee in the Queen's Hotel, where they were interviewed by Mr Frank Garriock, the Norwegian Consul, and Mr Adie from Voe. The *St Magnus* took the family to Aberdeen, where they took the train for London.

When the war ended, Oddvin's boat sailed from Aberdeen to Oslo with a cargo of much needed medical supplies.

Demobbed just after New Year 1946, Oddvin went back to Fanoy. The rest of the family had spent their time in London where Karstensen (senior) had worked as a supply officer. Sadly, Oddvin's two sisters did not survive the war. The remainder of the family took up their lives again as fishing folk on their remote little isle.

P.S. Oddvin and his brother Atle were on the quayside at Bergen in June 1981 when CFVA members Norman Hine, Les Taylor, Bill Cartwright, Ron Hunter, Hughie Greenstreet, 'Wiggy' Bennett and Charles Milner arrived to meet up with some of MTB 718's wartime passengers. Oddvin and his wife made a reciprocal visit to England later. Sadly Oddvin died in January 1988.

Tom Angus is a member of the Shetland Norway Friendship Society.

The MTB mentioned in 'Karstensen's War' by Tom Angus was MTB 718, with acknowledgement to the Commanding Officer, Lieutenant R. F. Seddon, DSC, RNVR.

Coastal Forces Veterans Remember

Leif Larsen

Leif Larsen, the legendary Norwegian fisherman who has died at
Bergen aged 84, won an astonishing variety of decorations—including a DSO, DSC, CGM, and DSM and Bar—for his gallant
sea-going exploits in the Second World War.

As a skipper in the Shetland Bus Service Larsen worked under the
auspices of the British Special Operations Executive to smuggle
Allied agents, arms and supplies into occupied Norway—and Norwegian volunteers and refugees into Britain—during some 50 ferry trips
across the North Sea.

Larsen's quiet, modest courage and his natural authority inspired
total confidence, and in the autumn of 1942, when the Royal Navy
sought to cripple the German battleship *Tirpitz* in Trondheim, he was
an obvious choice as the lynchpin of the operation.

He was given command of *Arthur*, a small 55-foot Norwegian
cutter, loaded with a cargo of peat for delivery to Trondheim conceal-
ing two Chariot two-man human torpedoes.

Larsen and his crew, together with naval personnel for the Chariots,
accordingly arrived in Norwegian waters where, equipped with forged
documents and current Norwegian magazines, they foxed a German
naval inspection at the entrance to the Trondheim fjord.

But when they were only five miles from the *Tirpitz* disaster struck.
Heavy weather snapped the cables towing the Chariots, which broke
away and sank. Larsen was forced to scuttle *Arthur*, though he and his
party reached the shore and set out on foot for Sweden.

They were eventually challenged by two armed policemen, and in
the ensuing gun battle Able Seaman Robert Evans fell wounded and
had to be left behind. Nonetheless Larsen led two of the Britons through
neutral Sweden to safety—the others escaped independently—and was
awarded the Conspicuous Gallantry Medal.

Lines from the Censor

Reading some of the letters we receive, I often wonder what some of our Censoring Officers must have thought when reading some of them.

Dear Son,

Just a few lines to let you know I'm still alive, I'm writing this letter slowly because I know you cannot read very fast. You won't know the house when you come home, we've moved. About your father, he has a lovely job, he has 500 under him, he is cutting the grass at the cemetery. There was a washing machine in the new house but it isn't working too good. Last week I put 14 shirts into it, pulled the chain and haven't seen them since. Your sister Mary had a baby this morning. I haven't found out if it's a boy or a girl so don't know whether you are an Aunt or Uncle. Your Uncle Dick drowned last week in a vat of whisky in Dublin Brewery. Some of his mates dived in to save him, but he fought them off bravely. We cremated his body and it took three days for the fire to go out. I went to the doctor's on Thursday and your Father came with me. The doctor put a small glass tube in my mouth and told me not to open it for ten minutes. Your Father offered to buy it from him. It only rained twice last week. First for three days then for four days. We had a letter from the undertaker. He said if we don't pay the last instalment on your Grandmother up she comes. I meant to put ten shillings in with this letter, but had sealed the envelope before I remembered.

Love, Mum

Motor Torpedo Boat 382—31st Motor Torpedo Boat Flotilla (Commanding Officer: Lieut. J. F. Russell-Smith RNVR; First Lieut.: Sub Lieut. J. F. Crewdson) Photograph taken off Felixstowe, 1944. Armament: Four 18" torpedo tubes; one × 2 20mm Oerlikon for'ard; two rocket flare projectors (on tubes); two × 2 0.303" Vickers (mounted on tubes).

Miscellanea

Impossible!

A hateful word, usually supplanted among good seamen by 'We'll try'.

London Marathon 1987
London Limbless Ex-Servicemen's Association

I am pleased to report that Dicky Bird, CFVA member number 30, aged sixty-two, ran the London Marathon in 4 hours 9 minutes for the above Association and received from the London Branch Sponsors the princely sum of £78.00 and from the North-East Lancashire Branch £14.00, making a grand total of £92.00.

Well done, Dicky and a big hand to the London and North-East Lancashire Branches.

Memories of '44

A late June morning, somewhere off Cap de la Hague, and a boat of the 35th, bows down, port side awash, crew perched on the wheelhouse, rum bottle seen off, waiting for the control frigate (*Duff*) to return after a chase, with remaining boats, of a group of S-boats leaving Cherbourg.

And later still—a July evening in the Assault area under way in company with an ML playing a Sinatra record over their loud-hailer— 'This is a lovely way to spend an evening'.

Next morning, coming back off the Trout Line, same ML, different record, or other side of same record: 'I didn't sleep a wink last night. Why did we have that silly fight?'

Member No. 1642 Bernard Griffiths

159

Preservation

The Swedish national daily newspaper *Svenska Dagbladet* of Sunday 19 April 1987, carried a very interesting article about Henry VIII's flagship *Mary Rose* and the problems of its preservation. Apparently the timber will be treated with polyethylglycol similar to the Swedish ship *Vasa* which was salvaged in Stockholm harbour after capsizing on 10 August 1628. The *Mary Rose* was earlier, in 1545.

Member No. 33 Lionel H. Blaxell, Stockholm, Sweden

Rolls-Royce Heritage Trust

The trust organised in Derby, the home of Rolls-Royce engine production during World War 2, would like to obtain any information, photographs and stories from any personnel who served in British Power Boats—Merlin powered MGBs No. 40–46 and 50–67 which served with the 3rd—4th—6th Flotillas. Also any information on MTB 105 lost off the Azores in 1942 whilst serving with HMS *Fidelity*.

Although Rolls-Royce withdrew from the marine side in 1941 (the Government decided it would prefer to see three Spitfires than one Motor Gun Boat propelled by Merlin engines) and that their involvement was short and of a minor nature, it is believed the Merlin powered boats did have success during their commissions.

It is hoped through your help and co-operation to be able to record this part of the Company's history as a lasting tribute to those who built the engines and those who served on the boats.

Nigel Lawson's Ties

I knew Nigel Lawson was coming out fighting when he chose to confront Sir Robin Day in a pink and green tie. The Chancellor's ties are a proven indicator, for which the Treasury should nowadays be grateful. At moments of caution he prefers a Royal Naval Volunteer Reserve tie—suggesting to his party faithful that he is just a retired naval officer maintaining a tradition of public service. The Garrick's colourful stripes, by contrast, carry a message of cheerful ebullience and readiness for argument, with few holds barred.

All at Sea with Nigel

I have been wrong all this time about Nigel Lawson's tie. Not, that is, his pink-and-green club tie for moments of ebullience, but the conservative effect in dark blue which signals caution. I thought and, the other day, wrote that it was the Royal Naval Volunteer Reserve tie. Not so—it is the far more exclusive tie of the Coastal Forces Veterans Association, whose 1,900 members (so the treasurer, Charles Milner, courteously explains to me) served in the Royal and Allied Navies in motor gunboats, launches, torpedo boats or in their shore bases. Most have wartime service, but Mr Lawson qualifies for his time in the 1950s as a naval Sub-Lieutenant in command of HM Motor Torpedo Boat *Gay Charger*.

Articles by Christopher Fildes,
The Spectator, November/December 1988.

The Poppy Emblem—How It Began

The Flanders Poppy was first described as the Flower of Remembrance by Colonel John McCrae who before the First World War was a well known Professor of Medicine at McGill University, in Montreal.

He had previously served as a gunner in the South African War and at the outbreak of the First World War decided to join the fighting ranks. However, the powers that be decided that his abilities could be used to better advantage, and so he landed in France as a Medical Officer with the first Canadian Army Contingent.

At the battle of Ypres in 1915, when in charge of a small first aid post and during the lull in the action, he wrote, in pencil, on a page torn from his despatch book, the following verses:

In Flanders fields the poppies grow, between the Crosses, row on row,
That mark our place: and in the sky, the larks, still bravely singing, fly,
Scarce heard amid the guns below.

We are the dead, Short days ago, we lived, felt dawn, saw sunset glow,
Loved and were loved, and now we lie, in Flanders fields.

Take up your quarrel with the foe, to you from failing hands we throw,
The torch, be yours to hold it high, if ye break faith with us who die,
We shall not sleep, though poppies grow, in Flanders fields.

The verses were sent anonymously to *Punch* magazine, and published under the title 'In Flanders Fields'.

Starboard Side

Because the Vikings shipped their star (steering) oar on the right hand side of their vessels, and called the side of the ship its 'board', the right hand side of vessels had ever since been designated as the 'Star-Board' side.

German *Schnellboote* (E-Boats)

Since it first started publication in February 1975 the CFVA News-letter has included many interesting accounts of Coastal Force actions and details of the boats and bases in many parts of the world during the Second World War.

Perhaps it is time, fifty years after the founding of Coastal Services, to consider the actions, design and bases of some of the German boats that opposed us.

The German *Schnellboot* or S-Boat was known to the British as the E-Boat. The origin of the British term is not fully understood as the British Admiralty usually referred to German ships by their German type names. A possible explanation is that one of the designers of the German E-Boats was the Lurssen boat yard and they developed a way of using the rudders which could produce a cavitation effect which tended to increase the maximum speed of the boat and reduce the stern wave, so that the boats remained almost horizontal at maximum speed. This feature was known as the 'Lurssen Effekt' and it is possible that the British Power Boat specialists referred to this 'Effekt' and that the term 'E'-Boat came into use because of this.

Though two fast boats had been built for the German Navy in 1928 they were not a success as their sea keeping qualities were not very good and they were discarded in 1931. In 1929 Lurssen yard built the first deep sea S-Boat which was commissioned on 7 August 1930 and was first numbered U.Z.16, later changed to WI (Watchboat) or Guardboat. Its details were 39 tons, 29 metres length, 4.5 metres beam and 1.6 metres draught. It was powered by three 900 h.p. Daimler engines which gave it a maximum speed of 32 knots. Later still it was re-numbered S1 and subsequent boats would continue the S designation. S2, 3, 4, and 5 were slightly heavier at 45 tons, had similar dimensions to S1 and were built in 1932. They also had Daimler Benz engines of 12 cylinders and 950 h.p. A Mayback engine was fitted to S5 for endurance running. All these first boats had petrol engines but S6, which was built in 1933 and could also do 32 knots, had three Mann diesel engines of 1,320 h.p. S10 to S13 followed with three Daimler Benz 16 cylinder diesel engines of 1,320 h.p. and were 78 tons displacement, 32.4 metres length, 4.9 metres beam and 1.7 metres draught.

A purpose designed depot ship, the *Tsingtau* replaced the tender *Nordsee* as an accommodation and depot ship on 26 September 1934. The new ship was almost 2,000 tons, heavier than all British destroyers until January 1944, when the Battle class destroyers were built.

S14 to S17 were built from 1936 to 1938 and were of 97 tons, 34 metres length, 5.26 metres beam, 1.67 metres draught and could do 37 knots; these boats were fitted with Mann diesel engines which were long and high and strained the base mounting plates which caused cracking of some parts of the engines. Daimler Benz diesels were used for all S boats after this. S18 to 25 had the same dimensions as S14 to 17 but 2,000 h.p. 20 cylinder V diesel engines were fitted. Much use was made of light metal and plywood in these new boats instead of the solid wood with strengthening plates used in the earlier boats. These boats became the standard design for *Schnellboote* and the change in structure meant that the new boats which were 85 tons displacement could do 39.5 knots. The last peacetime boat was commissioned in July 1939, and on the declaration of war in September 1939 there were eighteen boats in commission.

The pre-war S-Boats had their torpedo tubes mounted on the forward deck in front of the wheelhouse and there was a wheelhouse shield behind the tubes which extended to a point level with the aft end of the bridge. Designed armament was quite light and consisted of a 20mm. gun mounted on the stern, with machine guns on stands either side of the wheelhouse, on some of the boats. Practice exercises in peacetime had indicated that night attacks might give the best results and an off white camouflage was adopted which was thought suitable for day and night operations.

The wartime developments of torpedo tubes enclosed in the hull structure in front of an armoured cupola bridge, the fitting of Bofors guns, twin cannon in socket mountings which could be lowered below the decks, engine horsepowers of 2,500 and 3,000, the use of the boats for minelaying purposes as well as the hazard of too effective camouflage causing friendly collisions all lay in the future.

Member No. 628 Gordon N. Aldersley

The Price we Paid for Success

During the night of 15/16 April 1944, MGB 502 (Lieutenant Commander P. Williams, SO 15th MGB Flotilla) and MTB 718 (Lieutenant R. F. Seddon) rescued from the beach at Beg-an-Fray in Britanny, France a number of Allied airmen who had evaded capture and two young French ladies, SOE agents, who had escaped from the infamous German hostage prison at Castres.

After the successful pick-up from the 'pin-point', the two boats were intercepted off-shore by three enemy R-boats and both were hit. After the action ceased, Signalman George Colledge was despatched from the bridge of 502 to check for damage and stumbled over the body of AB William Sandalls who had been killed instantly.

Over the past year George has been tracing the whereabouts of his shipmate's final resting place.

'Let Light Perpetual Shine upon Able-Seaman William Sandalls.'

Sweeping the Ports
with the 19th Flotilla

I served on ML 906 which sailed from Queensborough along with ML 916, and after leaving Ostend we attempted to lay a smokescreen at Walcheren Island for the landing craft, but were kept at bay by an 80mm. German gun emplacement. As we laid off Walcheren it was a lovely sight to see two Mosquitoes make short work of the troublesome gun.

After laying our smokescreen along with ML 916 we proceeded sweeping the Scheldt followed by the MMS, BYMS, and Fleet sweepers from Antwerp. The Dutch pilot had a tricky job navigating the shifting sands and repositioned buoys. One of the first V2 rockets had exploded on Antwerp's dock that morning. The rest of our 19th Flotilla joined us after several days sweeping the surrounding canals; we were returning in line astern to Terneuzen when ML 916 was blown up by an acoustic mine.

Only two survivors were found, the bunting tosser and Skipper. The Skipper's legs were a terrible mess, and I understand he lost one completely. We landed him and he was taken to Ghent hospital for treatment. I have often wondered how he has survived, and also what happened to the Signalman who I heard suffered broken ankles. Apparently they were aft in the ward room when the explosion occurred, and they both dived through a hole in the ship's side.

Volunteers were called to act as pall bearers to bury the six bodies at a cemetery at Bergen-op-Zoom. I have several snapshots taken at this funeral ceremony. The Imperial War Museum tells me the names which can be read from a photograph in their possession are S/ L. D. B. Curtis and another: Rix.

We suffered a fire in the engine room caused by the donkey-engine overheating, which burnt the ship's side and deck-head, so we returned to Shoreham for repairs. I have never found anyone from ML 906 except for our Chief M/M Sam Wall. Perhaps this will find some others.

Member No. 2005, Ron Metcalfe

O my Kingdom for a Cuppa

It was during the very hot weather in North Africa in 1943, when a fair crowd of Coastal Forces staff were entrained at Algiers railway station for a move to Oran. The tops of the walls of the train were open to the weather, and we had to keep people posted (armed with a variety of clubs such as trench tool handles, etc.) to stop the Arabs from stealing our gear, because every time we stopped in the middle of nowhere dozens of Arabs would appear on the roof of the carriages, bent on knocking our gear off.

It was during one of the stops in the middle of nowhere that I took a hobing bucket, put in a couple of handfuls of tea and walked up to the engine. The train driver understood my pidgin French and promptly filled up the bucket with boiling water; he then moved the train until I was level with my carriage, I put my hand up and he stopped the train to let me climb aboard. Here we promptly opened a tin of condensed milk, added a bit of sugar and, lo and behold, we had the best cup of char for many a day.

P.S. Even though it tasted a wee bit soapy.

Member No. 1594 Ron Allwood, Melbourne, Australia.
Torpedo man. Mers-el Kebir Base Staff.

Five Day Visit to Ostend

On Tuesday 8 May 1990, several members along with their partners from the London, East Anglia, South London and Southern branches met in Ostend for a five-day visit to various venues. In the evening of the first day we were met by Colonel Noel Dedeken, formerly of the Belgian 10th Para-Commandos who briefed us on two events. Later John Harris, Secretary of the Royal British Legion, Ostend and District branch, arrived and made arrangements to visit and pay homage to Coastal Forces members including members of the 29th Royal Canadian Navy Flotilla who are buried in the Stuiverstraat Cemetery.

During the second day we were met by Captain J. C. Leinart (Rtd), Royal Navy Belgian section, who arranged to meet us on Thursday to escort us to the Ostend and Zeebrugge Naval base. At the base we were welcomed by the Commanding Officer and our National Standard Bearer made a triumphant circuit of the dining hall before we sat down to an excellent meal provided by the Ch/PO's mess. After lunch we were escorted by Captain Leinart around the finest Mine Museum in the world, which included one of 'our torpedoes' found in the mud at Ostend. Time then to the Ch/PO's bar to partake of more bevies. A Coastal Forces Veterans Association plaque was presented to the Mess President. At 7.30 a.m. on Friday the bus arrived to take us to Marche-les-Dames, near Namur, home of the Belgian Commando Centre (CEDo), to join the Belgian Commando veterans in their annual reunion—and what a reunion!!

At 10.30 a.m. we were met by the Commanding Officer, Lieutenant Colonel Engelen and Major General Baron G. Danloy (Rtd) at the officers' mess for a reception followed by a presentation, visit to the training ground and demonstrations. We were each escorted by a veteran who acted as our personal guide. A four course lunch was served in the officers' mess with wine and all the trimmings. A CFVA plaque was presented to Major General Danloy and also to Colonel Dedeken who organised the whole affair. Our thanks go to all concerned, in particular to our escorts for the day. Around 8 p.m. saw us back at Ostend where we were joined by Kathleen and Arie Van-Den-Dool who motored down from the Hague. Arie, a long standing member of Coastal Forces, has not enjoyed very good health recently and it was a pleasure to be with them once again. More friends were made; several celebrations were taking place on the Continent at this time and it was difficult to attend all of these functions.

Saturday at 2 p.m. was our big day when all assembled at the Stuiverstraat Cemetery along with members from the Royal British Legion, Ostend and District branch, the 10th 1a Para-Commandos Veterans, the Royal Navy (Belgian section) and the Belgian Royal Navy Association. All were headed by their Standards. Also in attendance were members of the public of Ostend who remembered the holocaust of 14 February 1945. An outdoor service alongside the graves was conducted by the English Church Warden, three wreaths were laid at the Cenotaph, one of which was on behalf of the Coastal Forces Veterans Association, the Last Post and Reveille were sounded and all Standard bearers conducted themselves in a reverent and professional manner. It was a beautiful day and some time was spent in silent tribute to former Coastal Forces personnel who died on that fateful day and during the rest of the war. The cemetery is well kept and a fitting resting place for those who laid down their lives. Several members of the Royal Canadian Navy 29th Flotilla are at rest there.

In the evening we were guests of the Royal British Legion, Ostend and District branch, at a social in their Headquarters Café Orbit which lasted until after midnight. Sunday saw us depart by various routes and ferries, seen off by Captain Leinart and Kathleen and Arie Van-Den-Dool. We arrived back at Dover at 2 p.m. Our sincere and grateful thanks to all who contributed to a memorable five days and we look forward to the next time.

Sydney J. Clifford (Social Secretary) London Branch

Sir Peter Scott

Sir Peter Scott, CH, CBE, DSC, FSC: an appreciation on his death a few weeks before his eightieth birthday.

In the fashion which is typical of his whole life, Peter Scott managed to cram an awful lot into his naval career from late 1939 when he joined as an RNVR (Supplementary List) Sub Lieutenant, till the summer of 1945, when he left to fight in the post-war General Election, by which time he was a Lieutenant Commander with an MBE, two DSCs and several Mentions in Despatches.

Peter came to us in Coastal Forces in the summer of 1942. He had been hoping to get command of a destroyer, but the Admiralty first gave him something smaller—a new Steam Gun Boat, SGB No. 9, which later on, when the class got names, was called *Grey Goose*, and at 150 ft. was much bigger than the rest of our MGBs and MLs, which together made up Coastal Forces.

Peter had *Grey Goose* for some eighteen months and for about a year he was Senior Officer of the SGB Flotilla, mainly operating from Newhaven (where my MTB flotilla was also operating for the early part of 1943). After taking part in the Dieppe raid in August 1942, Peter and the SGBs had a number of gallant battles in the Channel in the spring and summer of 1943.

In March 1944 he joined me on the staff of Captain Coastal Forces (Channel) to prepare and operate all the Coastal Force Craft in the Channel during Operation Neptune, the naval portion of Operation Overlord, the invasion of France.

On our small Coastal Forces Staff, attached to C-in-C, Portsmouth, Peter became a roving controller, spending some time in the assault area in France, and later on with the Americans in Cherbourg, operating their PT boats against the Channel Islands.

He was an invaluable staff officer, because the combination of his wide knowledge of Coastal Forces operation, his good brain and tactical sense, together with his considerable reputation, made him an excellent envoy and representative.

One of Peter's most noticeable characteristics as a sailor was his formidable determination that he must be the best at whatever he took on. When he got command it had to be the best boat ever, when he was given a flotilla it had to be the best of the lot. I always imagined that the determination sprang from an inborn need to keep up his father's immense reputation, since he had been brought up with the background of that great sailor and explorer's heroic journeys and death.

At the same time, in parallel with his firm ambition to succeed, he was undeniably and endearingly rather scruffy—his uniform tended to be pretty shapeless and he wore a grey cardigan underneath, which showed, and there was frequently some paint here and there, on him or his clothes.

In some respects the fact that when he joined the Royal Navy he was already a household name as a painter, author, naturalist broadcaster and Olympic dinghy sailor, was a disadvantage to him, in that his superiors were liable to expect him to be a cocky young so-and-so and his equals were liable to be jealous. However, one soon learned that, although he neither concealed nor paraded his determination and ambition as a dedicated sailor, he was a kindly and amusing messmate and companion, a most excellent shipmate in any situation and a very good friend.

He will be greatly missed by his many friends in all sorts of different occupations in many countries of the world, and most particularly in the various fields of conservation to which he has contributed so much in the years since 1945.

He was not a member of our association, because he really could not afford the time and he was incapable of doing anything half heartedly! Nevertheless he was proud of his time in Coastal Forces and was always a valuable advocate for us.

Commander Christopher Dreyer, DSO, DSC, RN (Rtd)

171

The German Point of View

Very well I remember 17 January 1942, since it was an extraordinary incident for us soldiers of the German Air Force. None of my crew had any naval experience. My Flak unit was stationed in Ostende, Zeebrugge and Ghent for quite some time and was transferred to the ferry boats, called *Siebel Fahre*, in summer 1941 for a special mission on coastal waters. We left Ostende on 3 January 1942 with a reduced crew to Dunkerke. Actually we should have left Dunkerke some days earlier, but due to MTB warnings the departure of the convoy to Boulogne was postponed. In the evening of 17 January we left the harbour of Dunkerke about 1700 to 1800 hours in a convoy consisting of two German patrol boats, four unloaded coastal cargo ships which were unarmed and operated by civilian crews, and a sea tug towing my Flak carrier (*Siebel Fahre* SF 110). This Flak carrier, not actually designed for sea going purposes, was equipped with one 37 millimetre automatic Flak, two 20 millimetre Flaks and two quadruplats 20 millimetre Flaks.

It must have been about 2130 hours when our convoy reached the position abeam Cap Gris Nez and our patrol boats opened fire in the direction of the open sea. Then the fire was returned by the British MGBs, 40 millimetre Beaufors Flak. We at the end of our convoy could not identify any one of the British MTBs and MGBs. At about 2145 hours a boat shadow approached us from the French coast side and on a distance of approximately 20 metres we opened fire, hitting the MTB 47 in the bow part. Then MTB 47 passed us on port with extreme slow speed at a distance of 12 to 15 metres. In this position MTB 47 was exposed with its broadside to the quadruplats of my carrier and had received more than 500 shots in a relatively short time. It must have returned fire by a machine gun, since we noticed some hits in the upper construction. First we saw smoke coming out of MTB

47 and finally it burned in an open fire, lying approximately 50 metres behind us, abandoned by its crew. When we entered the port of Boulogne we saw the fire. Its crew swimming in the cold water was rescued by both of our patrol boats and taken POW. After our arrival in Boulogne I saw the twelve British sailors sitting in blankets close to the engine room of patrol boat 1806, which was the convoy leader under the command of Lieutenant Ronniger. Owing to other obligations I could not find a chance for a talk with the CO of MTB 47. I also did not know his name, I only know he was in the rank of a lieutenant. Further I was not informed what has happened to this crew of MTB 47. So if the CO of this boat survived the war and will be still alive, I would highly appreciate getting his name and address, so I can get in touch with him. Perhaps we could find a chance for a personal contact; I really would enjoy this.

Last month I followed an invitation of a very good friend in Burbage, Wilts., and at this occasion I dropped in the Dauntsey's School, West Lavington, which I already knew from summer 1936 during an exchange of pupils. I might happen to come again to England to sightsee in London. At this occasion it could happen, that I will drop in your office to say hello and get acquainted with you also.

Adolph Schmidt

The Phantom of Algiers

We all experienced at sometime, being 'in transit', and to those who served in the Med during 1943 this usually meant a spell in Algiers, being billeted in HMS *Hannibal*, a former convent school taken over by the Navy as a base and transit camp for most branches of the service. The following is a true account of an incident that occurred while I had charge of 110 Mess, which was a large dormitory situated at the top of the building, exclusively for Coastal Forces ratings. Chiefs and POs were messed elsewhere in the building along with their counterparts from General Service, not as lucky as the lads.

During the winter of '43, a thief was at work in *Hannibal*; operating at dead of night he successfully raided everywhere, the officers' mess, chiefs', POs', other ratings' messes, even the Jaunty's cabin was not spared a visit, but, until the time this story refers to, 110 Mess had been spared, possibly because of our situation at the top of the building, or maybe it was simply a question of time?

PO Frank Barnard was the Coastal Forces 'Buffer'. He and I worked closely together; he organised working parties for the boats in the docks, while I carried out my duties as base AVGI. Frank came to me with a suggestion: would I organise the lads in 110 Mess on a voluntary basis, as night sentries, in an effort to catch the Phantom? I put it to the lads and they jumped at the idea, so a rota was made out and we settled down in earnest to 'thief catching'. It was certain that we would be raided, but the enthusiasm of the lads was beginning to wane as nights went by without a visit, although he was still raiding other parts of the barracks. There began to be talk of packing the 'sentry lark' in, but we did not.

And then it happened. Around two in the morning Leading Seaman John Simpson, an HDML Cox'n, was on watch, with AB Bob Smart and one other lad. Just a brief glimpse of a moving shadow and rustle of clothes alerted John Simpson, who, along with the lads on watch, gave out a terrific yell and switched on all lights. They managed to collar the intruder before he escaped down the stairs to freedom.

Examination of the Phantom was difficult. I did not envy the lads holding him. He stank to hell and high water, was as lousy as a coot, filthy dirty from head to toe, and dressed in billowing unkempt sheets. We at first thought he was an Arab. (*Hannibal* was on the edge of the Casbah, and it was assumed he came from there.) It was only when the barrack guard took over that it was discovered that the Phantom was a British matelot on the run. He had deserted from HMS *Maidstone* then laying alongside in port, he had been living in the Casbah for several months, thieving whenever possible, lying low in daytime. The Phantom was taken into a yard, hoses played upon him, and he was forcibly scrubbed with long-handled scrubbers. The lads spared him nothing. I never saw him after they finished but I am certain he was far from comfortable; only when the MO was satisfied did they ease up and forcibly cut his hair for him.

We in 110 Mess were jubilant. We had succeeded where others failed, we had caught the 'Phantom of Algiers'. Costly Farces had triumphed again. The Phantom was sentenced to a period in jail, I know not where, and dismissed the Service dishonourably.

Bob Smart is a fellow member of CFVA, Frank Barnard was a member of the Bromley RN Club and died about 1950, John Simpson died in the early fifties, I believe, having risen to a position of much responsibility and influence with what is now the Trust House Forte Empire.

Jack Davies, Base AVGI at Algiers and Brindisi

175

'The Wassenaars Slag' Remembrance Service

On 27 February 1989, a Remembrance Ceremony took place, in bitter cold weather, at the beach head called 'The Wassenaars Slag'. It was exactly forty-five years ago, in the same bitter cold weather, that a group of six very brave young French Commandos were launched into a dinghy, specially constructed for the occasion, on board MTB 617, which at that time was commanded by Commander Donald Gould Bradford, DSO, DSC.

The Commandos were to land on the enemy-occupied beach of Wassenaar, which is just north of Scheveningen, Holland. This carefully planned raid was carried out, the Commandos reached the shore, but alas, a tragic end, of which we shall never know the true facts, awaited these brave young men. The story has made history in Holland, but this would be better told by Commander Bradford.

It was a great honour to have Commander Bradford and his wife at the ceremony, along with our President of CFVA, Commander Christopher W. Dreyer, DSO, DSC, and Mrs Mark Stevens, whose late husband, Gordon Stevens, was the coxswain of MTB 617 at the time of the raid. Several other guests included Mr W. A. de Looze, RMWO (Netherlands VC), DSC, ex Commander 2nd MGB flotilla, Mr H. C. Jorissen, BK (Netherlands DSO), DSC, ex Commander 9th Flotilla and ex members of Commando 10 and SAS, many of whom are awarded with DSO and DSC. Many Netherlands officers and ex crews were also present. Flags were at half mast, speeches were given by the Mayor of Wassenaar and the Ambassadors of France and the United Kingdom. Wreaths were placed at the Monument by the Mayor, Ambassadors, Commander Bradford and Commander Dreyer, and for the Netherlands Navy, Commanders de Looze and Jorissen and Jack de

Mos. This was followed by the hoisting of the flags, accompanied by the playing of the national anthems by the Royal Netherlands Marine Band. It was a most impressive and moving ceremony. Many of us were later guests for a buffet lunch at the French Ambassador's residence. The evening of the same day, the guests from England were invited to a dinner, by the British Ambassador, at the British Embassy.

The following day, our guests were flown back to the United Kingdom, by military plane, accompanied by Dr Hans Hers and myself. May I add, that this whole organisation could never have taken place on such a great scale if we had not had the whole-hearted help and co-operation of our Honorary Member, Dr Hans Hers.

Jack de Mos

Motor Launch 104. Senior Officer's boat of the 50th Flotilla. Photograph taken off Dover. Armament: Six ground mines; one 3-pounder aft; two × 2 0.303" Lewis.

Secret Mission

It was Sunday 23 November 1941 and my pal and I had just returned from a visit into town for dinner. To our surprise, on boarding our boat, we were informed that it was putting to sea immediately. This was approximately 1330 hours; we had to wait fifteen minutes for two stokers who were adrift, but not being able to wait longer, a volunteer from another boat was taken in their place. So, with one hand short, and an extra officer, we cast off from Great Yarmouth. Ten minutes later we berthed further down the Rive Yare; here, to our surprise, we picked up three Allied Army officers, and then immediately cast off again, this time straight to sea. All this only took half an hour at the most, so it was approximately 1400 hours when we left harbour for an unknown destination.

Immediately upon leaving harbour the crew took up their defence stations. .5 machine guns and the pom-pom were manned. After travelling for about thirty minutes the guns were fired just in case of defects; there were none and everything was in order. From here our speed was increased to twenty knots, and was maintained for the next five and a half hours.

At 1500 hours the Skipper called the crew together on deck. He then revealed the purpose and cause of our sudden and very unexpected trip to sea, and impressed upon us the need for secrecy while on this mission. Up till 1930 hours the journey was quiet and uneventful, apart from spotting an occasional plane or ship, all of which were friendly, much to the disappointment of the gunners. One little thing did occur though: our ship's steering broke, and had to be steered by two hands on the tiller aft. This was a stroke of bad luck and very disappointing indeed, but as far as this particular job was concerned only a very minor detail.

According to our rough judgement, at 1930 hours we had travelled over a hundred miles and were within ten miles of enemy occupied territory. At this moment the cox'n came round to all the crew and told us that we were to be at action stations for at least the next four hours and on no account were we to leave our posts.

Ten minutes later the Skipper spoke to all the gunners individually. We were, he said, ten miles off land and were going right in to the shore, to land one of the Army officers. Silence must be maintained while this was being done, and reports from the look-outs were to be made in whispers. He then told us that the enemy had no heavy shore batteries in the vicinity, but anti-aircraft guns and searchlights. If by a stroke of bad luck we were discovered, our job was to put out the searchlights as soon as possible. This was to ensure that our landing was carried out in safety for those concerned, and in the utmost secrecy.

Our boat was then on the silenced centre engine; consequently it would be hard to hear from the shore. Our speed was decreased to ten knots, and tension reigned everywhere aboard.

Everything was in our favour. The weather was ideal for the purpose, the almost new moon kept being blocked out by fast travelling clouds; a heavy mist was fast rising. Not long after, a light was reported off the starboard bow. Everybody held their breath. What was this? ... an E-Boat or what? As far as we knew, the nearest base for E-boats was at least thirty miles away, but anything was possible in these waters, and we weren't leaving anything to chance. We drew slowly nearer and nearer to it, and, to our great relief, found that it was only a buoy. Blimey, we were glad to see that buoy, God bless it.

Slowly but surely we crept nearer the shore, and at a hundred and fifty yards from the beach we stopped and anchored. All was still and quiet; not a soul aboard moved. This was it. Shortly after, a light was seen flashing ashore. It soon disappeared from sight. 'Probably a coastal patrol,' said the Skipper.

The dinghy was then lowered, and the 1st Lieutenant rowed three Army officers ashore. We all waited in dead silence aboard, our nerves highly strung, and very excited; this for many of us was our first bit of real action. Believe me when I say that quite a few prayers were said at that moment; I myself for one, said one.

After about ten minutes we heard the dinghy again. Soon it was alongside. Then we heard to our bitter disappointment that the landing had been made in the wrong place, and that it had to be made again later. We all swore softly to ourselves, especially when we heard that it couldn't be made until the following morning owing to the three o'clock curfew imposed on that particular country. We then started up our centre engine again. To all upon the upper deck it seemed as though bedlam had been let loose. We soon arrived at the correct place and we lay there until 0300 hours, when landing was made, this time successfully, thank God. Our nerves couldn't have stood the strain much longer, and having been all this time at 'action stations' we were badly needing sleep.

The officer concerned was landed and the others returned after what seemed a hell of a time, an hour and twenty minutes to be precise. A signal was flashed from the shore and all was well. This meant we could go, and go we did, as fast as our one engine would allow. During the time we lay off the shore, this particular engine had broken down, but thanks to the efficiency of the engine-room staff it was quickly repaired.

As soon as the ten-mile limit was reached all the engines were started, and the course plotted for home. Once again, as far as we were concerned, the journey was uneventful.

But apparently the night had been busy for some, as we came across several of our destroyers on patrol. This was unusual in this particular part, but we were soon to know the reason why, as later we saw a destroyer standing by a merchant ship; only the bows of the latter were above water. A balloon was still flying from it unconcerned, ironically funny. Within the next half an hour the destroyer had sunk it completely.

Since leaving the ten-mile limit we had been travelling at twenty knots and over, all the time; this made use of a considerable amount of 'juice', to our disadvantage, as we learnt later.

At 1145 hours we sighted land and drew slowly nearer to it, to our

181

extreme joy as we were very tired and dirty. Many of us had only had an hour's sleep that night and kept a watch the previous night in harbour too. We were looking forward to turning into our beloved bunks again with much anticipation. But our luck was out, for just outside the harbour we ran out of petrol, and had to lie there waiting for a tow in. It seemed ages from when the signal was flashed until the ML arrived to tow us in. This was at 1400 hours, when we were towed to the fuelling berth.

Here we refuelled, then made our way to the base. Once in there we cleaned up the ship and all guns. After that everything was one mad rush; the one idea in most of our heads was to have a bath and turn in. Some, the watch ashore, went ashore, but not for long; sleep was more important to us all.

So ended a very memorable night in the history of MGB 320, a night that will never be forgotten by any concerned, least of all myself.

Member No. 120, Jack Davies

The original of this is in the Dutch War Museum (Netherlands Government War Documentation Bureau in Amsterdam) given to them by Erik Hazelhoff, one of the three Allied Officers mentioned, and author of the book *Soldier of Orange*.

Lieutenant Peter G. Loasby, RN was the skipper, Sub Lieutenant Bob Goodfellow, RNVR the 'Jimmy' and 'Sharkey' Peter Ward, the Coxswain.

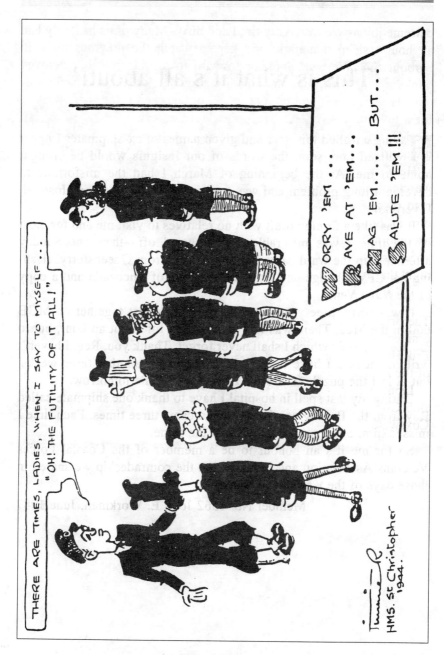

'This is what it's all about!'

Having enrolled this year and given names of ex-shipmates I never realized how soon the words of our insignia would be brought home to me. At the beginning of March I had the misfortune to develop a lung problem and was transferred to Broadgreen Hospital, Liverpool.

It was like a foreign draft with no relatives to visit me and for most of the time I was miserable and browned off—then one Sunday afternoon up the ward came one Reg Evans from Queensferry, flashing his CFVA badge and clutching a bottle of Lucozade and a copy of the *Navy News*.

It was forty-three years ago when we were last together on MGB 660 in the Med. There was lots of nostalgia for about an hour, but to me it was a tonic which I shall never forget. Thank you, Reg. I haven't written because I have been in Broadgreen for another three weeks, but at last the puzzle is over and I'm going home tomorrow.

During my last spell in hospital I have to thank one shipmate called Roy from the Broadgreen Branch, who came three times. Each time I missed him, but I got the grapes just the same.

So for me it's an honour to be a member of the Coastal Forces Veterans Association and to know that the comradeship we shared in those days of the war still remains.

Member No. 1562 John E. Workman, June 1987

So said the Great Admiral!

Reading the account of the exploits of MTBs 639, 633 and 637 makes one realise that the spirit of Nelson lives on. C. S. Forester could never have written a more hair-raising story. This episode confirms the effective role of the Fairmile 'D's.

May I quote from *A Sailor's Odyssey* by the illustrious Sir Andrew Cunningham, Admiral of the Fleet:

> I have mentioned the port of Bone and its value, and here, before long we were able to send reinforcements of British MTBs, and a few of their American counterparts, the PT Boats, though the former, particularly the 'D' Type, were lamentably slow and so full of gadgets and unnecessary amenities that they could hardly fulfil their functions.

So wrote the great Admiral, and continued some pages later:

> The MTBs from Bone and Sousse, with our aircraft, were a constant menace to Axis shipping. Hardly a night passed but they were off Tunis and Bizerta; mining, harrying the patrols, attacking and sinking vessels carrying stores, ammunition and petrol so badly needed by Rommel's Army.

He then went on to describe in detail Lieutenant P. F. S. Gould's exploits. He wrote: 'It was a praiseworthy exploit.' The day before this incident: 'I had made a signal to our Light Coastal Forces to the effect that I was following their excellent work with intense interest.'

The great Admiral certainly changed his opinion of the Fairmile 'D' in four pages!

As an ex-Coxswain of various 'D' types, I wonder about the 'gadgets and unnecessary amenities'. Where were they? Anyone know!

Member No. 1084 Frank Loy

A Funnel for ML 293

Those who call on Midland Branch member Norman Hine and his wife Cynthia at their lovely home in the Worcestershire countryside, have learned not to be surprised at what they find there. A tractor with an office swivel chair as its seat, the extensive garden 'dressed overall' with bunting, the CFVA Caravan Park with its own pennant, the 'fall out shelter' where Norman says he hides when he falls out with Cynth (but in reality his wine-cellar for all his home-brews) ... the list of unusual sights is endless.

Recent visitors, however, even before they had sampled the goodies in the wine-cellar, could be forgiven if they thought they were imagining things, when over the hedge they espied what was unmistakably a ship's funnel ... Surely Norman hadn't grown tired of gardening, wine-making, house alterations, caravan building etc., and gone and got himself his own ML?

Not quite ... but nearly!

When the Midland Branch paid a visit to ML 293 in Bristol Docks in April this year, comment was passed that she was minus the distinguishing feature of a 'B' Class Fairmile boat, the funnel. What better way of saying 'Thank you' to her owner for his hospitality than by offering to provide a funnel? And who better to construct it than the man to whom apparently, no job is too big, too small, or too unusual—'our Norm'?

The finished article is a super job and 293 will soon look like a real 'B' Class again.

Well done, Norman; what on earth are you going to tackle next?

Charles Milner

What a Liberty!

The East Coast convoy channel ran northwards from the Thames to south of the Haisborough Sands where it altered westerly to clear these and other banks before continuing on to the northern ports.

One night late in 1944, in calm weather with moderate visibility, a ship from the northbound convoy missed the crucial course alteration and, with others presumably playing follow my leader, ran aground on the Haisboroughs. Information reaching FOIC Great Yarmouth was confused and RML 512 was despatched to signal an on-the-spot situation report.

At 2230, near the South Haisborough buoy, the RML contacted an escorting trawler shepherding several ships back into the swept channel after they had managed to come free of the sands. However, one vessel remained stuck fast. This was the SS *Samnethy*, a liberty ship with a cargo of iron, and Cromer lifeboat under the redoubtable Cox'n Harry Blogg was alongside. The ship was undamaged and her master expected to refloat at high water around 0100 next morning.

512 duly reported this to base and was instructed to remain on station as guard boat and to report developments.

Shortly before high water, *Samnethy* began running her engine astern and continued until well after the peak of the tide but to no avail. But the master stayed optimistic of success at next high water in the afternoon. On this being reported, FOIC arranged for a tug from the Humber to assist at the next refloating attempt. At 1100, the ocean tug *Samsonia* joined the party and, when the time came, added her great strength to the power of *Samnethy*, but without effect. We had to wait a further twelve hours and try again.

Later in the day the weather, which had stayed reasonable throughout, began to deteriorate and towards midnight FOIC warned of an imminent gale and for *Samnethy* to be abandoned, the master and crew to return with the lifeboat to Cromer, RML 512 to return to base and the tug to remain on station.

The gale arrived and blew all day and aboard 512 in harbour the mood was one of gloom at the thought of a fine ship being pounded into scrap by wind and wave. This seemed to be confirmed, when, early in the morning on the day after the storm, the plot at FOIC HQ indicated that *Samnethy* had broken up and a section was a drifting hazard to shipping somewhere beyond the convoy channel.

With the Port Salvage Officer aboard, RML 512 was ordered out to find and report the position and condition of the hulk. After the gale there was still a strong breeze, though the skies were cloudless and visibility excellent. On the 'guestimate' of direction of drift and assurance that any sizeable object might be spotted at extreme distance, the RML crossed the convoy channel east of Great Yarmouth and continued eastwards for some time before what might be a vessel's topmast showed on the horizon. Shortly afterwards a second mast showed, then a funnel and gradually into sight came a complete and apparently undamaged liberty ship *Samnethy*. Unseen by the tug, which had withdrawn clear of the sands at the height of the storm, she had freed herself and allowed wind and tide to take her to where she now was, perilously close to the East Coast mine barrier.

The Jacob's ladder used when she was abandoned still hung overside so that when 512 went alongside it was no trouble for the Salvage Officer and some of the RML's crew to climb aboard to make an assessment of damage.

In due course the ship's position was radioed to base together with the information that with dockyard attention she could be returned to service. (Upper deck plates were severely distorted and the main shaft was damaged but the hull was sound.)

By this time the tug *Samsonia* hove into sight and her people took over from the RML crewmen for the tow into Great Yarmouth roads with 512 a diminutive escort.

We made one more visit to *Samnethy* when we took the master out to rejoin his ship for the long tow to a northern dockyard from which, some months later, she returned to duty. As maids of all work, MLs

188

tended to pick up all manner of odd jobs. The case of the liberty ship that took its description literally is one of the odder ones!

P.S. RML 512 was of further interest in that her original CO was 'Jas' Tait who was one of the few survivors of the St Nazaire operation and his successor Patrick Troughton will be remembered by many readers as 'Dr Who' of the TV series at one time, and many other TV plays.

Member No. 1500 Don Mackintosh

The Three Stranded E-Boats at Unie
– January 1945

The moon cast its cold light down from the dark canopy of the sky in a broad path of burnished silver. It lit up islands and sea alike, making the white cottages and tiny church of Molta village stand out with a ghostly radiance.

At the mouth of the narrow inlet and merged in the shadow of a small cliff lay a Harbour Defence Motor Launch. Her task was to guard the Macnare Channel, the main gap in the chain of rocky islets which fringe the Dalmatian coast, and through which passed all the munitions and supplies for the campaign against the occupying Germans. Enemy E-Boats and F-lighters had made many attempts to mine this Channel, and so successful had they been that the Naval HQ at Zara had decreed that there should be a nightly patrol to discourage this activity.

As Peter, Sub Lieutenant RANVR in command, rested his elbows on the bridge of his tiny craft, every now and again sweeping the horizon to seaward with his binoculars, his thoughts must have often strayed to happy days spent surfing and sunbathing on Bondi and Manly beaches in his far away Dominion.

Suddenly the sound of a high pitched engine note broke through his reverie, and as his finger pressed the alarm buzzer for Action Stations, the dark shapes of four E-boats in close formation came sweeping round the point. Peter must have known that he stood very little chance in a fight with four opponents, each armed with four torpedoes, and weapons which included 40 mm. and quadruple 20 mm guns, but nevertheless he shouted down the voice pipe to his wireless operator to bang out an enemy report, rang full ahead on his telegraphs and ordered his two single Oerlikons to open up. There could only be one result to this very brazen and gallant action, and that came swiftly.

The leading E-boat fired a torpedo which struck the little HDML amidships, blowing her up in a sheet of flame, the explosion causing the alarmed villagers to tumble from their beds and gather outside their homes. It was just as well for some of them that they did so, for as they watched the flames of the shattered HD on the water, they were horrified to observe the foaming wakes of six torpedoes churning up towards them in the narrow waters of their harbour, three of which exploded a minute later with an enormous flash and thunderous bang which reverberated from the Veliebet Alps in the east to the Istrian Highlands in the north, and which completely destroyed three or four of their houses.

With a final savage burst from their guns, aimed in the general direction of the village, the E-boats departed, no doubt highly satisfied with their night's work. Had they been able to call upon the services of one of their Führer's celebrated crystal-gazers their satisfaction would have been short lived ...

The crews of his Majesty's MTBs 699, 706 and 698 were tired, wet and well and truly fed up! To use them for a dull patrol like the Macnare, with the Venice-Pola convoys just asking to be attacked, was surely just plain silly! The E-boats would be unlikely to return after their success of the recent night and their Ustachi spies would most certainly have informed them that the patrol now consisted of three MTBs, a very different proposition to the solitary Harbour Defence ML. Yes, a complete waste of time and a most uncomfortable way of spending it, searching the blackness of the wet night for a non-existent enemy.

At about five o'clock in the morning the Senior Officer of the unit heard the voice of his 'Sparks' calling up the voice pipe to the bridge, 'Signal for you, Sir, it's headed "immediate": Partisan reports enemy vessels aground Unie Island, locate and destroy.' As if by magic every trace of lethargy and fatigue vanished and within a minute the MTBs were foaming their way north-westward up the Adriatic.

They reached the island just as dawn broke, and as they rumbled past Unie village with its white, red-roofed cottages, the golden ball of an early morning sun crept over the horizon, suffusing the island and its background of mountains with a warming glow. The sea was

191

calm and visibility excellent, revealing with a disturbing clarity the wireless mast and fortifications of Pola a few miles away. With a silent prayer that the Hun would be so overcome with his misfortune that he would be sound asleep and that the stranded vessels were not destroyers, the SO continued slowly down the coast, eagerly scanning the beach with his binoculars. As the unit reached a small lighthouse the voice of Philip came over the intercom: 'There they are, Monty, just to the left of the Point,' and there, shining in the sun, lay three E-Boats, all in perfect station, well and truly stranded on the beach. As the MTBs wheeled to port to close their range, a burst of fire from the nearest vessel was swiftly silenced by the arrival of one of our 'fish' which detonated with a colossal explosion, shaking the neighbourhood for miles around and sending figures running from the boats to seek the somewhat meagre shelter of a ploughed field. In a few minutes what once had been three fine examples of the German hundred-foot E-Boat were a blazing shambles, as shell after shell from six-pounders, Oerlikon and Point Fives poured into their hulls. From a clump of what looked like gorse bushes came some spasmodic return fire, but it too fell silent after the arrival of a well placed six-pounder shot.

'Right Philip, Mike,' came the SO's voice over the intercom, 'We'll pack up now, I reckon, we've had enough target practice for to-day.' And as they journeyed homeward, every now and again turning to observe a further explosion as torpedo after torpedo blew up on the flames of the three E-Boats, one thought was uppermost in our minds: that Peter and his gallant ship's company had been in a small way avenged.

The following signal was made by Captain J. F. Stevens following the Stranded E-Boats incident:

SEC

Subject HMMTBs 699, 706 and 698 report of proceedings on night of 15/16 January 1945 – Destruction of 3 stranded 'E' boats on Unie Island.

FROM ... The Captain Coastal Forces, Mediterranean

DATE ... 22nd March, 1945, No. C.F. 8118/018/156

TO ... The Commander in Chief, Mediterranean.

(Copies to: The Flag Officer, Taranto and Adriatic, The Senior Naval Officer Northern Area, The Commander Coastal Forces, Western Mediterranean, The Senior Officer, 59th MTB Flotilla).
References:

The Senior Officer 59th MTB Flotilla's Report dated 10th February, 1945. The Commander Coastal Forces, Western Mediterranean's Minute II No. CFW4573/0130 dated 13th March, 1945.

To finish off these boats placed it beyond the means of the enemy to recover any material intact and was well worth while.

Subsequent reconnaissance, both surface and air-photographic, showed all three enemy craft to have been most thoroughly destroyed.

J. F. Stevens, Captain

The Chicken Run

In January 1941 I joined ML 114 2nd Flotilla as a L/MM taking over the engine room after one round trip. We were escorting the channel convoy and Chatham to Pompey was our lot, later changed to Ramsgate to Pompey.

Those days we lay at Petrol Pier in Haslar Creek and came under HMS *Dolphin*.

The 'hinterland' between the pier and main gate (the submarine escape training tower has since been built there as well as other things) consisted of allotments, chicken runs, garages and anything else you can imagine with nondescript paths leading to *Dolphin* and the main gate.

It must have been some time in February or March when, returning rather late, an additional aroma to the usual sea boots, stockings, etc. was apparent as I descended to the galley flat. It was not an improvement. In the galley was L/Seaman Wilkie and Geordie the cook, both stripped to the waist, literally covered with feathers which they were busy plucking from four decapitated chickens. Needless to say, the galley was far from devoid of feathers. A hasty retreat to my bunk in the Coxswain's cabin seemed the best course of action.

The Ship's Company was awakened by the early arrival of the *Dolphin* Master-at-Arms with henchman looking for the missing poultry (I believe this is the correct description of a dead chicken), the M-at-A being left in no doubt of this as the four heads were left in the run or pen.

He was assisted in his endeavours by a convenient trail of blood which led to our trot of four boats and seemed to peter out at 114 which was lying outboard.

Believe it or believe it not, they found not a trace of the missing birds, not even a feather. I can confirm this; the only thing that was unusual, and this only applied to the crew, was how remarkably clean and tidy the galley was.

The owner of the missing birds was, I believe, the Captain of Dolphin.

The aftermath is best left to the imagination: no words committed to paper by me would be adequate to describe the event. It was not helped by the fact that we were storm-bound for two days, instead of sailing that day.

The flotilla's standing with Dolphin, especially the officers, was not greatly improved by this incident.

Assistance by the civilian police was of no avail and we finally sailed, without the mystery being solved, eventually arriving at Ramsgate.

There was no NAAFI those days at Ramsgate, the International Stores acting as agents for them. The M/M off 113 (Len Garforth, if my memory is correct) and myself used to visit the Municipal Bath House in Ramsgate as soon as we were safely berthed in the inner harbour, sometimes calling on our way back to see if the stores were ready to be picked up from the International, which we duly did. The manager enquired if all the caterers had gone mad as they had all asked for chicken on their orders. What would have been the result of any chicken arriving in the ward room of any ML is open to speculation.

P.S. I understand the offending birds were in a .5 ammunition box which was freely moving about the upper deck the whole time the search was being conducted. Their contents were wisely laid to rest in mid Channel about midnight.

Member No. 123 R. Dawson, DSM

1667—Navy Rum—1970

At ten to twelve each forenoon
Since the Navy first began
Jack drinks the health of Nelson
From Jutland to Japan.

He's always done his duty–
To country and the throne
And all he asks in fairness–
Is to leave his tot alone.

Requiem

You soothed my nerves
and warmed my limbs
And cheered my dismal heart
Procured my wants, obliged my whims
And now it's time to part.

And so the time has come, old friend,
To take the final sup.
Our tears are shed. This is the end.
So goodbye and bottoms up.

31 July 1970

Memories of Naxos

I was 'sparker' on ML 360, our skipper, Lieutenant John Ford was SO, 'Jimmy the One' was Lieutenant R. Steel, Cox'n was CPO 'Syke' Turner and PO Tony Jarrett was our Motor Mechanic. He also had on board several Army officers and the War Correspondent who wrote the article reproduced in the newsletters, so it was 'hot bunks' in the wardroom.

The capture of the German garrison commander was memorable. The two little Greek boys who rowed him out were overjoyed when they discovered we were the Royal Navy. They jumped on board, rushing from one crew member to another, kneeling and kissing our hands, somewhat to our embarrassment. Our prisoner was accommodated in the mess deck for the next few days, where he almost became one of the lads. He quite willingly did the mess deck chores and the spud bashing. In civilian life he was a farmer from the Hamburg area and produced the usual photographs of his wife and children. We even taught him to play 'uckers'.

After the refusal of the surrender terms by the German second-in-command we opened fire with everything. The very first shot from the Bofors struck the flag post over the German positions and brought it and the swastika tumbling down. Later, further proof of the ML's accurate fire was demonstrated when the two German float planes flew in. George Wood on the midships Oerlikon put a full pan into the nearest one. There was an unconfirmed report that it had crashed on its way back to base. Certainly we could clearly see the tracer thumping into its fuselage.

After surrender of the garrison the MLs had to give passage to them back to Chios and we had sixty to seventy German troops sheltering under an awning on the foredeck for the overnight trip.

When I came off watch I went up top for a look-see and found Lofty Metcalf, who was supposed to be guarding them, busy souvenir

197

hunting while his Hotchkiss was left lying on the wash deck locker. The Skipper never knew about that one.

The small tanker called the 'EMS' was a great boon as the MLs could be refuelled from it, instead of the long, hot and slow process of refuelling from four-gallon jerricans which had been our lot until then.

Mention of jerricans also reminds me of the occasion early in the Dodecanese campaign when ML 360 was running short of fresh water. We were hiding out in one of our secret bases on the coast of Turkey at the time. We rowed ashore in the dinghy and filled jerricans of fresh water from a small stream, watering ship in the manner of the Navy of old. All the MLs carried around fifty jerricans lashed along each side of the engine room casing and most useful they were for carrying extra supplies of water and fuel.

Member No. 951 Bill Mavor

Motor Torpedo Boat 496 22nd Motor Torpedo Boat Flotilla. (Commanding Officer Lieutenant Alex Foster, RNVR. First Lieutenant Sub Lieutenant John Lake, RNVR.) Photograph taken off Lowestoft, May 1945. Armament: One 6-pounder for'ard; one × 2 20mm. aft; two × 2 0.303" Vickers; Two × 18" torpedo tubes.

How Naxos was Liberated

From the *Sunday Times of Malta*, 7 January 1945

Among the unpublicized but none the less important events of the War in the Mediterranean in 1944 was the freeing of the Aegean Islands. In October 1944 British forces liberated the island of Naxos. Here, for the first time, is the report of how a little party of British MLs helped in the liberation.

The mountainous island of Naxos, some ten miles long and eleven miles broad, lies in the centre of the southern Aegean about a hundred miles to the north of Crete.

At 3.24 a.m. on 13 October, ML 360, Lieutenant John Ford, RNVR, anchored some 200 yards off a beach on the west coast of the island of Naxos, not far from the town and harbour of Naxia, which was clearly visible in the moonlight. ML 354, Lieutenant Michael Foore, RNVR, secured alongside and by 4.15 they had completed the landing of a number of men of the Greek Sacred Squadron who were to attack the German garrison at dawn. The MLs then closed to within half a mile of the harbour and steamed slowly up and down waiting for the signals showing the attack had started. No signals came. The attack was not made as planned, for when daylight arrived, it was found that the Greeks had been landed on a beach about two and a half miles from Naxia.

At 6.30 a small dinghy was seen coming out of the harbour towards the MLs. It contained four civilians and one German standing up in the stern. Leaving ML 354 to cover, Ford took his own ship towards the dinghy. The wind at the time was blowing towards the harbour, so that the White Ensigns of the MLs were difficult to make out.

When the dinghy was close alongside the awful truth dawned on the German. It looked, as Ford says, as though he were going to have an accident. The Greek rowers gave him no chance. With so many guns levelled at him the German could not draw his revolver, and had to surrender. He thought the two MLs were German craft come to evacuate the garrison. Judicious questioning elicited the fact that there were about two hundred German troops on the island.

At 7.30 there were still no signs of the attack by the Greek landing parties. The Germans ashore, however, were becoming restive and were busy erecting a mortar on top of the old castle. so the two MLs headed out to sea, three mortar shells being lobbed at them before they were out of range. To conceal his intentions, Ford then took his two MLs to the neighbouring island of Paros where he made contact with the Greek patrol there, and also managed to get into wireless touch with the commandos previously landed on Naxos.

He learned that they were in contact with the enemy and after firing a few shots were about to open negotiations for the surrender of the German garrison. Considering that the sight of his MLs off the harbour would lend emphasis to the negotiations, Ford decided to return.

He was back off Naxia at 11.35 and on arrival was met by a small boat with a man waving a white flag. It was treated with great circumspection until it was seen to contain the British Army Liaison Officer, two Greek soldiers and two Germans, all armed.

The situation was peculiar. It transpired that the German officer on board ML 360 was, indeed, the garrison commander, and the Greek landing party had allowed the two Germans to come out and talk to him in the presence of an interpreter. The enemy ashore refused to surrender to a Greek force for fear of reprisals from the civil population.

As a sign of good faith, Ford therefore decided to enter the harbour with his ML and cover the Germans with his guns while they marched down to the quay with Greek troops to protect them. This being translated, the two Germans promptly asked their captured officer for orders, to which he replied that being a prisoner he could give none. The Germans were then given until 1.40 p.m. to hoist the white flag and their representatives were sent ashore to explain.

At 12.50, leaving her consort off the entrance as cover, ML 360 moved into the harbour and anchored about 200 yards from the shore.

While there they could see the enemy's mortar, machine guns and riflemen constantly being moved into new positions. Time drew on with no sign of surrender so, at 1.35, Ford weighed his anchor, ran out of the harbour and joined 354 outside.

At 1.40 precisely both MLs opened fire with their heavy guns at a range of about 1,000 yards. The sea was calm and the shooting very good, at least three shots out of every four falling into the target area. After a five-minute burst our craft ceased firing to allow their guns to cool. The enemy machine guns were deserted but presently the MLs were fired upon with rifles. The Germans were treated to another dose after which there was no reply. At about 2.20 Ford withdrew his boats to make contact with the Greek troops. The situation was something of a stalemate. Though the Germans could not get out, the Greeks could not storm and capture the enemy position, the castle walls being too thick to be breached by light shell.

Later that day Ford took his ship to Paros to embark the Greek patrol from there. He found that they had been unable to concentrate, so after arranging to pick them up next day, he returned to Naxos, where 360 and 354 spent the night close inshore near Naxia keeping a careful watch for any enemy attempt to reinforce the garrison.

Early next morning, 14 October, the MLs landed food and ammunition for the Greek troops on shore, and at 10 a.m. Ford was informed that the enemy had opened fire with their mortar at the Greek forward positions. He was asked to silence it, so both MLs moved to Naxia, where they were met by what is described as a hail of fairly accurate rifle and machine gun fire. Unable to locate the mortar, Ford took his two craft out to a range of 1,500 yards and opened fire. It sent the Germans to cover. All their fire ceased.

Later that day, leaving 354 off Naxia, 360 again visited Paros, embarked the Greek patrol and their equipment and landed them on Naxos. Nothing further happened that night, which the MLs spent at anchor as before.

At 3.30 a.m. on the 15th, ML 1385 arrived and discharged stores, and three hours later Ford had a message from the Greeks asking the MLs to close the harbour. Then two Dorniers appeared to the westward and disappeared after being fired upon. Meanwhile the MLs received considerable rifle and machine gun fire from the shore. By 7.00 the Greeks ashore were using their three-inch mortar to great effect, the MLs joining in the battle by an effective bombardment lasting fifteen minutes. The Greek attack started at 11.00 and to send the enemy to ground the MLs were bombarding enemy positions at the rate of a round a minute. Aircraft of the RAF had been seen earlier but, at 2.45 p.m., four Beaufighters appeared and attacked with rocket projectiles, the MLs closing the shore and bombarding during each run by the aircraft. At 3.15 the Beaufighters attacked the enemy with cannon shell, keeping it up for ten minutes.

A little later the MLs ceased fire to allow attack by the Greeks. Their three-inch mortar did good work and presently a large enemy-occupied building started to smoke and then burst into flame. At about 4.30 p.m. came the welcome news that the enemy had surrendered, so the MLs entered the harbour, embarked the prisoners and their Greek guard, and landed them elsewhere early next morning.

Lieutenant John Ford had done a good job. During those four days of complicated operations he had in the words of a Senior Officer, 'Shown great initiative and judgement and used his force to the fullest effect.'

Naxos was liberated as the result of a combined operation between sea, land and air; but the lucky capture of the German garrison commander, and the presence of the Motor Launches and their accurate supporting fire were important contributory factors to the success of one of the many little sideshows in the Aegean in which the smaller vessels of the Royal Navy have played so important a part.

Member No. 2000 Jack Park

Captain Peter Dickens
DSO, MBE, DSC

From the Chairman

The summer started in tragic circumstances for our Association with the sad death of our President, Peter Dickens. I was very proud that so many of our members were able to attend the funeral at Withyham. At the last meeting of the national committee it was agreed that a memorial service be held at which a seat with an inscribed plaque would be unveiled in memory of Peter Dickens. I am very pleased to report that Mary Dickens has agreed to our request and our secretary and treasurer are organising both the provision of the seat and the memorial service. I hope we shall have a good attendance for the occasion, the date of which will be notified to you as soon as it is arranged.

I am very pleased to hear that the branch in Wales has made arrangements for their official inauguration. I wish them well in their endeavours and if possible I hope to be able to attend their function.

Whilst writing about branches I should like to wish good fortune to Ron Woods in his efforts to start a new branch in West Sussex. There are many members in that area and I hope they will support him in the work he is doing.

Bill Cobby

Captain Peter Gerald Charles Dickens, DSO, MBE, DSC, RN (Rtd)

Peter Dickens, President of the Coastal Forces Veterans Association, passed peacefully away on the morning of 25 May 1987, having fought a long battle with illness. We are, as an association, always saddened and diminished by the loss of an old friend or comrade, the loss of our President, a grievous blow! Many of our members were proud to have served under him in wartime; he was proud to serve us all as our President.

204

The funeral service and interment took place on a lovely day in the beautiful setting of the parish church of Withyham, Sussex, with which Peter was closely connected. The Association were well represented by at least forty members and the ladies; it was naturally to be expected that for many of our members attendance was impossible; they can be assured that they were represented by those of us able to attend! I must add that there were present those who had travelled many miles to attend. The service, as can be imagined, had been pre-arranged by Peter himself and reflected his great Christian outlook and his wonderful sense of humour! In a personal letter to the officiating priest, his cousin, he mentioned that they had, in the past, had many a friendly argument over the hereafter, etc. The letter continued that he, Peter, would by now be in full possession of the truth! At the end of the service, the coffin was carried from the church to the lovely words of the *Nunc Dimitis*: 'Lord, now lettest thou thy servant depart in peace.' Peter was laid to rest on the north side of the church, overlooking the lovely Sussex scenery.

Mrs Mary Dickens kindly invited those of us who attended to go back to the family home to partake of refreshment where we were kindly received by her family. I can only conclude by saying that, at no time, did one get the feeling that Peter had departed; his wonderful personality seemed to be with us all. We remember with pride, his Presidency, his interest in all that went on and his kindness to all of us in contact with him; we remember above all, his attendance at the Sunday of our AGM at Lowestoft: sadly, he could not give his usual address but he came! That outward sign of a great Leader and Friend.

'May light perpetual shine upon him'.

Len A. Bridge, Secretary CFVA

Captain Dickens as CFVA President

It was at the Association's first AGM, held in the Victory Club, RNB, Portsmouth on 23 February 1975, that Captain Dickens accepted the invitation to become President.

To be elected President of any organisation is to be accorded the highest honour that Members can bestow on one of their number. It was so obvious to those present that in the case of the then newly-formed Coastal Forces Veterans Association, such an honour was due to the one man who epitomized what Coastal Forces accomplished during the War.

The unanimous choice of Peter Dickens was, over the ensuing twelve years, to prove time and again that we had the right man at the top. Never obtrusive, always available, regularly in attendance with his charming wife Mary at Association functions, he took pride in the CFVA, and we in him. Despite his many achievements and well-deserved honours, he remained essentially a very modest man, and who amongst us will ever forget the unfailing courtesy that he extended to each and every one, be they Royalty, brother officers, or those of us from 'the front end of the ship'?

Throughout its existence, our Association has been fortunate in its friends, and was thrice-blessed to have had Captain Peter Dickens, DSO, MBE, DSC, as its first President. We who are left must honour his memory in the way that he himself exemplified, by keeping alive the comradeship we had in Coastal Forces during our formative years, and helping one another as the going gets harder. One can almost hear him saying those well-remembered words ... 'Carry on' ...

Charles Milner, National Treasurer.

Peter Dickens' Testament

My primitive theology goes something like this. It's derived from observation, not convention; nor, I fear, much practice, but so far as that has gone, it fits. I believe in a God of Love, who created us with independent minds and wills to lead active, creative, and above all loving lives in his greater glory. But he is also a God of battles, who demands that we stand up and fight against evil when goodness would otherwise be destroyed. We can and should seek his guidance and help, but he prefers initiative and courage to cringing subservience. This is just as well since we can't possibly understand more than a mite of his infinite vastness and purpose; in this instance whether or not he has ordained an afterlife, which I for one certainly don't know. If he has, good; if he hasn't, equally good, goodness being what he ordains; so let's leave that one to him. But if there's any love in Withyham Church today, that's palpably, wonderfully, divinely real;

and please count me in on it because I have, as strongly as my feeble nature allowed, loved you.

16th July 1987

My Dear Friends,

Please forgive me writing to you in the Newsletter, and not individually; but as you may imagine, I have had so many letters about my Dearest Peter and so many splendid and well deserved tributes paid to him, that it would be many months before I could write to you all; and answer your comforting letters and cards. Thank you for them and for your generous donations to Withyham Church; and above all for coming such a long way to say 'Goodbye' to your President. It was wonderful that so many of you were able to come to the heart-warming Service, which was a thanksgiving so well-earned, for a life so well-lived. Your presence was a great support to me and the family.

Thank you for asking me to be an honorary member of the CFVA. This is a great compliment which I gladly accept as another tribute to Peter. I am so pleased to think that I won't lose touch with you all, and I hope you know that there is always a welcome here for anyone who comes this way. We'll raise a glass to Peter and remember happy times together.

Your suggestion of a Memorial seat in Withyham churchyard is very appealing, because he loved it so much and worked hard on the trees which added to the beauty of that peaceful place. We will be able to make arrangements for the dedication when Mark returns to the surface early in September, and we will always be happy to go along with any other suggestions for a Memorial you may have.

I enclose a copy of Peter's testament which Harry read out at the funeral, because several people have said that they would like to have it. I think that it gives us the essence of a true and honest man whom we all loved and admired, and of whom we are all so proud.

Bless you all and my Warmest Thanks for everything.

From Mary (Dickens)

Mark at the present time is serving in nuclear submarines with the Royal Navy – Editor.

Mary Dickens donates Research Material

I am sure that all Peter's shipmates will be very glad to know that I have donated the files on *Narvic*, *Night Action* and *HMS Hesperus*; and the original draft of *Night Action* and *Jungle Frontier* to the Imperial War Museum. These contain the action reports from both British and German Commands, which are unique; and there is a copy of Peter Scott's own story of Coastal Forces in Normandy after 'D' Day.

I am very proud that my Peter's work has received such splendid recognition and I know how thrilled and delighted he would be.

I enclose a copy of the letter I received from Roderick Suddaby, Keeper of the Records, who would welcome visits from members of the Coastal Forces Veterans; so I do hope that some of you will go along there. If you give him twenty-four hours' notice he will be glad to see you and show you the documents.

Then you can come here and see me afterwards!

Best wishes to you all from Mary.

An Appreciation from R. W. A. Suddaby, Keeper of the Department's Documents, Imperial War Museum

Dear Mrs Dickens,

I was very pleased to meet you and one of your daughters at the splendid lunch party at Commander Gaunt's London flat and to be able to accept from you in person your donation to this Museum of your husband's research materials for his two Second World War books and the profile of *HMS Hesperus* and the final draft of *The Jungle Frontier*. I must say at once how impressed I am by Captain Dickens' meticulous organisation of his research notes and I am certain that this will be greatly appreciated by all those who have occasion to consult the collection in the future. I am confident, too, that these very extensive materials will prove a most rewarding source for researchers since they include much detailed testimony gathered by your husband from those who took part in the operations about which he was writing as well as, in the case of *Night Action*, his own contemporary records. Captain Dickens' papers, which will now be placed in the Museum's archive under his name, are therefore a valuable addition to the collection of documents held here on the nation's behalf.

Roderick Suddaby, Imperial War Museum

Motor Gun Boat 108 (Became Motor Torpedo Boat 418 in September 1943)—9th Motor Gun Boat Flotilla—Dover. Commanding Officer: Sub Lieutenant Ronald Barge, RNVR. Armament: One × 2-pounder pom-pom; one × 2 20mm. Oerlikon; two × 2 0.303" Lewis; two depth charges.

Our Founder
Gordon Alfred Charles Stevens
1918–1988

Chief Petty Officer, DSM, MiD

Gordon Stevens had an idea in 1974 after his demobilisation from the Royal Navy; he discussed this idea with his wife Marc who in turn contacted Radio Solent. Radio Solent rang Gordon at his home and broadcast his 'idea' live. The response was immediate and far greater than Gordon envisaged even in his wildest dreams. He thought that the comradeship shown by personnel in 'Little Ships' could be fostered and extended in civilian life—he was right—the need was apparent. By June of that year there were 16 members; in September, 190; in October, 260; and by the first Annual General meeting on 25 February 1975 the membership had risen to 300.

Who would have guessed in those early days that seventeen years later on 19 April 1992 at the Annual General Meeting at Mill Rythe Holiday Village, Hayling Island, Portsmouth, Hampshire the total membership excluding wives and associates had reached the figure of 1,890 and was still rising. 'His idea' has developed into what we now reverently refer to as The Coastal Forces Veterans Association.

In the embryo stage Gordon was talking and thinking all his waking hours, almost an obsession, to plan and organise an Association entirely devoted to his aspirations, the desires of ex-members of Coastal Forces to meet together to foster the 'comradeship' being the main feature. Now twenty branches of the association thrive throughout the length and breadth of the United Kingdom including: Scotland; North-East; N.E. Lancs; Leeds; Merseyside; Fleetwood; Staffordshire;

North Midlands; East Midlands; Midlands; Wales; East Anglia; South London; London; South-East Essex; Southern; West Sussex; South-West; Cornwall.

We mourn the loss of our founder; may his dreams continue to flourish. We salute you, Gordon.

Harold Pickles DSM

Supreme Headquarters Allied Expeditionary Force

Soldiers, Sailors and Airmen of the Allied Expeditionary Force! You are about to embark upon the Great Crusade, toward which we have striven these many months. The eyes of the world are upon you. In company with our brave Allies and brothers-in-arms on other Fronts, you will bring about the destruction of the German war machine, the elimination of Nazi tyranny over the oppressed peoples of Europe, and security for ourselves in a free world.

Your task will not be an easy one. Your enemy is well trained, well equipped and battle-hardened. He will fight savagely.

But this is the year 1944! Much has happened since the Nazi triumphs of 1940–41. The United Nations have inflicted upon the Germans great defeats, in open battle, man to man. Our air offensive has seriously reduced their strength in the air and their capacity to wage war on the ground. Our Home Fronts have given us an over-whelming superiority in weapons and munitions of war, and placed at our disposal great reserves of trained fighting men. The tide has turned! The free men of the world are marching together to victory!

I have full confidence in your courage, devotion of duty and skill in battle. We will accept nothing less than full Victory!

Good luck! And let us all beseech the blessing of Almighty God upon this great and noble undertaking.

Winston Churchill

213

Two trips to Sando

Sando is a small island, a mile long from north to south, and at its widest point is just over a quarter of a mile across; it lies in the Skagerrak, nineteen miles east of Lindesness at the south-west tip of Norway, two and a half miles off the Norwegian mainland. There is a smaller island, Odden, separated by a narrow channel from, and just south of, Sando.

My first trip started when MTB 718 (Lieutenant R. F. Seddon, DSC, RNVR) left Aberdeen on Operation 'Lola' at 22.00 hours on Monday 12 February 1945 – object: to land two Norwegian agents who were to set up an observation post and W/T Station. 718 carried a heavy deck load of stores, 2,000 gallons of petrol in jerricans, and a Norwegian surf boat additional to her own SN6 which was the usual conveyance for putting down and picking up agents on these operations to German-occupied Norway and, previous to then, France.

Immediately the MTB was clear of the sheltered waters of Aberdeen harbour she was into rough weather. Water came into the W/T office, there were flashes from the newly-installed TGY receiver and we had thus lost our wireless receiving gear. From then on, we had to rely on the short range TCS set normally used only for R/T work, but on this occasion manned for W/T, and this surprisingly produced a range of 150 miles, until it, too, failed owing to further sea water infiltrating.

It took two and a half hours to empty the 2,000 gallons of petrol, and hole and jettison the jerricans in a very rough sea.

The first navigation lights off south-west Norway were sighted, twenty-three hours after leaving Aberdeen: Ryvingen Light at 21.06 (13th) and Songvaar Light at 21.53. These were the first fixes for two hundred miles and the ship was within two miles of track. The enemy

214

convoy route was crossed at 22.24 in heavy snow squalls which reduced visibility to nil at times. The Norwegian pilot aboard suggested abandoning the operation in view of the weather conditions, but the Captain would have no truck with such ideas.

The small island of Odden, at first difficult to identify because of the snow having altered its outline, was first sighted only thirty yards abeam to port at 23.30 hours. At 00.22 hours on Wednesday 14 February, the northern tip of Sando was identified and fifteen minutes later, 718's anchor was dropped fifty yards off the 'pin-point' on the north-east side, where the two agents were to be put ashore with their stores.

The surf boat, SN6, with Lieutenant Guy Hamilton, DSC, RNVR in command and one of the agents, Muller, accompanying, pulled away, but they reported by 'walkie talkie' that the south-westerly swell made a landing too hazardous, so they were recalled. The MTB weighed anchor and was slowly moved through the rocky channel round the north of Sando, the way being 'felt' by use of the lead line, A/B Ron Hunter lying on the foc'sle for this operation.

A suitable alternative landing place was found on the north-west corner of the island, and the extremely laborious task of landing stores commenced just after 01.30 hours in difficult conditions of snow squalls, swell and poor visibility, with 718's anchor dragging at one stage. We lost a torch, a watch and the Norwegian surf boat; we almost lost our Newfoundlander, A/B Hayward Rockwood, who jumped into the water too soon at the new pin-point and landed in several fathoms of very cold water, but he swam ashore. (A very tough character this 'Rocky', who, the previous year, was left behind in Occupied France with Lieutenant Guy Hamilton and Leading Seaman Albert Dellow, DSM; his handling of the King's English as he split the infinitives and stuffed into them his own rich brand of original expletives made him a joy to listen to.)

Because the Norwegian surf boat, waterlogged, drifted away, the MTB's own SN6 was left with Muller and Larsen. In common with most of the ship's company, the two agents had been sea-sick for most of the passage from Scotland, and a last minute request for some

215

'bread and water' meant hastily preparing sandwiches for them in the galley and also putting a water container into their boat. From then on, the two Norwegians had to be left to their own devices and 718 set off on the long trip home.

In the Skagerrak, sea conditions were quite good by comparison to what was met when once again the North Sea was reached, and the Captain's report rightly described them as 'atrocious'.

When the first QH fix was obtained exactly forty-eight hours after leaving base, the ship was found to have been driven fifteen miles off track. Most of the return journey was at only six to eight knots, later increased to eleven. The boat was taking water in the forward bilges and the engine room, and here continual pumping by PO M/M Bill Cartwright, DSM and his staff could not prevent the water level rising above the twenty-four-volt batteries and the circuit had to be broken. All the remaining W/T apparatus was U/S from this time.

718 sighted Peterhead eventually and only with great difficulty, because of the weight of the water in the bilges, was she manoeuvred alongside at Aberdeen around 08.30 on Thursday 15 February.

The Captain's Report on 'Lola' concluded:

> I must wholeheartedly commend the spirit, resourcefulness and conduct of the officers and men under my command during these two and a half days of appalling conditions – conditions far in excess of the normal requirements of these small craft, and as physically exhausting to the men as to the boat.

He made special mention of the skilful navigation of Sub-Lieutenant K. O'Brien, RNVR which was indeed superb. The Admiralty acknowledgement endorsed what our Captain had said, but rightly made the point that all the qualities described would have been of no avail without Lieutenant Seddon's leadership and determination, and the greatest credit was due to him. None of RFS's crew would disagree with that; he took us there, did the job, and got us safely back, and only God knows how he did it during those fifty-eight hours at sea, fourteen of them at continuous 'Action Stations'. Meanwhile, confirmation was received that Muller and Larsen had set up shop and were operating successfully over there in Norway.

My second trip to Sando took place during a holiday in Norway, on 6 August 1976 to be precise. Leaving the car at the end of a rough road on the island of Skjerno, which is linked to the mainland near Kristiansand South, and armed with chart, binoculars and camera, and wife dutifully bringing up the rear, we proceeded in 'single line ahead' for the south-east corner of Skjerno. The sun shone, the sea was calm and there, a mile away, was the pin-point where we left Muller and Larsen 31½ years before, and it all seemed almost unbelievable that Trip Number One ever happened.

It must have done, and all those other operations too. Or else why do the Ship's Company of MTB 718 seek out each other in their middle age and re-kindle the embers of their wartime comradeship, conveniently forgetting the many times they cursed the sea, the war, the Andrew, and each other – and wished they had never joined?!

C. W. Milner, DSM (Ldg. Tel. MTB 718)

(Eleven former members of 718's Ship's Company, including Captain and First Lieutenant, are CFVA members and one Telegraphist, Les Taylor, serves on the National Committee.)

Motor Anti-Submarine Boat 57. Completed September 1940 prior to being redesignated Motor Gun Boat 57 in January 1941. 4th Motor Anti-Submarine (later Motor Gun Boat) Flotilla. Normally based Portland. Commanding Officer: Sub Lieutenant The Hon. Mark Tennyson, RN (now Lord Tennyson). Armament: one 20mm aft; two × 2 0.303" Lewis; two depth charges.

Dalmatian Incident

The morning sun streamed in through the window on the desk where I sat, doing my best to concentrate on completing the report. Outside I could see the blue waters of the Adriatic, upon whose ruffled surface the sunlight danced and sparkled, while the air was cool and filled with the mingled scent of spring flowers and wood smoke, a scent which seems somehow or other to belong only to the Continental countryside. The white sheet of foolscap was bare apart from the opening sentence, which read: 'Sir, I have the honour to report on the loss of HMMTB 697 by striking a mine ... '

There my brain seemed to halt. How could a string of typewritten words convey to admirals in Naples and in far away Whitehall the horror of that night? How could any words of mine do justice to the courage and heroism of those officers and men from that small MTB when from out of the darkness came that deafening explosion and sheet of terrifying flame? The bald official statements which Their Lordships would expect would give so inadequate a description. As I gazed at those tranquil waters outside my window, my thoughts took me back to the events which led to our being there ...

I was in the operations room of Navy House one day in April 1945, when Chris came bounding into the room. Chris was a young Lieutenant RN, filled with an enthusiastic energy which, if it had been allowed full rein, would have had us approaching Pola harbour in broad daylight to put a 'fish' into the E-Boat pens. He was Operations Officer and very often came out with us on the expeditions he had suggested. This morning he was in his usual high spirits.

'Hullo there!' he said. 'Big stuff to-night: The Jugs are going to attack Krk and we have lined up a trip for you and the boys. We want you to go up the west side of the island and give any of the Huns who might be deciding to evacuate the full treatment. SNONA [Senior

219

Naval Officer, Northern Adriatic] is still at Rab in the landing craft HQ chatting with Commissars and other Jug worthies; so you can pay them a visit there first, and get the very latest information on the party to-night.

'By the way,' he continued, 'I have two Jug pilots outside who have done some mine-spotting for us. They are attached to the RAF at the local field here and fly Hurricanes.'

At that moment in they came, and we were soon poring over the chart of the area in question.

'You will go in between Krk and Cherso,' said Chris, his dividers stabbing sections of the chart, criss-crossed with signs indicating 'Heavily Mined'. I had just opened my mouth to protest vehemently that the 59th had already lost two of its ships within the last fortnight on an area not marked as a minefield, and that I had no intention of taking my chaps through a spot actually confirmed as one, when Chris broke in saying:

'Hold on a minute; these chaps have just done a "recce" and have reported seeing mines there, but only in the middle of the channel. Close into the Krk side, they say, none was visible, and if you keep well into the shore, you will be as right as rain. There aren't any rocks or shallows, and the water's quite deep right up to the beach.'

I nodded rather dubiously ...

It was one of those delightful April days with a clear blue sky, bright sunlight, and a slight nip in the air which seemed to perk up everybody's spirits, and it was a cheerful trio of His Majesty's MTBs which left Zara that afternoon. I was travelling with Rover in 658 accompanied by Dennis Booth, DSC, RNVR in 697 and Frank in a recently repaired 633. As we rumbled up the narrow channel at some 25 knots, with our exhaust notes booming and reverberating, it was not very long before the look-out shouted: 'Rab ahead, Sir!' – and there, up a narrow inlet, lay the town, with the landing craft tied up alongside the jetty and with SNONA standing on deck to greet us.

After SNONA had given me an idea of how the night's attack would develop, he suggested that I should go only as far as I considered wise, but upon no account was I to try and visit Fiume unless I saw the *Scharnhorst* or something like that!

220

'Off you go,' he said. 'Have your supper and be ready to sail about 19.15. Good luck to you. I'll be on the LCH's bridge to wave you goodbye.'

The Bosun's pipe sounded off and the crew came to attention while we saluted the figure of SNONA, etched sharply against the outline of the LCH in the dying sun. We headed into the smoke, with the water foaming and swirling about our hulls. Yes, we were off, and it was good to be alive.

Very shortly we were out on the broad waters of the Mali Kvarner on our way to Plavnic, which lay about forty miles to the north, where I intended to lie until the young sliver of a moon had disappeared. Coming to within six miles of Plavnic, we reduced speed to about six knots, put in our silencers and called the crew to action stations. As we closed on the dark shape that was the island, I hoped fervently that the night would get darker. About ten yards from the beach, we stopped and lay together, merged into the deep black shadow of the island. Plavnic was still nominally in enemy hands and was covered on one side by the battery in the town of Krk, and the side we were on by the 210mm. guns of Stojan Point.

The moon seemed reluctant to go down; the hours passed slowly. However, about 2 a.m. some clouds crept up from the north-east and in about an hour things looked a little better. We moved off on what was the equivalent of MTB tiptoes, slow ahead on one engine, and in a few minutes reached the narrow gap which separates Plavnic from Cherso. Rounding this point, we made a 90° turn to starboard and steered for Krk Island, making for Burisca Bay. As we slowly crept along the coast I was hoping desperately that our shapes had not been made out and that there would be no Hun patrol, lying huddled round their machine gun, waiting to pour a stream of lead into us as we passed, a mere stone's throw from the rocks and shingle.

We had just reached Spena Point when from ahead on our port bow on the Cherso Island side came a flickering light with the challenge letters 'AA-AA-AA-AA'. The point was a shore battery, and as soon as I saw the light a host of thoughts chased through my mind. To stop, to turn round, to carry on ... Alas, the decision was made for me. There occurred one of the most sickening sensations I have ever experienced: a tremendous bang, followed by a blinding flash and a great blast of hot air swept across our bridge with a frightening sound.

Turning round, I saw to my horror that 697 appeared to have been blown to pieces from the mast aft, leaving only the bow portion floating, surrounded by a sea of flame. My first thought was that it had been a direct hit from a shore battery, but in the brilliant light caused by the flames, which lit up the mountains, shore and sea for miles around, I made out the black shapes of two large mines floating half under the water about forty yards away, and realised that 697 had hit one.

Trying to keep the tremble out of my voice, I called up Frank, who was third in line, on the intercom, telling him to go alongside the floating remains, while Rover slowly turned 658 round to allow us to make for the Carley float, upon which one man was lying with two others clinging to its side. As we slowly closed the float, some of the crew ran up forward with lines and a scrambling net, and, working thoroughly and with great coolness, they heaved in the men, all of whom appeared to be in poor shape. Meanwhile Frank and his crew were doing a magnificent job in rescuing 697's men, who must have felt overjoyed when 658's bow nosed her way alongside, enabling them to leap nimbly aboard.

'Survivors aboard, Sir,' came the quiet, unflurried tones of Rover. 'Two of them are pretty badly hurt and I've laid them out on the charthouse deck. In the meantime Tony is giving them a shot of morphia each. Incidentally, we have George aboard.' I turned round to see the dripping figure of 697's navigating officer still wearing his cap and saluting. He had flung the confidential books overboard and dived into the water, where he helped to put one of his crew on the float and supported the other, who had a broken leg.

A minute or so earlier I had asked Rover to lower the dinghy, as I was convinced there might possibly be survivors somewhere in the water, and at that moment he reported the dinghy was ready afloat, but the rowlocks couldn't be found. 'Well, we'll just have to imitate our Redskin friends,' I remarked. 'Tony, come with me and we'll see if there is anyone left in the water.'

Together we lowered the oars into the tiny dinghy and, seizing one each, we paddled off in the general direction of the flaming wreckage.

We carefully skirted the worst spot and headed to where we were sure we could hear the cries of someone in the water. As we drew near, we saw in the light of the flames a cork life jacket from which emerged the head of a man surrounded by wreckage. He was screaming in a most piteous fashion and his oil- and blood-covered face made him look scarcely human. He appeared at first glance to have half his jaw missing, while one of his arms appeared to be badly injured. To get him into the dinghy was the next problem, and in our first two attempts we nearly succeeded in joining him. He was so completely covered with oil that our hands kept slipping as we tried to get a grip. All this while he kept up a horrible animal-like howling, despite our reassuring cries of, 'Take it easy, old boy. We'll have you back on board with a nice tot of rum inside you in no time': a sentiment we were far from believing ourselves. I personally was in a state of complete terror, as we were fairly close to the now-abandoned remains of 697's bow, which was blazing fiercely, with ammunition blowing up in great style, fortunately mostly in the air. After what seemed an eternity, we finally dragged the man on board, nearly drowning the poor fellow in our waterlogged dinghy, as his head got jammed under one of the thwarts. At last we started off, paddling Indian-fashion.

That return journey is a nightmare which will live with me for the rest of my life, an agony I cannot describe. Eventually willing hands climbed down the scrambling net to take our precious cargo up on deck and finally to haul us up too. Our dinghy, which was half filled with water, promptly sank. Taking our duffle coats off, we joined Rover on the bridge, to be rewarded with a large cup of hot soup each. 633 lay about fifteen yards off and a group of men were standing by the depth charges on the stern, trying to hoist their dinghy on board. They were evidently having a very hard task, as there appeared to be someone lying in it. One man was in the water alongside the dinghy, trying to keep the waterlogged boat afloat. I shouted to Frank, asking him to speed up as I was very anxious to get out of the area in case either of our ships struck another mine or the strangely silent shore battery decided to open up.

In reply Frank yelled, 'I'm trying my hardest, but it's hellish difficult, as I think the poor fellow's back is broken and we can't lift him without the dinghy.'

'All right,' I said, 'Try your best, but be as quick as you can.'

After about ten minutes or so Rover shouted: 'It looks as if their dinghy's sunk,' and, to everyone's despair, that is exactly what had happened; despite their Herculean efforts, the man was lost.

It was with a sad heart that I then decided to head for home, as I felt that we had rescued everyone we could, and with the flames lighting the area like a gigantic bonfire, there seemed little possibility of anyone else being alive either within the inferno or on its edge. The mine must have struck 697's engine-room and after petrol compartments, which contained well over three thousand gallons, bringing a speedy death to the half dozen men who were below.

As we covered the miles southward to Zara, we could see from our bridge the flames from the burning wreckage, with exploding ammunition making neat parabolas high into the night sky. Even when we were fifty miles away that flaming glow could still be seen like an enormous torch flickering against the background of mountains, to be replaced when dawn came by a pillar of black smoke reaching upwards for hundreds of feet.

... I gazed down at the typewriter, and slowly the lines took shape:

> Survivors were taken aboard 658 and 633, while a thorough search was made of the area. It is regretted that no sign could be found of the ten missing ratings. The conduct of officers and men was exemplary, the injured behaving with great fortitude. It is considered that the safe with the confidential books has been destroyed.
>
> I have the honour to be, Sir, your obedient servant ...

There, it was finished. As I stood up my eye caught the sight of our rows of ships moored alongside the quay with their White Ensigns fluttering in the breeze. Yes, their sacrifice had not been in vain:

> *If a good death be virtue's noblest crown,*
> *This we achieved when Fortune struck us down,*
> *Who strove for Hellas' freedom held the fort,*
> *And here lie deathless in men's good report.*

Norwegian and British Reunion at Dover

The British 50th and the Norwegian 52nd ML Minelaying Flotillas based at Dover from 1941–44 met together for the first time in forty-five years.

The Norwegian party of six and their wives led by Christian Gysler met the British contingent of six and their wives on 30 November 1989. Needless to say, it was a momentous occasion when we all recognised each other after all those years.

It was the Norwegian party who promised the town of Dover a Christmas tree for 1989 in appreciation of the kindness and hospitality they received during the war from the people of Dover and it was on this occasion, 30 November, that the Christmas tree was duly sited in the middle of the Market Square to be lit and presented to the Mayor of Dover.

A reception prior to the light of the lighting of the tree was held in a room overlooking the Market Square where before three or four hundred local people Christian Gysler on behalf of the Norwegians thanked the people of Dover for their kindness to which the Mayor replied. The large crowd joined together to sing the National Anthems of both countries, after which everyone participated in the countdown to the lighting of the tree.

The Mayor of Dover then invited both parties to the Town Hall where, in company with other members of the Dover District Council, we were entertained to a buffet supper. The evening was concluded by a short speech of welcome by the Mayor after which he presented to each member of the Norwegian party a memento of their visit. Christian Gysler replied and thanked the Mayor on behalf of the British and in passing was able to recount several stories in appreciation of our Norwegian friends' escapes from Norway during the war.

In conclusion may we thank Christian Gysler for his effort in bringing us together, nor would it be amiss for me to add that through the efforts of Christian Gysler and his party there is in Norway a museum of Norwegian Naval activities during the war. It was he who approached the British Naval Attaché in Oslo to ask whether he could obtain the results of the minelaying operation carried out by the 50th and 52nd ML Flotillas from 1941–1944. The Naval Attaché arranged through the Admiralty for the records to be made available at the Records Office at Kew for Christian Gysler. The records show that fifty-six ships were sunk, thirty-four damaged, for the loss of four MLs out of eight, two out of each flotilla.

The passage of German shipping through the Strait of Dover was drastically reduced.

Member No. 1368 H. R. Boyd

Motor Torpedo Boat 97. Joined 24th Motor Torpedo Boat Flotilla, later to Mediterranean. (Commanding Officer Lieutenant Nicko Poland, RN.) Photograph taken on trials 1942. Armament: Two 21" torpedo tubes; one × 2 0.5" Vickers.

A Glossary of Words and Sayings from the 'Andrew'

Anchors – from Greek word for hook or crook.

Andrew – The Royal Navy. Andrew Miller was a very zealous officer who, at one time, worked in the press gang.

Apron – protects the leadsman's clothing when heaving the lead.

Banyan party – an outing ashore.

Barrack stanchion – a rating who somehow managed to wangle a berth in Royal Navy barracks and seemed immovable.

Beef chit – slang for menu.

Bee's knees – the two eye bolts at the end of the boat boom for the lazy painters.

Bitter end – turn of cable eased out little by little, around the bits, and the part which must stay in-board is the bitter end.

Black dog for a white monkey – something for nothing.

Blood bucket – ship's lifeboat.

To bone – means to steal – a Lieutenant Bone convicted of theft at the beginning of the nineteenth century.

Brass monkeys – cold weather (the term 'cold enough to freeze the balls off a brass monkey' from the days of fighting sail, when cannon balls, being iron, contracted with the cold so much that they became loose in their brass tacks, 'the monkeys', and so fell off and rolled around the deck).

Bumbluff – an incipient beard.

Cackleberries – eggs.

Chokka – fed up, exasperated (from chock-a-block, when a rope is hard up against its block).

Cottage – old hands' slang for mess.

Damager – the NAAFI canteen manager, a civilian even on board ship.

Doggo – ugly.

Fitted to an affigraphy – denotes a perfect fit.

Gaff – house or flat.

Gondola – hammock.

Nelson's blood – rum. After he died, Admiral Nelson's body was placed in a barrel of rum to preserve it. It was sent back from Trafalgar to Plymouth in the fast frigate HMS *Pickle*. On the way home the matelots in *Pickle* tapped the barrel and drank the rum.

'Pipe down' – the order to turn in to sleep (from the days of the fighting sail, when the seamen put their smoking pipes away for the night).

'Pipes out' – the order to return to work.

Sons of Guns – in the days of fighting sail matelots were not allowed ashore. Their womenfolk were brought on board, and loved with their men in their berths between the cannons. Some women gave birth to babies on board and the male babies were brought up on board and spent their whole lives in the Andrew. They were 'sons of guns'.

Top your boom – addressed to an unwanted person means to 'go away'.

Work your ticket – to wangle your way out of the Andrew. The most common way was to pretend insanity.

Endpiece: the Naval Career of our President

I got my second stripe in December 1939, and joined MTBs in HMS *Vernon* in January 1940. At that time the 1st MTB Flotilla, of twelve 60 ft. British Power Boats, was based at Felixstowe, having returned from Malta through the French canals; the 2nd Flotilla of six similar boats was in Hong Kong; and the 4th Flotilla of 70 ft. Vospers was forming at Portsmouth.

In March I was given command of MTB 102, the Vosper prototype 70-footer, and became SO of the 3rd Flotilla, which consisted of 102 and 100. We spent our days and nights training officers and men for the new boats being built.

On 1 April we commissioned HMS *Hornet* and moved the boats over there. Very soon after this the Germans invaded Norway, and then Holland and Belgium, and the war hotted up considerably.

At the end of May the Dunkirk evacuation took place, and I took 102 to Dover, where we took our part in that epic adventure, together with some MA/SBs and several smaller Thornycroft MTBs.

In June 102 took part in the blocking of Dieppe, and then, in July, I was given command of MTB 30, a new Vosper MTB built by Camper & Nicholson. I took her to Felixstowe to join the 4th Flotilla (which then consisted of 22, 24, 25, 29, 30, 31, 32 and 34). We did a number of anti-invasion patrols and offensive patrols to the Dutch coast, without any action, but early in September I was ill and was invalided from MTBs and I was awarded the DSC in the Dunkirk Honours List.

For the rest of 1940 and 1941 I was the First Lieutenant of an ex-American destroyer, HMS *Ludlow*, trained soldiers in landing craft at Inveraray and did a Long Torpedo Course at Roedean in 1942. In

July 1942 I returned to MTBs as SO of the 5th and 6th Flotillas in Dover (35, 38, 42, 43, 45, 48, 218, 219 and 221), and became SOMTBs there when the Dutch 9th Flotilla was moved to Dartmouth. I was awarded a bar to my DSC in 1942.

In January 1943 I was moved to Newhaven as SO of the new 24th Flotilla of Vosper 70-foot boats (81, 85, 86, 89, 97, 226, 242 and 243) and we operated from there for that winter and early spring, doing many patrols without finding any enemy. In April we were moved to the Mediterranean, being shipped out to Algiers from Liverpool and Glasgow.

We reformed the Flotilla in Bone in May 1943 and then moved to Malta in June, ready for the Sicilian invasion in July. For that we operated many patrols in the Messina Straits, from Malta and then from Augusta. I again became sick and was invalided home to UK in September. I was awarded the DSO for the Sicilian invasion.

After sick leave I was sent to the Admiralty to write the CB on Coastal Force Warfare, and then in February 1944 I was appointed Staff Officer to the Captain Coastal Forces (Channel), who was appointed to the Staff of C in C Portsmouth to operate all CF Craft in the Channel for the Invasion. I became the Senior Staff Officer of this organisation for the period of the Invasion, working in Fort Southwick on the Portsdown Hills, where the main controlling Plot for the Portsmouth Command was sited.

After the Invasion, in the autumn of 1944, I was returned to General Service; but in 1947 I came back to HMS *Hornet* as Senior Officer, MTBs for two years, and then in 1950 I went to the Admiralty in Bath for two years, co-ordinating the technical departments in the design and maintenance of all CF Craft.

In 1950 and 1952 I was lent to the Royal Swedish Navy for some months as adviser on MTBs and shore control of Light Forces, and in 1953 I was made a Chevalier of the Order of the Sword of Sweden.

From there, in 1953, I was sent to HMS *Ark Royal*, stood by her for two years and then had a year in her as Commander for her first commission in 1955. I was invalided out of the Navy from *Ark Royal* with chronic brucellosis (or Mediterranean fever), a dreary plague which I originally caught as a midshipman, eating ice creams in Malta!

After leaving the Navy I had some twenty-two years working for Vosper, selling their MTBs and other patrol boats and warships to many navies of the world, till the firm was nationalised by Mr Wedgewood Benn and made part of British Shipbuilders in 1977.

Commander Christopher W. S. Dreyer, DSO, DSC, RN (Ret.)

Story of HAROLD THOMPSON
an evading U.S. airman evacuated from L'Aber Vrac'h
on 1-2 December 1943

July 1943

When we returned to our base at Knettishall the morning after our rescue from the North Sea, we were debriefed, then issued new flying gear, we would not be going back to the States. The policy had been changed that allowed crews picked up from a ditching to call it a tour; so we had another 23 missions to go. After several days of hanging around, we were flown to a depot near Liverpool to pick up our new plane. This was the same model as the one we lost, but it had several improvements to make it more battle worthy - such as bullet proof glass in the cockpit, nicknamed coffins; still, better than what we'd had, which was nothing.

We started flying again about mid-August and between missions I was flying transition flights to get checked out as pilot. Both Major Chamberlain, the Squadron Commander, and Capt. Bynum, the Operations Officer, certified that I was ready to take over a replacement crew and on 8 Sept, with Bynum in the co-pilots seat, flew my one and only mission as an aircraft commander. It was a short four hour flight to the buzz bomb staging area in France. Next morning as they were waking up the crews for the day's mission, Bynum told me that my crew had come in during the night and the pilot would take my place on Lt. Del Porter's crew. Something didn't seem right, and I realised the "Wee Bonnie" would be getting a guy flying his first mission who'd had only a couple of hours of sleep. I asked why I couldn't take over my crew when I got back in the afternoon? Bynum said it was fine with him so I scrambled after Del and the others making their way to the chow hall.

The target that day turned out to be the Renault truck works just south of Paris. Our approach to the Initial Point was uneventful. We were leading the second element of the lead squadron of the group leading the whole division to the target. We'd gone through the usual flak at the

233

French coast, and about 40 miles from the outskirts of Paris, I noticed a single fighter plane flying at our attitude and several hundred yards to our right on a parallel course. I thought he would be giving altitude information to the flak batteries around Paris. He finally pulled out and turned in for a head-on attack of the lead ship in our formation; When he came in range, all our guns opened up on him and single puffs of smoke came out of the centre of his propeller when he fired. He had a large bore gun as the shells would explode in a large ball of smoke and flame. He missed the lead plane but hit us right at the point where the main spar and the other wing are riveted together. It felt almost like hitting a wall, the plane's nose started down and we slid right out of formation; we could only see a strip of metal sticking up outside of the #1 engine. It didn't take long to realise we had no directional control of the plane even after dropping the bombs and trying to use the engines by alternating power. The outer wing had dropped down and back, the air speed dropped to less that 100 MPH, and we were in a hopeless position. So Del hit the bail out switch. When everyone had jumped, I gave him his chest chute and headed for the escape hatch below the flight deck. Took only seconds to go out head first with only one thought; to see how far I could drop before I pulled the rip cord. I thought the closer I could get to the ground the better my chances of getting away. As I was heading down I could feel and hear the rumble of explosions right below me and thought I was heading into the target area so I waited for just a few seconds more and pulled the rip cord. The chute opened with a pop, I swung back and forth for awhile, but this gave me a chance to see where I was, not over the target, which was a big relief. I counted eight chutes way above and behind me. I thought I was around 12,000 feet. A fighter plane was flying in a huge circle around the string of parachutes. I was sure he was letting the troops on the ground know where were likely to land.

As I got closer to the ground I could see the Eiffel Tower almost close enough to reach out and touch, but still miles away in reality. I thought a school yard in the direction I was drifting would be my landing point but I was still much too high and kept going. The area below me was residential with people out in the streets watching the air show. About this time I noticed two men in German uniforms with rifles slung on their backs pedalling furiously down a street parallel to the one under my descent. When they realised they would not reach my landing spot before I did, they stopped, unslung their rifles and fired at me. In a flash I remembered all the horror stories about how in some areas they did not take prisoners, and I was sure that was what would happen to me if they got me. Their aim was way off, I did not hear the bullets zinging past but the flash and sound of their guns galvanised me, as nothing else could, to do all within my power to see they didn't get their hands on me. I could see they would be two blocks away from my landing spot, so I looked ahead to see where I would come down and had only time to lift my legs up to miss the roof of a house. In this legs-up position I landed right in the middle of a small apple tree. It helped break my fall but it broke in two and my parachute was draped all over the standing half of the tree. I bounced up, supercharged, unbuckling my parachute harness and ran around the small yard looking for a way out. Finding no gates, I picked what looked to be the weakest part of the rusty chicken wire fence and crashed through it head first breaking through easily. On my hands and knees in the next yard, I headed down through the weeds toward a small chicken house. While I was doing this, the two soldiers on bicycles came down the street, asking everyone where I had gone. The Frenchmen pointed down the street in the direction of the soldiers were headed, at the corner the soldiers asked again, and soon they were directed completely out of the area.

In the meantime I was digging, with my hands, a small crawl space under the chicken house. I had just gotten settled in when I heard a soft whistle coming from the area where I'd landed. It was a young teenaged boy motioning me to come back. When I did he made me understand by using hand gestures that I was to follow him into the house next door. I knew he wanted me to get rid of my flying gear, so when I'd take something off, he would throw it over the fence into the yard where my chute was. When I was down to my sweatshirt, khaki pants and G.I.

shoes, he led me out of the house and settled me under a bush next to the fence of the yard with all my flying gear. No way was I staying there. I crawled along the fence to the big wall out front. The people standing in the street suddenly stopped talking, so I looked out and saw a man in a black suit, black bowler, smoking a pipe, slowly coming in my direction. No one said a word to him so I figured he would be no friend of mine. It was this fellow's chicken house I had dug my little tunnel under. I was told later he was the only German National living in the area. When he came to the house that had my chute and gear in the back yard, he opened the front gate and walked down to the back of the house. As soon as he was out of sight I dashed through the next door gate onto the street. No one I approached was ready to take a chance, openly, to help me. They seemed more concerned that I get rid of the small hunting knife on my belt. We carried these to deflate our Mae West in case it activated under our parachute harness. I took the knife out of the scabbard and tossed it over into someone's yard - which set off a scramble by several young boys to see who could reach it first.

Anyway, realising the man in the black suit would be back out, I headed down the street in the direction the soldiers had come from. I'd gone by several houses when I saw a road between the fenced yards which led to a huge garden, probably half the size of a football field. At one end was a number of small apple trees, and beyond, a small vineyard. I headed for the apple trees and found a depression next to the tall fence with all the grapes on it. I lay down and covered myself with grass, thinking I was as well off there as anywhere, anyone coming into the garden would have to be on top of me to see me. I had been there maybe 10 minutes when I could see and hear someone in the yard next to me. Finally a white haired lady, very frail, worked her way to the fence opposite me. She was pretending to be snipping dead leaves from the grape vines overhead. She reached in the top of her dress and pulled out a small white slip of paper and pushed it through the fence just above my head; I took it and read, "Welcome to France. You are safe where you are. We will have instructions for you later. Don't leave your place." This boosted my spirits to the limit. The lady held her hand out near where she'd put the message through so I gave it back to her. She smiled at me for the first time and I smiled hack. We were buddies. I'd been in my hide-out for maybe an hour when I heard troops come marching from the direction the two soldiers had taken. When they got to the house where my chute was, they stopped and I could hear orders being given. They scattered in all directions in the block of houses where my chute was. I could hear them yelling from one house to another; after a lengthy search, they assembled and marched off. In a very short while the old lady appeared - but none of the snipping. Now she walked right up to the fence and handed another note through, then reached into her apron and pulled out a huge sandwich. I read the note, handed it back and proceeded to devour the sandwich - brown bread filled with soft cheese and ground meat. The note told me they were working out how to move me to a safe place far away from this area but I was to stay where I was, not to move around. So I like to say that I relaxed and had a little nap, but I was too hyped up to nap. A little later, I saw two men working down from the other end of the garden. They would seem to finish what they are doing in one area, then move to another. Before I knew it they were right next to the apple trees and by now they could see where I was. They looked all around and one came over to me, reached into a pocket and pulled out an "AGO" Card - Officers Identity Card - belonging to our navigator Henry Cabot Rowland. Well I was flabbergasted; this meant they had "Rollie" under their wings. He held out his hand and pointed to the card, meaning he wanted mine. I dug it out and gave it to him. We all smiled and they took off with my card. About twenty minutes later they were back marching straight down to me, and said, "Come", only word they knew. I followed them out to the garden to the street trying to walk behind them but they would not have any of that, insisting we walk arm in arm right down the middle of the street. No traffic, so I guess it was alright. My concern was that they were 5 foot 2 or 3 inches tall and I towered between them very conspicuously.

We were soon in the centre of town, Sartrouville, a suburb of Paris, to the north west. Everything pretty quiet, so we headed into the first bar in sight. My guides said something to the bartender, big smiles all around and cognac poured in small little glasses. The French were all talking at the same time, more smiles, more cognac, then on to the next bar with same declarations, same smiles, more cognac. Finally quit after three bars and headed to the house where Rollie was being kept. I now know the address as 6 Allee des Lilas. The cognac hadn't loosened me up a bit; when I saw the condition Rollie was in, I really lit into him about putting these people's lives in jeopardy by getting drunk. Rollie was immediately contrite and pledged, sobbing, that he'd never take another drink in France. Our hosts were alarmed and couldn't understand what was going on between us so they quickly moved us into separate rooms.

We all carried "escape" photos with us which were to be used to make bogus identity cards. They showed me the one they had made up for Rollie and wanted my photos - but I didn't have them. They must have been with my gear where I had landed. So I needed a picture taken and that meant moving me to another part of town. The first stop on the way was a barber shop - had to make me look more French. My guide on this trip was a middle-aged man who knew everyone. Before we went to the barber shop he made a sign that I interpreted to mean "don't say anything to anyone." As it turned out, the fellow getting a haircut in the other chair was a big black-market racketeer and a collaborator. He did his damnedest to try and get me to respond to his questions and comments. After my hair was trimmed and marvelled, we picked up a couple of bicycles and headed across town, finally stopping at a bar that was closed. The guide knocked several time and finally the owner came from the back and let us in. We sat around a table and drank red wine and dipped grey bread in it; found out later this was the only way they could eat the bread. The Germans took all their good bread flour for themselves. Later Rollie and Andre, the fellow whose house we first got together in showed up and we had some more wine. Rollie had sobered up and were were telling each other how we got away from the

Germans; he'd had a much closer call that I had. So our hosts started to relax, seeing we were buddies again. Something happened to the photographer and he could not come until after the evening supper, so we had to move to a house nearby and wait, as the bar had to open to the public at the regular time.

This house had a big courtyard with shops all around for processing meat; their speciality was pate. We had a big dinner with much champagne and many toasts. Finally the photographer showed up and I had my ID photo taken, afterwards more toasts. Rollie land I were not in their drinking league and soon found ourselves helpless. (The next day we resolved never to try and stay up with their drinking, and we didn't.) Our host started up his panel truck and we were carried out and tossed in with the bicycles on top of us for the ride back across town. I was dropped off at a new place and Rollie went on to Andre's house.

I woke up mid-morning the next day hearing a baby cry; did that ever sober me up. No way was I going to let a couple with a small baby shelter me. I tried to make the young mother understand that I had to get out of there. In a short time, her husband appeared and he knew I was upset about something. Finally a school boy came in who understood some English. He made me understand that, yes I would be taken from there as soon as I had my French ID card - which they were expecting at any time. Actually it was late in the afternoon before someone brought it - then a long walk following a guide to Andre's house.

This house was typical of the houses in the area, with the traditional heavy wrought iron fence in front and lesser fencing on the other three sides. The house had two big bedrooms upstairs, living and dining room same size on the first floor. Rollie and I slept in a large bed in one of the rooms and our host slept in the other. Each morning he would bring us a tray with toast, marmalade and tea, a perfect start to any day. We would spend our days reading English novels they brought us or in visiting the many friends and relatives of Andre.

One day someone brought a large bag of home grown tobacco and a small cigarette making machine. Rollie was beside himself with joy as he could not smoke their regular cigarettes. He quickly asked me to light one up too, so they would think they were furnishing enough tobacco for two. So each time someone was with us I would smoke one cigarette for show. But it wasn't long before I was smoking as many as Rollie, and when a fresh bag of tobacco would come in, we spent our time carefully dividing the tobacco into two piles. The cigarettes were better when freshly made, so we each had our own can.

We spent seven weeks in Sartrouville. The weather for the most part was dry and warm, we would go for bike rides with Andre who was used to getting around on a bicycle as he had no car. We would stop at friends for lunch, sometimes dinner. Andre wasn't too keen on travelling at night on our bikes, so we would usually get back to his house about the time it was getting dark. We had only one close call while were there with him.

He had arranged for two young college age kids to take us for a canoe ride on the Seine river. It was a Sunday afternoon, the beach area, and boathouse had a big crowd of young people enjoying time off and the nice weather. We rode over to the place on our bikes, our helpers got the canoe out of the boathouse and we were having a nice quiet canoe ride, when some guy on the bank started yelling at us and following us as we moved down the river. He finally got a gendarme to blow his whistle and order to come to shore. Our two guides were panic stricken for they knew as soon as either one of us tried to say anything we would be taken. So they quickly decided to land at a dock up ahead, and the one who could speak some English told us to stay put, that one of them would get out at the dock and explain to the gendarme how they came by the canoe, while he was doing this the other fellow would shove off and beach the canoe farther on, and we were to quietly get lost in the crowd. Once we had cleared the area were were to walk back to our bikes and head for Sartrouville, we'd be on our own. It seemed the man making all the fuss actually owned the boat and didn't know that someone else had given our guides a key to the locker in the boathouse, where it was kept. The owner was supposed to have been out of town that day. Our luck was still with us and it worked out just as they hoped it would. We were long gone by the time the gendarme got over to the canoe. We picked up our bikes and were some distance from the river, not sure we remembered the way back, when one of the guides came rushing up behind us. Now he was laughing about the whole affair. That was last time we went anywhere in Sartrouville without Andre.

Every couple of days, someone who was fluent in English would come and spend some time with us explaining what was going on, and Andre would be able to converse with us. He was a veteran of trench warfare in World War I, wounded a couple of times, and absolutely fearless. A couple of days before were were moved along the escape line, he took us to Paris for a little sightseeing. We left in the late afternoon and had a nice dinner, for wartime Paris, in a crowded restaurant, then walked around in the dark stopping at the opera and other big buildings in the centre area, rode the subways part of the way back to the main train station, then back to Sartrouville. While riding the subway, I did a very dumb thing. I went into a different car from one Andre and Rollie took; they could see me so it was OK, except that in my car was the most beautiful blonde German woman in officers uniform. She was sitting opposite me and I couldn't keep my eyes off her. When she realised I was staring at her, she became visibly upset, started looking around at every station for someone who could deal with me. My friends caught on to what was happening and signalled me to get off at the next stop. It wasn't where were were supposed to get off, but Andre had thought of a safe way to the main station - walk.

Andre took us to Paris the night of our first move. Before leaving, a fellow who had visited us many times, and fluent in English, came by and briefed us on what was going to happen once we got to Paris. Andre would turn us over to a guide who would be responsible to see that we got to our destination. We arrived early at the rendezvous, a theatre, the streets, quite dark in the blackout. Andre told us to promenade around and return every 5 minutes or so but to keep walking; everyone on the streets seemed to be going somewhere. I saw a group of four or five men bearing down and thought one of them was wearing a gendarme's cap. I quickly crossed the street and continued in the same direction. I knew Rollie had asked Andre where he could relieve himself so I expected them to be well behind me. First thing I heard was a funny whistle sound, then this group fanned out in all directions, grabbing people and holding them in small bunches. Finally when they had about twenty people under their control they would shout out the districts or towns the people came from, according to their ID cards. When it was apparent that everyone was from a different place, they let them go; all except Rollie, whom they had up against the side of a building with a flashlight shining in his face. They caught him with his pants open but no puddle on the ground. He had given them his ID card which showed him to be deaf and dumb, so when they tried to ask him what he was doing he rolled his eyes and made weird noises. He kept it up until they decided he was a harmless dummy walking the streets with his fly open.

While this was going on, I moved hack down the street and watched his ordeal. I could only see the flashlight go out and the whole group moved off. I thought for sure they had Rollie. After another turn around the block, I made my was back to the theatre entrance. No one in sight, I figured they had Andre too; so I paced back and forth thinking the guide coming to pick us up would speak some English and approach me—my only hope. Someone came up behind me and tapped me on the shoulder, it was Andre. He was beside himself, saying "Rollie kaput," so I thought he had seen them take Rollie away. Minutes later I saw this 'white as a sheet' face that seemed familiar glued against the wall. It was Rollie without his beret. I rushed over to him, congratulated him on his performance and asked what had happened to his beret. he said, "Can't you see I'm in disguise!"

Andre came up and pounded Rollie some more on the back, everyone happy again, finally the guide showed up. We shook hands all around and followed this fellow who looked like the Hollywood version of a big city newspaper reporter. He was wearing a white trench coat and large felt hat stuck on the back of his head, cigarette hanging out of his mouth.

He had already bought our tickets. When we approached the gate, in the train station, the guide stepped up to the conductor, held up the tickets, shoved his arm across the conductor's chest and waved us through. The conductor started yelling and chasing after us, shouting that he had to punch our tickets. By this time a small crowd had gathered to see what was going on; I'm thinking: after two months of evasion, it's only taking this guy two minutes to get us caught. But after the tickets were punched we headed for a car on the train. The train was jam packed, we wound up in the only place left with standing room. There was no seats or benches in this area so we would bump into each other every time the train hit some rough track. It turned out that everyone in our end of the car was either a guide or an evader, but until we were nearly into Cherbourg, none of the evaders said a word. The guides were talking to each other, finally one of them started whistling "Yankee Doodle," one evader after another would smile and nod, or flash a "v" for victory with his fingers.

At Cherbourg our guides opened the door that faced away from the station and led us across the tracks to another train. We piled into a car that was almost empty—a special car for German officers. There was a handful of them asleep in compartments at one end of the car and we were trying to sleep in the other end. The train pulled out and a fresh set of guides, four in number, were spending their time making out new passes for us. We need the passes to explain our presence in the area we were being moved to. Also needed work permits showing us as members of the Todt organisation, which was building the "West Wall" beach fortifications on the Brittany coast. They used our French ID cards to copy our phony names properly. We took turns visiting their compartment. Sometime in the early morning, before we got to Landerneau, we moved to another car before the German officers had to be awakened. We were told that we would have to go through a checkpoint where we would have to show our papers—not to say a word and we'd have no trouble, we were all deaf and dumb according to the papers. The French gendarme in charge of the station made it possible for us to go through without being questioned. I didn't know until years later that he was the head of the Resistance in this section of France. At each checkpoint a German officer or NCO was observing the gendarmes and would ask for the papers of anyone they thought they should look over themselves. The whole station was filled with German troops in full field gear, some arriving, some departing.

After clearing the station, we followed our guides who would stop, once we were several blocks from the station, and put us in a house, one or two at a time. The lady of the house where Rollie and I were dropped off was expecting us. She had a large tray of sandwiches and hot tea. We made short work of this meal, then she showed us where we would stay (in the wood shed) until someone came to move us along. It had a couple of stacks of dry grass, so we took turns dozing off. Sometime in the early afternoon one of the guides came to the shed and told us to follow him. He took us eventually to a long steep road leading out of town. A panel truck came along and without completely stopping, the rear doors opened and someone beckoned us to hop in. This was repeated until all the evaders were in the truck, about twelve or thirteen. We were wedged in like sardines and the springs were so weak the tyres hit the top of the wheel well at every big bump. I think we all had the same thought, "Don't know where we're going but it better be soon." It was an early 1930's vintage truck whose engine coughed and sputtered all the way.

We had to stop at two German checkpoints, which was scary in that if they required the two Frenchmen in the cab to open the back so they could see the cargo, our number would be up. Both men had .32 calibre Colt pistols hidden under a sweater on the seat between them so someone was going to get hurt if it all came down. Again we were lucky and got through OK. We made a stop in one of the town squares so a phone call could be made, never knew what it was all about. When we looked out of the front curtain in the truck, all we could see were German troops and equipment, it seemed they had taken over the whole town. We eventually reached a farmhouse out in the middle of nowhere but near the water. Here the truck stopped, we all piled out and were led to two huge haystacks near the house.

We were divided up and once in, through a small opening, found each stack hollowed out and, though dark, quite comfortable. After awhile a man came by who spoke poor English but made us understand we would have a long walk on the beach to a certain large rock where we would be picked up by a boat without the Germans seeing us. The boat would take us to a nearby island named Guenioc. He explained that we would have to carry our shoes, tied together, to make the Germans think we had buckets, and pretend to be picking up seaweed and shellfish as the locals habitually did.

We were to stay close to the water's edge, single file, and keep the man ahead of us just in sight. We were taken one at a time to the road leading to the beach. Once out in the sand the first thing I saw was a big flat orange object sticking up out of the sand—a land mine with a pencil sized trigger sticking up from its centre. That gets the adrenaline moving. I kept a sharp eye out to make sure I didn't pop one of those triggers with my bare toes. The walk to the big rock turned out to be at least one mile, all the time under the watchful eyes of the Germans manning the gun positions on the banks above the beach. About half way there, I could hear a band playing in a small field near the cliff. An infantry platoon was marching to music, doing some sort of drill. I didn't try to get a close look, but the guy behind me was heading right up their way; later he said he had lost sight of me and thought I'd gone off in that direction. When he got to the top of the sand dune, he found he was close enough to fall right in their formation; said he turned around and headed toward the water expecting a shout to halt or a bullet. Neither came and he soon spotted me up ahead.

When we got to the rock we found a small fishing boat. The fisherman would load five or six of us, throw some lobster crates on top of us, and motor to Guenioc, off the coast of North Finistere near the mouth of the Aber Wrac'h. Once there, he landed us behind another huge rock and when we all had been assembled, we were told to stay put until dark, then we could move about the island which was some twenty

245

acres in size. They told us we would be taken by small boats to a submarine that would come close to the island after dark. We couldn't believe our luck, tomorrow we'd be safely landed in England. They told us they would contact the submarine by radio at an agreed upon time. Once it was dark we went bouncing around, everyone in high spirits, our ordeals over, only a quiet ride in a submarine ahead of us. The frolicking got to a dangerous point, we were making so much noise, so one of the guides rounded us up and put us in three groups at three different places on the island. We had instructions to stay put.

At about three or four in the morning we all gathered quietly on the seaward side of the island to try and find out what had gone wrong, where was the sub? It turned out the radio was actually a flashlight and they'd had no answering flashes all night. Just before daylight we were told to go back to our three hideouts and not move all day, they would try again that night to raise the sub. So we stayed put all day and as soon as it was dark we headed for the sheep dip in the centre of the island; being dark helped us think the water was clean. It wasn't, and tasted like sheep dip. Actually it was a shallow depression that collected rain water and when sheep were put on the island they would use it for sit baths as well as for a place to drink.

We could never decide whether being thirsty or hungry affected us the most. But food was on hand; at the end of our first day on the island the French showed us that the rocks and boulders near the water's edge were loaded with cone shaped limpets. All we had to do was take a knife blade or thin stick and pry them loose, extract the animal, swallow them whole; after eating a couple of dozen we'd feel almost like we'd had a meal. They warned us only to eat the grey fleshed ones, any having pink colour should be thrown away, they were poisonous. It didn't take us long to clean out all the limpets in sight. Before we left the island we were eating any shellfish, any colour, and still felt hungry. The weather wasn't all that good, at night the sheep dip would coat over with ice and there would be frost on the grasses. Then it started to rain so everyone was thoroughly soaked for we had no cover of any kind. The morning of the third day, one of the Frenchmen signalled to a fishing boat that was close to the island and asked him to return to the port and call someone to tell them their friends were in a bad way and needed to be taken back to the mainland. The boat turned around and headed in the direction of the port. We could only hope he wouldn't tell the Germans we were on the island. In the early afternoon he and another man came back, bringing food in the form of bread and cold cuts of meat, also some wine and blankets. Our group was only given a small amount of bread and meat, at least we thought so, but no wine or blankets. We expected they would return later in the day and start ferrying us back to the mainland. We later learned they couldn't find the fishermen who had taken us to the island, so it was the next morning before the boat with the lobster pots showed up. We had moved to the big rock after it was dark and we were able to huddle together and stay somewhat warm with the blankets; still, it was the most debilitating experience any of us had ever had.

Once back on the beach we moved, shoes in hand, single file, to the farmhouse. We waited in the haystacks until the old truck appeared and took us to the chateau, Penmarc'h, about 10 minutes away. They had a big fire going in a huge fireplace and soon several pots of stew appeared with lots of cookies and good things to eat. The ladies who had been preparing everything soon disappeared; found out later they feared for their safety, as they described us a bunch of uncivilised wild men. Took us well into the night to get dry and warm. Most of us slept on the floor as close to the fire as we could get. Next day a bunch of clean clothes, soaps and razors were brought in and we spent the day getting cleaned up and refitted. My dress on the island was a summer weight jacket, pants, and a light turtleneck sweater, so I was looking for some warmer clothes to get into. The trouble was there were very few large sizes of anything. I kept my sweater, pants and found a wool suit coat that would have to do.

In the afternoon we were all gathered together and told that a fishing boat had been purchased to take six evaders to England. Almost everyone wanted a chance to go, so we drew for high cards from a deck spread out on the table. I drew the ace of hearts so I knew I was going. After everyone who wanted to go had picked a card, we had our group. Then we got together and decided we'd better be prepared to feed ourselves for three or four days at sea. Each of us set about looking for food in the kitchen. By this time several cars had come and picked up everyone else to take them to Brest to await another rendezvous with a British rescue boat. The six of us had the place to ourselves, plenty of warm blankets, out spirits were high.

Next morning a car took us to the farmhouse again; this time no French guides or instructions other than that we were on our own to proceed to the big rock on the beach and wait for a boat. So back on the beach with shoes in hand, only this time we all looked like distorted figures with things bulging out all over us. I had two bottles of wine, two baguettes, a huge hunk of pate, and cookies in every pocket. We all felt we could last for several days on what we had. We arrived at the rock, still undetected by the Germans. At noon we had a small snack and shared a bottle of wine, mid afternoon another light snack, another bottle of wine—still no sign of the fishing boat. When it became apparent that the boat wasn't coming, we decided we were not going to leave all that wine so we drank as much as we dared, knowing we had nearly a mile to walk before reaching the farmhouse. But our luck was still with us and the exercise cleared our heads, it was our only relaxed beach walk. The fisherman had informed the Resistance people that he changed his mind, so they had a car waiting at the farmhouse to take us to the chateau, where we spent another comfortable, warm night on the floor by the fire. Next day Dr. and Mme. de la Marniere came and drove five of us to Brest where we were dropped off at several houses. The sixth man stayed somewhere near the chateau, I think he had been put up there earlier.

I was assigned to Colonel Scheidhauer's apartment. It was a large one with big rooms that took up the whole floor. There were four apartments in this one building. We were on the second floor, with a known collaborator on the first floor and a German major on the floor above us.

There were no toilets in the apartment; they were located on the landings between the floors. With six evaders staying with the Colonel it got to be pretty hectic to keep the toilets available for the other tenants. We finally got our systems adjusted so that we would go in the middle of the night.

We stayed about three weeks with the Scheidhauer's, waiting for the next period of moonless nights. No sightseeing, no trips on the outside, but we had plenty of visitors; what was nice for us was that about everyone could speak or understand some English. Dr. and Mme. de la Marniere were especially fluent, so we learned a lot about how ready the Resistance people were for the invasion to start. The Colonel and I played chess whenever he was home. He was the mayor of Brest, appointed by the German occupation authorities so he was almost above suspicion. This enabled the Resistance people to have access to all kinds of passes and permits; the Colonel's secretary was a key figure and very clever in getting things done. The Marnieres' daughters would bring their girl friends over to learn how to jitterbug with the evaders. As a lady told me at an AFEES meeting in Los Angeles a couple of years ago, "You would never dance with us because you were always playing chess with the Colonel." That was true and I was nice enough not to point out that they were only in high school and I thought them too young to dance with; plus the fact that I didn't jitterbug that well anyway.

We had some excitement one day, all the anti-aircraft guns in the city opened up and we heard a plane, B-17, flying low overhead but it happened so fast we never saw the plane. It turned out that it crashed outside the city and two of the crew escaped, rest being killed or captured. The plane was being ferried to England from , North Africa and had lost its way.

On the 1st of December another rescue attempt had been laid on and assorted cars and trucks took us back to the Aber Wrac'h area late in the afternoon. A new plan had been formed to take us off the beach by the big rock. A kayak would be launched after dark and contact the rescue boat, then show them where we were waiting near the big rock. Six of us were picked to carry the kayak, in the dark, from a farmhouse about a mile from the beach. When we got to the farmhouse, after a small meal, we picked up the kayak which turned out to be made of wood so it was heavy. We finally figured out the best way to carry it was on our shoulders. To avoid detection by the German patrols we travelled from one field to another, shoving the boat over the top of hedgerows. I have no idea how far we carried it before we got to the water, but it took us over two hours. When we finally went down the path to the beach we were dragging the boat along the ground. French helpers took it over from us once we were on the beach, and the French Resistance leader, L'Mao", headed out alone in it to contact the British Motor Gun Boat 318. We then proceeded to the rock and once there sat around, about 20 of us, very quiet and apprehensive that this might be another failed mission. After midnight it started raining again and the wind began to pick up about the time that three dinghies from the MGB quietly came ashore to our part of the beach. ("Mao" came ashore at the same time as the dinghies, thoroughly exhausted by his efforts in the kayak). The stores they were bringing in for the Resistance people were quickly unloaded and the evaders scrambled into the boats, making sure they would not be left behind. It was only a few minutes until we were all sorted out, so that the boats had about the same number in each. The weather could not have been worse. We were all soaked to the skin as it had been raining off and on since we left the farmhouse with the kayak. The winds got stronger as the night wore on. The sea conditions seemed to make it impossible for the boat to gain any headway, as they were wide abeam and not too long, maybe about 12 feet. Within a few minutes of pushing off the beach, the three boats were far apart.

I was in the boat of Lt. Uhr-Henry, the officer in charge of the three rescue boats. We were supposed to be leading the way back to the MGB, but it was impossible to see where the others were; it was pitch black, with only the rocks sticking out of the raging sea being blacker. The other two boats quickly met the fate we feared, one hit a rock and sank, the other capsized in the mountainous waves. All aboard were able to get back to the beach and were successfully hidden until three weeks later when taken off the same beach by MGB 318. How we missed the rocks was one of the miracles occurring that night. There was a string of others. For example, our boat had a leak in the bottom that took in about the same amount of water that came in with every crashing wave. Someone had the bright idea that we could use our shoes to bail the water out. This kept the evader's minds off how hopeless the situation was and gave us a feeling that we were helping to get the little boat back to the big boat. It wasn't long before the two young sailors pulling on the oars gave out. The officer asked for two volunteers to man the oars; two evaders quickly took their places and for a few minutes did OK, but not being used to that kind of work, they soon tired, with another two taking their place. It was apparent to the British officer that he had only two passengers with any skill at rowing, so it settled down that these two would relieve the sailors when they needed a rest. Everyone else continued to bail, hoping to keep from going under. The wind kept getting worse during these two long hours with still no MGB in sight.

I was wedged in the high bow of the boat and would every so often twist around and scan the black sea ahead for any sign of a light. The officer had said earlier that the big boat would be showing a light just above the water line so that it could not be seen from shore. After all this seemingly hopeless rowing in the raging sea, spirits among all of us, except for the officer, started to sink; so I decided to pick up our spirits by giving a positive answer when they asked again "Do you see the light, Tommy?" "Yes I see the light!" What happened then, I'm convinced, made the rescue possible. For they all ignited, and started shouting "We're over here!" The sailors on the MGB who were on lookout duty heard us above the roar of the wind and waves. The skipper gave the order to ease toward the noise and then we could hear the boat's engines which gave everyone more lung power; finally a most beautiful sight for us was the outline of the boat's stern easing slowly towards us. It would be nice to say that we closed the gap, but actually the fellows rowing were too tired to do much more. When we came along side, rope ladders were thrown down and the scramble up began. Most memorable to me was watching our fearless boat commander getting chewed out by the skipper. I thought he'd be given a "Well done" at least, but he was told he'd really blown it by losing the other two cockboats and crews. We got under way immediately and after being given dry clothes were dispersed under the deck with pads to lie on. The crossing back to England, I found out later, was the roughest trip that any of the MGBs made during the war; the sea conditions were several points above what the boat had been designed to withstand.

Only one evader, Sgt. Duane Lawhead, wasn't seasick on the trip home; he could be seen cheerfully eating everything brought down for us by the crew. We arrived at their secret base in the late afternoon and were assigned to barracks and given clean British fatigues, hot showers, almost anything our stomachs would keep down, and clean beds. Next day we were escorted to a train station and taken under escort to London. There were given US uniforms and assigned a debriefing time, restricted to the building we were in until cleared by a member from our Squadron who could identify us. Once all this was over with, we were paid and had only to await orders sending us back to the States.

"WEE BONNIE" CREW LIST FOR 9 SEPTEMBER 1943

PILOT, DEL PORTER - POW Exchanged, Medically Disabled, through Sweden 1944
CO-PILOT, HAROLD THOMPSON - Evader
NAVIGATOR, HENRY ROWLAND - Evader
BOMBARDIER, VERNON ADAMS - POW
TOP TURRET GUNNER, JOHN MOFFIT - POW
RADIO OPERATOR, JOHN ASH - POW
BALL TURRET GUNNER, RALPH MALLICOTE - Evader
WAIST GUNNER, CLEMENT MEZZANOTTE - POW
WAIST GUNNER, ROSWELL MILLER - Evader
TAIL GUNNER, IVAN L. SCHRAEDER - Evader
"STARS AND STRIPES" PHOTOGRAPHER,
ALPHONSE SULCHINO -POW